THE FLIGHT
OF THE IGUANA

By David Quammen

Nonfiction

Natural Acts
The Flight of the Iguana

Fiction

To Walk the Line
The Zolta Configuration
The Soul of Viktor Tronko
Blood Line

THE FLIGHT
OF THE IGUANA

A Sidelong View
of Science and Nature

DAVID QUAMMEN

**Delacorte
Press**

Published by
Delacorte Press
The Bantam Doubleday Dell Publishing Group, Inc.
1 Dag Hammarskjold Plaza
New York, New York 10017

Library of Congress Cataloging in Publication Data
Quammen, David, 1948–
    The flight of the iguana.

    Bibliography: p. 279
    1. Natural history—Miscellanea. 2. Zoology—Miscellanea.
I. Title. 279
QH45.5.Q358   1988   508   87-30578
ISBN 0-385-29592-8

Manufactured in the United States of America

June 1988

10 9 8 7 6 5 4 3 2 1

BG

to Kris
In view of Baboquivari

CONTENTS

INTRODUCTION

A Mouse Is Miracle Enough

The pageant of nature: Sometimes it seems like a freak show. You hear the nasal chant of the barker, you follow the pull of a prurient curiosity, you pay the dime, step through the flap of the tent into musky darkness and nose-flute music and when your eyes have adjusted you see there, sure enough, these garish living shapes. The spoon worm. The okapi. The red-footed booby. The plant that eats frogs. The chambered nautilus, ancient and unrecognizable, hovering in its aquarium, a snail-like critter with octopus arms who gazes back at you quizzically from two squinty eyes. The scorpion, armed and dangerous, glowing a luminescent blue-green. The rogue bedbug *Xylocaris*, with its almost unspeakable (though we will speak of them) sexual practices. But nature is *not* a freak show.

And this is emphatically not a book full of geeks, though in places that impression may offer itself.

Please don't be misled. There will be giant earthworms, yes, there will be dogs without voices and chimpanzees talking in sign language, yes, there will be an iguana that sails through the air, needless to say, but the whole point of exhibiting such creatures is not for us to peer shudderingly at some sad monsters, or to examine the quirks that result when natural processes go haywire. On the contrary, the point here is simply nature itself on a good day. On a *normal* day. Quirks and haywire don't even enter into it. These unpopular beasts I seem to have gathered here, for your contemplation, are the natural and true-born practitioners of life on this planet, the legitimate scions of organic evolution, as surely as are the white-tail deer or the parakeet or the puppy. If we ourselves can fathom them only in the context of carnival canvas and hootchy-kootchy music, the problem is probably our own.

One name for that problem is *xenophobia:* fear or hatred of what is foreign or strange. The term is applied most often in connection with attitudes toward folk of the wrong skin color, but it's applicable also to nonhuman characters with the wrong number of legs or eyes, the wrong shape of face or jaws, the wrong sexual or alimentary deportment.

And I certainly don't exempt myself from this problem. You are in the company here, as you'll see, of a fellow who is guilty of a lifelong and deep-seated revulsion toward spiders. Mere spiders. Harmless innocent beneficial unassuming house-and-garden spiders, as well as the other kind.

Which brings us to *Latrodectus mactans,* a spider but definitely no mere one. *Latrodectus mactans* is the black widow. Among other superlatives, it is America's most famous and possibly most venomous arachnid. Having just forced myself to reread the book you are holding, I've discovered somewhat to my surprise that *Latrodectus* appears recurrently throughout it. Sometimes in a featured role, more often in cameos. There's a reason for that. The black widow is not just a spider, not just a poisonous spider, not just a poisonous spider that happens to have a high degree of menacing but undeniable beauty; it is all those things and more. To me it's a synecdoche, representing its own vivid self as well as other and broader meanings. Dangerous but not malicious, exotic-seeming but in truth rather common, ruthless as a mate, tender (and sometimes again ruthless) as a mother, death-dealing and life-seeking, fierce and vulnerable, gorgeous or hideous depending upon how we happen to see it, the black widow spider *is* nature.

Two primary subjects tangle their ways throughout this book: first, the surprising intricacies of the natural world, and second, human attitudes toward those intricacies. I've been intrigued for a long time not only by the sinister beauty of the black widow but also by my own—and your—reactions to it. I'm fascinated not only with the Galápagos marine iguana, as it sails through the sky on page 161, but equally with the young Englishman who got it airborne, and with the cluster of human ideas and attitudes closely connected to that flight. Facts are important to the appreciation of nature, because "appreciation" without comprehension is often a shallow and sentimental whim; and the essays that follow do contain, I think, their reasonable share of facts. But many of those essays are also full of opinion, bias, personal emotion, and what I offer as an earnest—if highly unsystematic—examination of attitudes. Within the term *attitudes* I include both emotional affinities and questions of principle. Not to wax portentous, but it seems to me that almost nothing bears more crucially upon the future of this planet than the seemingly simple matter of human attitudes toward nature.

Human attitudes toward the black widow spider and the marine iguana, if you like. It is all ineluctably connected.

Apropos of the matter of attitudes, this is the place to insert a quote. "I think I could turn and live with animals, they are so placid and self-contain'd," wrote Walt Whitman, "I stand and look at them long and long." It's from "Song of Myself," of course, that great epic hug bestowed on mid-nineteenth century America by our crazy-wild poet of inclusiveness and enthusiasm. The full section is worth remembering:

*I think I could turn and live with animals, they are so
    placid and self-contain'd,
I stand and look at them long and long.*

*They do not sweat and whine about their condition,
They do not lie awake in the dark and weep for their sins,
They do not make me sick discussing their duty to God,
Not one is dissatisfied, not one is demented with the mania
    of owning things,
Not one kneels to another, nor to his kind that lived
    thousands of years ago,
Not one is respectable or unhappy over the whole earth.*

Walt Whitman never met a snake or a sea cucumber that he
didn't like, and this Whitmanesque attitude toward nature is exactly the one that seems to me exemplary. It is highly unscien-
tific, it tends toward anthropomorphism, but then scientific ob-
jectivity and abstention from the anthropomorphic metaphor are
not absolute virtues; those two forms of cold intellectual purity
can help us understand nature, sure, but they shouldn't necessarily define our relations with it. The Whitman view is more
inclusive, more daring, and ultimately more salubrious for all
concerned. Few of us lesser souls, though, are fully capable of it.
Some of us come to the sticking point over spiders, some over
grizzly bears, some over rattlesnakes, or cocker spaniels, or house
cats. But we can try. More about all that in the essays that follow.

In recognition of the Whitmanesque ideal, I considered at one
point labeling the present volume for the title of the essay about
scorpions and their feeble eyesight, "See No Evil." But it wasn't
right. There's too much *human* nature in this book for that title
to apply generally—as you will have sad occasion to see in Part
IV, "The Moral Ecology of a Desert."

You will also find some quiet and mundane creatures that

don't seem at all like they might ever be mistaken for freak-show attractions. The common European earthworm *Lumbricus ter-restris*. The tepary bean of Sonoran agriculture. The nameless tree that grows from a sidewalk pit on West Forty-fourth Street in New York City. The Canada goose. In my personal view, each of these has the same import and the same mysterious resonance (though in more elusive ways) as *Latrodectus mactans* or the marine iguana, and each raises the same sort of questions about our relations with nature and with each other. Each one is a set of Chinese boxes, seemingly only more complicated and sus-penseful as we work down toward that hidden center. The mys-tery and magic we're chasing in this collective entity called na-ture is really everywhere; like the God of the pantheists, it inheres somehow in every leaf, every mite, every cell. In that connection, it's time to quote Whitman again:

> *I believe that a leaf of grass is no less than the journey-work*
> *of the stars,*
> *And the pismire [ant] is equally perfect, and a grain of sand,*
> *and the egg of the wren,*
> *And the tree-toad is a chef-d'oeuvre for the highest,*
> *And the running blackberry would adorn the parlors of*
> *heaven . . .*
> *And the cow crunching with depress'd head surpasses any*
> *statue,*
> *And a mouse is miracle enough to stagger sextillions of*
> *infidels.*

This book is a gathering of portraits and questions and thoughts. It is populated with a spectrum of creatures that, to my own eye, constitute the biological and aesthetic and philosophical equivalent of tree toads, pismires, leaves of grass. If it doesn't somewhere among these pages make you angry, and somewhere else make you laugh, and somewhere still else make you sad or worried or vaguely inclined to rethink some matter of attitude, I will be disappointed. I don't ask for sextillions of infidels. But I'll be very gratified if the mouse is enough, on closer inspection, to stagger you.

AUTHOR'S NOTE

Each of these essays was first published, in similar or slightly different form, in a magazine. But that is not quite the same, please note, as saying that they were all *written for* magazines. On the contrary, most of them were written to be eventually part of this book. At least, they were conceived and shaped—though for magazine publication initially—with this book ultimately in mind.

The large majority appeared first as installments of the monthly column I write, under the title "Natural Acts," for *Outside* magazine. It's probably not possible for me to state adequately the depth of my indebtedness and my gratitude to the people of *Outside,* but here's a concise attempt: extreme. I've had unimaginable freedom and opportunity as *Outside*'s natural-science columnist these past six years. And when I mention that gratitude toward "the people of *Outside,*" I have in mind not just a few editors, not just them plus the owner and publisher, not just the whole staff at *Outside* world headquarters in Chicago, but also and preeminently the magazine's readers, who seem to me an interesting and mentally vigorous group of folks, and who have certainly made this book possible. Thank you for the dialogue, people.

xvi AUTHOR'S NOTE

As with a previous volume of these essays *(Natural Acts,* 1985), I have resisted the temptation to try to update every fact or statement, changing numbers, adjusting for inflation and entropy, making follow-up calls about matters that are best left unfollowed-up. So it should be understood that a reference to "now" or "the present" in an individual piece might refer to any time between 1984 and 1987, and that any temporally contingent assertions made will reflect the state of things at that given time. Some of the situations may have since changed incrementally, but not, I believe, drastically.

Thanks are due most especially to John Rasmus, Larry Burke, and Renée Wayne Golden, the three good souls most responsible for giving me rope enough to move between subjects like a kid on a Tarzan swing. If the rope has also occasionally been used to hang myself, that's not their fault. Thanks also to Marc Barasch, David Hirshey, Lee Eisenberg, Lewis Lapham, Gerald Marzorati, Barry Lopez, Jackie Farber, Loretta Barrett, Tom Parrett, John Fife, Jim Corbett, Peggy Hutchison, Phil Willis-Conger, Bob Hirsh, Bill Roberson, John Crawford, Dick Murless, Marc Young, Allan Ostling, E. Jean Carroll, and of course Steve Byers.

First publication of each of the pieces was as follows: "The Face of a Spider," *Outside* (March 1987); "Thinking About Earthworms," *Outside* (June 1986); "The Thing with Feathers," *Outside* (September 1985); "Nasty Habits," *Outside* (February 1987); "Stalking the Gentle Piranha," *Outside* (January 1986); "See No Evil," *Outside* (April 1985); "Turnabout," *Outside* (November 1984); "The Selfhood of a Spoon Worm," *Outside* (December 1985); "The Descent of the Dog," *Outside* (August 1985); "Street Trees," *Outside* (April 1987); "The Ontological Giraffe," *Outside* (October 1984); "The Lonesome Ape," *Outside* (June 1987); "Stranger than Truth," *Outside* (August 1986); "Deep Thoughts," *Outside* (November 1985); "Island Getaway," *Outside* (October 1985); "Talk Is Cheap," *Outside* (July 1986); "Icebreaker," *Outside* (June 1985); "Agony in the Garden," *Outside* (February 1986); "The Poseidon Shales," *Mercedes* (Spring 1987); "The Beautiful and Damned," *Outside* (July 1985); "Provide, Provide," *Outside* (May 1985); "The Flight of the Iguana," *Outside* (July 1987); "The Beaded Lizard" (as "Knowing the Heart of a Stranger"), *New Age Journal* (August 1984); "Drinking the Desert Juices," *Outside* (November 1986); "The Desert Is a Mnemonic Device," *Harper's* (December 1986); "The Miracle of the Geese," *Outside* (September 1986); "Swamp Odyssey," *Outside* (January 1985); "The Siphuncle," *Outside* (January 1987); "The Same River Twice," *Outside* (May 1986).

I
FACES
UNLIKE OURS

THE FACE
OF A SPIDER

*Eyeball to Eyeball with
the Good, the Bad, and the Ugly*

One evening a few years ago I walked back into my office after
dinner and found roughly a hundred black widow spiders frolick-
ing on my desk. I am not speaking metaphorically and I am not
making this up: a hundred black widows. It was a vision of
ghastly, breathtaking beauty, and it brought on me a wave of
nausea. It also brought on a small moral crisis—one that I dealt
with briskly, maybe rashly, in the dizziness of the moment, and
that I've been turning back over in my mind ever since. I won't
say I'm *haunted* by those hundred black widows, but I do remember them vividly. To me, they stand for something. They
stand, in their small synecdochical way, for a large and important question.

The question is, How should a human behave toward the
members of other living species?

A hundred black widows probably sounds like a lot. It is—
even for Tucson, Arizona, where I was living then, a habitat in
which black widows breed like rabbits and prosper like cock-
roaches, the females of the species growing plump as huckleberries and stringing their ragged webs in every free corner of every
old shed and basement window. In Tucson, during the height of
the season, a person can always on short notice round up eight or

ten big, robust black widows, if that's what a person wants to do. But a hundred in one room? So all right, yes, there was a catch: These in my office were newborn babies.

A hundred scuttering bambinos, each one no bigger than a poppyseed. Too small still for red hourglasses, too small even for red egg timers. They had the aesthetic virtue of being so tiny that even a person of good eyesight and patient disposition could not make out their hideous little faces.

Their mother had sneaked in when the rains began and set up a web in the corner beside my desk. I knew she was there—I got a reminder every time I dropped a pencil and went groping for it, jerking my hand back at the first touch of that distinctive, dry, high-strength web. But I hadn't made the necessary decision about dealing with her. I knew she would have to be either murdered or else captured adroitly in a pickle jar for relocation to the wild, and I didn't especially want to do either. (I had already squashed scores of black widows during those Tucson years but by this time, I guess, I was going soft.) In the meantime, she had gotten pregnant. She had laid her eggs into a silken egg sac the size of a Milk Dud and then protected that sac vigilantly, keeping it warm, fending off any threats, as black widow mothers do. While she was waiting for the eggs to come to term, she would have been particularly edgy, particularly unforgiving, and my hand would have been in particular danger each time I reached for a fallen pencil. Then the great day arrived. The spiderlings hatched from their individual eggs, chewed their way out of the sac, and started crawling, brothers and sisters together, up toward the orange tensor lamp that was giving off heat and light on the desk of the nitwit who was their landlord.

By the time I stumbled in, fifty or sixty of them had reached the lampshade and rappelled back down on dainty silk lines, leaving a net of gossamer rigging between the lamp and the Darwin book (it happened to be an old edition of *Insectivorous Plants,* with marbled endpapers) that sat on the desk. Some dozen others had already managed dispersal flights, letting out strands of buoyant silk and ballooning away on rising air, as spiderlings do—in this case dispersing as far as the bookshelves. It was too late for one man to face one spider with just a pickle jar and an index card and his two shaky hands. By now I was proprietor of a highly successful black widow hatchery.

And the question was, How should a human behave toward the members of other living species?

The Jain religion of India has a strong teaching on that question. The Sanskrit word is *ahimsa,* generally rendered in English as "noninjury" or the imperative "do no harm." *Ahimsa* is the ethical centerpiece of Jainism, an absolute stricture against the killing of living beings—*any* living beings—and it led the traditional Jains to some extreme forms of observance. A rigorously devout Jain would burn no candles or lights, for instance, if there was danger a moth might fly into them. The Jain would light no fire for heating or cooking, again because it might cause the death of insects. He would cover his mouth and nose with a cloth mask, so as not to inhale any gnats. He would refrain from cutting his hair, on grounds that the lice hiding in there might be gruesomely injured by the scissors. He could not plow a field, for fear of mutilating worms. He could not work as a carpenter or a mason, with all that dangerous sawing and crunching, nor could he engage in most types of industrial production. Consequently the traditional Jains formed a distinct socioeconomic class, composed almost entirely of monks and merchants. Their ethical canon was not without what you and I might take to be glaring contradictions (vegetarianism was sanctioned, plants as usual getting dismissive treatment in the matter of rights to life), but at least they took it seriously. They lived by it. They tried their best to do no harm.

And this in a country, remember, where 10,000 humans died every year from snakebite, almost a million more from malaria carried in the bites of mosquitoes. The black widow spider, compared to those fellow creatures, seems a harmless and innocent beast.

But personally I hold no brief for *ahimsa,* because I don't delude myself that it's even theoretically (let alone practically) possible. The basic processes of animal life, human or otherwise, do necessarily entail a fair bit of ruthless squashing and gobbling. Plants can sustain themselves on no more than sunlight and beauty and a hydroponic diet—but not we animals. I've only mentioned this Jainist ideal to suggest the range of possible viewpoints.

Modern philosophers of the "animal liberation" movement, most notably Peter Singer and Tom Regan, have proposed some other interesting answers to the same question. So have writers like Barry Lopez and Eugene Linden, and (by their example, as well as by their work) scientists like Jane Goodall and John Lilly and Dian Fossey. Most of the attention of each of these thinkers, though, has been devoted to what is popularly (but not necessarily by the thinkers themselves) considered the "upper" end of the "ladder" of life. To my mind, the question of appropriate relations is more tricky and intriguing—also more crucial in the long run, since this group accounts for most of the planet's species—as applied to the "lower" end, down there among the mosquitoes and worms and black widow spiders.

These are the extreme test cases. These are the alien species who experience human malice, or indifference, or tolerance, at its most automatic and elemental. To squash or not to squash? Mohandas Gandhi, whose own ethic of nonviolence owed much to *ahimsa,* was once asked about the propriety of an antimalaria campaign that involved killing mosquitoes with DDT, and he was careful to give no simple, presumptuous answer. These are the creatures whose treatment, by each of us, illuminates not just the strength of emotional affinity but the strength, if any, of principle.

But what is the principle? Pure *ahimsa,* as even Gandhi admitted, is unworkable. Vegetarianism is invidious. Anthropocen-
trism, conscious or otherwise, is smug and ruinously myopic.
What else? Well, I have my own little notion of one measure that
might usefully be applied in our relations with other species, and
I offer it here seriously despite the fact that it will probably sound
godawful stupid.

Eye contact.

Make eye contact with the beast, the Other, before you decide
upon action. No kidding, now, I mean get down on your hands
and knees right there in the vegetable garden, and look that snail
in the face. Lock eyes with that bull snake. Trade stares with the
carp. Gaze for a moment into the many-faceted eyes—the win-
dows to its soul—of the house fly, as it licks its way innocently
across your kitchen counter. Look for signs of embarrassment or
rancor or guilt. Repeat the following formula silently, like a man-
tra: "This is some mother's darling, this is some mother's child."
Then kill if you will, or if it seems you must.

I've been experimenting with the eye-contact approach for
some time myself. I don't claim that it has made me gentle or
holy or put me in tune with the cosmic hum, but definitely it has
been interesting. The hardest cases—and therefore I think the
most telling—are the spiders.

The face of a spider is unlike anything else a human will ever
see. The word "ugly" doesn't even begin to serve. "Grotesque"
and "menacing" are too mild. The only adequate way of commu-
nicating the effect of a spiderly countenance is to warn that it is
"very different," and then offer a photograph. This trick should
not be pulled on loved ones just before bedtime or when trying to
persuade them to accompany you to the Amazon.

The special repugnant power of the spider physiognomy derives, I think, from fangs and eyes. The former are too big and
the latter are too many. But the fangs (actually the fangs are only

terminal barbs on the *chelicerae,* as the real jaw limbs are called) need to be large, because all spiders are predators yet they have no pincers like a lobster or a scorpion, no talons like an eagle, no social behavior like a pack of wolves. Large clasping fangs armed with poison glands are just their required equipment for earning a living. And what about those eight eyes—big ones and little ones, arranged in two rows, all bugged-out and pointing every-whichway? (My wife the biologist offers a theory here: "They have an eye for each leg, like us—so they don't *step* in anything.") Well, a predator does need good eyesight, binocular focus, peripheral vision. Sensory perception is crucial to any animal that lives by the hunt and, unlike insects, arachnids possess no antennae. Beyond that, I don't know. I don't *know* why a spider has eight eyes.

I only know that, when I make eye contact with one, I feel a deep physical shudder of revulsion, and of fear, and of fascination; and I am reminded that the human style of face is only one accidental pattern among many, some of the others being quite drastically different. I remember that we aren't alone. I remember that we are the norm of goodness and comeliness only to ourselves. I wonder about how ugly I look to the spider.

The hundred baby black widows on my desk were too tiny for eye contact. They were too numerous, it seemed, to be gathered one by one into a pickle jar and carried to freedom in the backyard. I killed them all with a can of Raid. I confess to that slaughter with more resignation than shame, the jostling struggle for life and space being what it is. I can't swear I would do differently today. But there is this lingering suspicion that I squandered an opportunity for some sort of moral growth.

I still keep their dead and dried mother, and their vacated egg sac, in a plastic vial on an office shelf. It is supposed to remind me of something or other.

And the question continues to puzzle me: How should a human behave toward the members of other living species?

Last week I tried to make eye contact with a tarantula. This was a huge specimen, all hairy and handsomely colored, with a body as big as a hamster and legs the size of Bic pens. I ogled it through a sheet of plate glass. I smiled and winked. But the animal hid its face in distrust.

THINKING ABOUT
EARTHWORMS

An Unpopular Meditation
on Darwin's Silent Choir

Somewhere between the ages of thirty and forty each of us comes
to the shocking realization that a lifetime is not infinite. The
world is big and rich, options are many, but time is limited. Once
that dire truth has revealed itself, everything afterward becomes
a matter of highly consequential choices. Every hour of cello
practice is an hour that might have been spent rereading Dos-
toyevski, but wasn't; every day of honest work is a day of lost
skiing, and vice versa; every inclusion is also an exclusion, every
embracement is also a casting aside, every *do* is also a *didn't.*
Then presto: Time is up, and each *didn't* goes down on the scroll
as a *never did.* Yikes, why is he punishing us with this platitudi-
nous drivel? you may ask. It's because I've just spent the entire
first week of my thirty-ninth year thinking about earthworms.

Now I ask you to give the subject ten minutes. That figure
includes a small margin, I hope, for divagations concerning television, the Super Bowl, the philosophy of Teilhard de Chardin,
the late space shuttle *Challenger,* and other closely related matters, not least of which is the far-ranging curiosity of Charles
Darwin.

Darwin spent forty-four years of his life, off and on, thinking about earthworms. This fact isn't something they bother to tell you in freshman biology. Even Darwin himself seems to have harbored some ambivalence over the investment of time and attention. In an addendum to his autobiography, written not long before he died, he confided: "This is a subject of but small importance; and I know not whether it will interest any readers, but it has interested me." The interest had begun back in 1837, when he was just home from his voyage on the *Beagle,* and it endured until very near the end of his life. He performed worm-related experiments that stretched across decades. Finally in 1881 he wrote a book about earthworms, a book in which the words "evolution" and "natural selection" are not (unless I blinked and missed them) even mentioned. That book is titled *The Formation of Vegetable Mould, Through the Action of Worms, With Observations of Their Habits.* By "vegetable mould" he meant what today would be called humus, or simply topsoil. It was his last published work.

Darwin seems to have found something congenial about these animals. "As I was led to keep in my study during many months worms in pots filled with earth," he wrote, "I became interested in them, and wished to learn how far they acted consciously, and how much mental power they displayed." Among his typically methodical observations of wormish habits was the following: "Worms do not possess any sense of hearing. They took not the least notice of the shrill notes from a metal whistle, which was repeatedly sounded near them; nor did they of the deepest and loudest tones of a bassoon. They were indifferent to shouts, if care was taken that the breath did not strike them. When placed on a table close to the keys of a piano, which was played as loudly as possible, they remained perfectly quiet." It's an image to be inscribed on all human memory, I think, as an antidote to pomposity and aloofness: Charles Darwin, alone in his study with a tin whistle and a bassoon and a piano, trying to get a rise out of his worms. Under the category "Mental Qualities," he stated, as though regretfully: "There is little to be said on this head. We have seen that worms are timid." Later in the book, though, he described some experiments—designed to distinguish instinct, in their leaf-gathering behavior, from judgment—that inclined him to credit them with "a near approach to intelligence."

But what mainly concerned Darwin was the collective and cumulative impact of worms in the wild. On this count, he made large claims for them. He knew they were numerous, powerful, and busy. A German scientist had recently come up with the figure 53,767 as the average earthworm population on each acre of the land he was studying, and to Darwin this sounded about right for his own turf too. Every one of those 53,767 worms, he realized, spent much of its time swallowing. It swallowed dead plant material for its sustenance, and it swallowed almost anything else in its path (including tiny rock particles) as it burrowed. The rock particles were smashed even finer in the worm's gizzard, mixed with the plant material and the digestive juices in its gut, and passed out behind in the form of "castings." The castings contained enough natural glue to give them a nice crumb structure, characteristic of good soil, and were also biochemically ideal for nurturing vegetation. Collectively, over years and decades and centuries, this process transformed dead leaves and fractured rock into the famous and all-important "vegetable mould." But that wasn't all.

At least some of those species of earthworm had the habit of depositing their castings above ground. A worm would back tail-first out of its burrow and unload a neat castellated pile around the entrance. As a result, Darwin recognized, soil from a foot or more underground was steadily being carried up to the surface. In many parts of England, he figured, the worm population swallowed and brought up ten tons of earth each year on each acre of land. Earthworms therefore were not only creating the planet's thin layer of fertile soil; they were also constantly turning it inside out. They were burying old Roman ruins. They were causing the monoliths of Stonehenge to subside and topple. On sloping land, where rainwater and wind would sweep their castings away and down into valleys, they were making a huge contribution to erosion. No wonder Darwin concluded: "Worms have played a more important part in the history of the world than most persons would at first suppose."

His worm book sold well in the early editions. By one account, in fact, it was a greater commercial success for him than *The Origin of Species.* Nowadays the book is generally ignored by everyone except soil scientists—who themselves nod to it devoutly but don't seem to take its contents too seriously. Sometimes these scientists mention that Darwin rather overstated the role of worms while he underestimated such other soil organisms as bacteria, fungi, protozoa, and subterranean insects. *The Formation of Vegetable Mould, Through the Action of Worms* is nevertheless a readable volume, mild and affable and modest in tone, containing a few curious facts and some telling glimpses of the author's fastidious methodology. But the most interesting thing about the book, in my view, is simply that this particular man took the trouble to write it. At the time, evolution by natural selection was the hottest idea in science; yet Charles Darwin spent his last year of work thinking about earthworms.

And thank goodness he did. That sort of stubborn mental contrariety is as precious to our planet as worm castings. It is equally essential that some people *do* think about earthworms, at least sometimes, as it is that *not everyone* does. It is essential not for the worms' sake but for our own.

More and more in recent years, we are all thinking about the same things at the same time. Electromagnetic radiation is chiefly responsible; microwaves, macrowaves, dashing and dancing electrons unite us instantly and constantly with the waves of each other's brain. We can't step out into the yard without being bonked by a signal that has come caroming off some satellite, and when we step back inside, there's Dan Rather, ready with the day's subject for thought. One day we think about an explosion in the sky above Cape Canaveral. Another day we think about a gutshot pope. On a designated Sunday in January we gather in clusters to focus our thoughts upon the Super Bowl. Occasionally we ponder a matter of somewhat less consequence, like the early returns from the New Hampshire primary or the question of who shot J. R. Ewing. Late in the evening we think about what Ted Koppel thinks it's important we think about. Over large parts of the planet we think quite intently about the World Cup soccer final. My point is not that some of these subjects are trivial while others are undeniably and terrifyingly significant; my point is that we think about them together in great national (sometimes global) waves of wrinkling brows, and on cue. God himself has never summoned so much precisely synchronized, prayerful attention as Mary Lou Retton got for doing back flips. And maybe God is envious. Of course now He too has His own cable network.

The Jesuit philosopher and paleontologist Pierre Teilhard de Chardin gave a label to this phenomenon. He called it the *noosphere,* and he considered it just wonderful. In Teilhard's view, the noosphere (*noös* being Greek for mind, and the rest by analogy with lithosphere, biosphere, atmosphere) was the ultimate product of organic evolution, the culmination of all nature's progress toward man and perfection—a layer of pure homogenized mind enwrapping the Earth, hovering there above us as "the sphere of reflexion, of conscious invention, of the conscious unity of souls." It was prescient of him, I think, to have shaped this idea back at a time when even radio was an inestimable new toy. But in my heartfelt opinion, his enthusiasm was misguided. Too much "conscious unity of souls" is unhealthy, probably even pernicious. It yields polarized thought, in the same sense that a polarized filter yields polarized light: nice neat alignments of attention and interest (which is different from, but a step toward, unanimity of opinion), with everyone smugly in agreement that such-and-such matters are worth contemplation, and that the rest by implication are not. Such unity is a form of overall mental impoverishment. For just one particular instance, it tends to neglect earthworms.

You will have sensed by now that I am a self-righteous crank on this subject. I believe that unanimity is always a bad thing. The prospect of all five billion of us human beings getting our alpha waves into perfect sync appalls me. My own minuscule contribution to the quixotic battle—the battle against homogenization of mind, the battle to preserve a cacophonous disunity of souls, the hopeless fingers-in-ears campaign of abstention from the noosphere—lies chiefly in not owning a television.

Pitiful, I know. It sounds like the most facile sort of pseudointellectual snobbery, I know. It is backward and petulant, and I am missing lots of terrific nature documentaries on the high-minded channels, I know. It's grim work, but somebody's got to do it. Anyway, I am not at all opposed to television. I am merely opposed to the notion that *everybody* should be dutifully, simultaneously plugged in. Maybe someday, for some unforeseeable reason, society will have need of a person who has never seen, say, a video replay of the space shuttle explosion. If so, I'll be ready. It's a personal sacrifice that I've been quite willing to make.

On the other hand, so as not to sound too tediously righteous, I want to confess that I did watch the Super Bowl this year, on a friend's set, thereby merging for three hours my somnolent brain with those millions of somnolent others. It was a sublime waste of time, and I'm glad I did it. Next year I won't.

You yourself can join in the good fight without even unplugging your television. Just take a day or an hour each month to think carefully about something that nobody else deems worthy

of contemplation. Break stride. Wander off mentally. Pick a subject so perversely obscure that it can't help but have neglected
significance. If everyone else is thinking about the sad and highly
visible deaths of seven astronauts, think about the Scottsboro
Boys. If everyone else is thinking about the Super Bowl, think
about a quiet little story called "The Loneliness of the Long-
Distance Runner." If everyone else is busy despising Ferdinand
Marcos, devote a few minutes of loathing to Fulgencio Batista.
Or think about earthworms.

Think about the Australian species, *Megascolides australis,*
that grows ten feet long and as big around as a bratwurst. Think
about *Lumbricus terrestris,* familiar to soil scientists as the common European earthworm and to generations of American boy-
hood as the night crawler, nowadays gathered at night by professional pickers on Canadian golf courses and imported into the
U.S. for a total value of $13 million per year. Think about how
hard it is to tell front from rear, especially so since they can back
up. Think about the curious reproductive arrangement of earthworm species generally, hermaphroditic but not self-fertilizing,
so that each one during the act of mating provides sperm for its
partner's eggs while receiving back the partner's sperm for its
own eggs; now imagine having a full sister whose mother was
your father. Think about the fact that these animals can regener-
ate a lost head. Think about the formation of vegetable mould,
and the relentless swallowing, digesting, burrowing, and casting
off of waste by which earthworms topple and bury the monu-
ments of defunct civilizations while freshening the soil for new
growth. Think about how sometimes it's the little things that
turn the world inside out.

THE THING
WITH FEATHERS

Is It a Bird,
Is It a Dinosaur,
or Is It Much More?

For today, a brief verbal Rorschach: What is the thing with feathers?

Don't rush your answer. Take some time. Allow your mind to billow and glide. If you've already said "A bird, of course. A bird is the thing with feathers," your test results indicate a latent aptitude for work as a punch-press operator. The question is just possibly a good bit more complicated.

Hope, according to Emily Dickinson, is "the thing with feathers" that perches in the soul, singing a tune without words. Woody Allen disagrees. "How wrong Emily Dickinson was!" he has written in a published selection from the Allen notebooks. "Hope is not 'the thing with feathers.' The thing with feathers has turned out to be my nephew. I must take him to a specialist in Zurich." It can get highly confusing, as you see, and even more so when you consider that an international group of distinguished paleontologists convened during the summer of 1984 in the small town of Eichstätt, Bavaria, to haggle among themselves on the very same issue. What *is* the thing with feathers?

Those scientists, divided raucously on particulars, did have one point of consensus. They were all concerned with a creature called *Archaeopteryx.*

Archaeopteryx is simply the oldest thing with feathers that mankind has ever unearthed. It was an animal. It is known from just six fossil specimens. It lived about 160 million years ago, in the heyday of the dinosaurs. It was first discovered in the early years of the Darwinian revolution and played a crucial role in giving impetus to that revolution, yet it remains today one of the pivotal unsolved riddles of paleontology. It had a long bony tail, it had teeth, it had the skeletal anatomy of a small dinosaur—and it had feathers, exactly like those of a modern bird.

This much is indisputable, literally written in stone. Say anything more about *Archaeopteryx,* and you have taken a controversial position.

There is no question today, among paleontologists, that birds evolved originally from a line of reptilian ancestors. Skeletal anatomy alone is enough to show a close kinship between modern birds and certain primitive reptiles. But the intermediate stages in that transmogrification are rather more of a mystery. No one knew what sort of creature might have been the missing link between reptile and bird—until the discovery of *Archaeopteryx.*

The first *Archaeopteryx* specimen ever recognized was just the impression of a single feather, preserved with startling precision in a piece of limestone. It turned up in 1861 at a rock quarry near the Bavarian village of Solnhofen, not far from Eichstätt, and announced itself to the world like the portentous opening chord of an overture to a wild opera. It had defied the odds, that feather, captured with photographic fidelity in the same fine-grain limestone that made Solnhofen rock highly valued for lithographic printing. It was the size and shape of a primary feather from the wing of a pigeon, and one German scientist wrote of it blandly as evidence of a fossil bird. Then almost immediately there came a related find from the same area of Solnhofen limestone. This one was a full skeleton, thoroughly fledged with the same sort of feathers; the anatomy otherwise, though, seemed purely dinosaurian. It was dubbed *Archaeopteryx*, a reasonably safe formulation meaning "ancient wing."

The Origin of Species had been published just two years before, and the notion of a transitional form between reptiles and birds (between *any* two groups of creatures) was as provocative as any idea in European science. To the anti-Darwinists (mainly church-men and conservative scientists) *Archaeopteryx* had to be either a bird, period, or a reptile, period, or else it was some sort of sick-minded hoax. To the Darwinists it was precisely the sort of miss-ing-link evidence that could give dramatic support to their the-ory. What *is* the thing with feathers? The disputation began.

In 1877 a second complete *Archaeopteryx* was uncovered, again from the Solnhofen quarries. Evidently the animal had been fairly abundant in this area during the late Jurassic period, when those fine-grain limestone strata were being laid down. This second full specimen—preserved in a natural pose, showing ex-cellent detail on both bones and feathers—was recognized as a rare scientific treasure and snatched up for a museum in Berlin. One expert has said of it: "The Berlin *Archaeopteryx* may well be the most important natural history specimen in existence, per-haps comparable in value to the Rosetta stone." Maybe so, but the hieroglyphics in question here still haven't been conclusively deciphered.

Three more specimens have been found in this century, none nearly so graphic as the Berlin fossil, but all nonetheless precious. The second of those had actually been dug up back in 1855 (near Eichstätt, once again) and incorrectly identified for 113 years as a pterodactyl. The last showed only the faintest feather impres-sions, which were overlooked, and it spent two decades mistak-enly labeled as *Compsognathus*, which is a small dinosaur.

To say that *Archaeopteryx* is known from "just six fossil speci-mens" might be somewhat misleading. For such a delicate crea-ture, a species with small bones and fragile feathers that disappeared 160 million years ago, six decent specimens amounts to a lot. Thanks to a convergence of accidents—six individual deaths, occurring at just the right place and time to be preserved within fine-grain sediments, and later discovered largely because mankind had a commercial reason for excavating those same sediments—*Archaeopteryx* is exceptionally well represented within the fossil record. Between it and the next-oldest bird or bird-like fossil there stretches a gap of ten million years, and not nearly so much is known about that next-oldest relative. Disproportionally well documented, *Archaeopteryx* nevertheless (or maybe therefore) raises a disproportionate number of questions.

To paleontologists this creature is by now a familiar riddle. But, familiar or not, it's still very much a riddle.

How did flight begin among birds?

Why did it begin?

Were the dinosaurs warm-blooded or cold-blooded?

Is a chicken more closely related to a crocodile or to *Tyrannosaurus rex*?

Did feathers come into existence for aerodynamic reasons or as insulation to keep body heat in—or maybe to serve as adjustable reflectors that kept heat *out*?

Were the predecessors of birds runners or tree climbers? Were they jumpers or were they gliders?

Did warm-bloodedness evolve two separate times—once in our mammal lineage and once among birds—or did we all inherit that handy attribute from a frisky two-legged dinosaur?

Did the dinosaurs ever really go extinct? Or do they survive among us today, in discreet and more humble forms such as *Turdus migratorius,* the robin? Are feathers merely the means that allowed dinosaurs, while becoming smaller, to stay warm?

If a bird can fly, why can't I?

* * *

To each of those questions the *Archaeopteryx* evidence is central. But that evidence is as resonantly ambiguous as a good haiku poem. Read from it what you will. Prove with it what you can. That's what the scientists have been doing with it for a century and a quarter. And it isn't their fault that *Archaeopteryx* lies there, sphinx-like, on its beige limestone slabs, granting many answers but no certainty.

The runners-versus-climbers controversy is a good example. From the time of Darwin right up through the Eichstätt conference in 1984, this has been one of the most fundamental dichotomies within the range of interpretations of *Archaeopteryx*. Some paleontologists have insisted that *Archaeopteryx* evolved from a tree-climbing dinosaur, which jumped from its high perches, then later developed gliding ability, then finally flew. Others have argued that *Archaeopteryx* came from the ground up, a fleet bipedal runner that stretched out its arms, leaping and sailing, until it developed the wing power to get airborne. These two schools of opinion know themselves respectively as the *arborealists* and the *cursorialists*. If you are an arborealist on the subject of *Archaeopteryx*, your professional attitude inclines toward polite but dogmatic scorn for all misguided cursorialists. And vice versa.

The arborealists point out that flight of some kind or another, from modest gliding to powered flapping, has evolved separately no less than sixteen times among the nonavian vertebrate animals —that is, in four distinct groups of flying fishes, in one frog, in two groups of extant reptiles as well as the pterosaurs, in two kinds of flying squirrels, in bats, and in three kinds of marsupials, not to mention a few other weird little kamikaze mammals that neither you nor I have ever heard of. Among those sixteen instances, all but the flying fish and maybe the pterosaurs are known to have gotten their start as tree climbers. The force of statistical probability, as well as the force of gravity, seems to favor the arborealist side.

So what? say the cursorialists. Evolution is not roulette. And besides, they say, the case of feather-assisted bird flight is obviously a drastic exception to the general pattern—peregrine falcons and hummingbirds are spectacularly proficient, after all, while those poor cloddish "flying" frogs and lizards and squirrels are still careening down half out of control and slamming themselves into tree trunks. Furthermore, say the cursorialists, it is hard to imagine *Archaeopteryx* doing much tree climbing with those long primary feathers sticking way out past its foreleg claws. Try opening your car door while wearing an outfielder's mitt on each hand, and you'll appreciate the problem.

To all of which the arborealists, of course, have ready rebuttals.

The first of the arborealists was none other than Othniel C. Marsh, a preeminent figure in American paleontology during the nineteenth century, and one of the two principals behind the great wild dinosaur wars that were fought out between rival collectors in frontier Montana and Wyoming. (The other paleontological warlord was Edwin Drinker Cope, and it's a bizarre story all to itself.) Concerning the evolution of flight, Marsh argued: "In the early arboreal birds, which jumped from branch to branch, even rudimentary feathers on the forelimbs would be an advantage as they would tend to lengthen a downward leap or break the force of a fall." Arguing the other view, among the first of the cursorialists, was Franz Baron Nopcsa von Felso-Szilvas, an elusive but unmistakably demented Hungarian who happens to be my own personal favorite in the paleontological pantheon. Baron Nopcsa was a brilliant prodigy who made significant contributions toward the study of *Archaeopteryx* until certain other interests pulled him aside toward Albania, motorcycle touring, and death.

Nopcsa was born in Transylvania, always a good sign. He published his first paleontological monograph as a university freshman, and thereafter turned into an arrogant snot. Somehow he became infatuated with the geography and ethnography of Albania. He learned the dialects, amassed a huge library of books about the country, made many visits; eventually he offered himself for the position of King of Albania, based on what he considered his surpassing competence for the job, but the Hapsburg overlords picked someone else. During World War I he served the Austro-Hungarian Army as a spy along the Romanian border, letting his hair grow and dressing as a Romanian peasant. He spoke the languages. He passed. Much later, when he was bored and impoverished, his baronial lands having been confiscated in the peace settlement, he took off on a long motorcycle ramble with his male lover, an Albanian named Bajazid. Finally, in April 1933, for reasons we'll never know, Nopcsa came to the end of his tether. He slipped Bajazid a mickey, shot him through the head, then put the pistol to himself. But before he died—in fact, it was way back in 1907—Baron Nopcsa had published a paper titled "Ideas on the Origin of Flight." The central datum was of course *Archaeopteryx*.

Nopcsa wrote: "We may quite well suppose that birds originated from bipedal long-tailed cursorial reptiles which during running oared along in the air by flapping their free anterior extremities. By gradually increasing in size, the enlarged but perhaps horny hypothetical scales [would] . . . ultimately develop to actual feathers; this epidermic cover would also raise the temperature of the body, and thus help to increase the mental and bodily activities of these rapacious forms."

Nopcsa was just deranged enough (well, maybe more than enough) to be a bold, original thinker. In suggesting an earthbound *Archaeopteryx* that flapped its feathered arms to help itself gain speed as it ran, he had broken through a basic assumption in the debate over whether feathers evolved first for insulation or for gliding—the assumption that, if those earliest feathers served *any* aerodynamic purpose, the purpose must have been flight. But ground travel too involves aerodynamics. Ask any designer of racing cars; ask anyone who rides touring motorcycles.

For three quarters of a century Nopcsa's view was dismissed as nonsensical. Ground-travel aerodynamics seemed an unlikely precursor to feathered flight since, as soon as the animal made that next little evolutionary leap, becoming airborne, it would have lost all the running leverage from its legs; losing that leverage, it would have achieved a net *decrease* instead of a net increase in speed, and therefore also a net decrease in its prospects of survival. The gap between feather-assisted running and feather-assisted flying seemed evolutionarily unbridgeable. But now again the notion of ground-travel aerodynamics is being given some careful thought.

One of the hot new ideas on the subject, as of the 1984 conference in Eichstätt, is that maybe *Archaeopteryx* used its arm feathers as *rudders,* for changing direction erratically as it ran along. Assisted by aerodynamic rudders, this little beast might have streaked out a wild zigzag path across the floor of Cretaceous forests, escaping from bigger and faster predators.

The cursorialists at Eichstätt were intrigued. The arborealists were not swayed. The disputation goes on.

What is the thing with feathers? It might be a dinosaur dressed for warmth in a chicken suit. It might be the earliest bird, hot-blooded and flapping its way from tree to tree. It might be your nephew or mine or Woody Allen's, in need of a visit to Zurich. It is a mystifying cross between fowl and reptile, a chimera sculpted in fossil stone—an oxymoronic creature that actually lived and died, rather like Baron Nopcsa himself.

It perches on the soul, this thing, singing a tune without words.

We call it *Archaeopteryx.* The name is Latin, standing for: *Thank God there are some riddles we can't solve.*

NASTY HABITS

An African Bedbug
Buggers the Proof-by-Design

A fellow named Duane T. Gish was in town here last week, playing his practiced role in a debate on the subject of "scientific creationism" versus evolutionary theory. I didn't go. It was dollar night at the movies. But now I regret having missed a precious opportunity, since just the next day, in my random reading, I came upon an account of the startling deportment of the hemipteran insect *Xylocaris maculipennis,* an animal that demands pondering by creationists and evolutionists alike. A question-and-answer period followed the debate, but with me off watching *Peggy Sue Got Married* and pushing popcorn into my face, the important *Xylocaris maculipennis* question never got asked of perhaps the one human being most qualified to attempt an answer. Namely, Duane T. Gish.

Duane T. Gish, as it turns out, is a famous (some would say, notorious) man, vice president and leading spokesman of the Institute for Creation Research, which is a fundamentalist think tank based in Santee, California. He travels across America arguing the creationist viewpoint—that the Earth is only 10,000 years old, that evolution is an atheistic delusion, that the myriad types of plants and animals which some of us think of as evolved species were all in fact created individually by God—and according to most reports he is a glib and effective debater, a man of some charm, good with crowds and capable of making fools of opponents who underestimate his intelligence. He holds a doctorate in biochemistry and seems possessed, if the photos do justice, of a bad toupee. A *country slicker,* is what you might call him. *Xylocaris maculipennis* is an African bedbug. There had to be more than blind coincidence involved in bringing this man and this insect both into my purview during the same week, but the precious opportunity nevertheless slipped past me. Dr. Gish was packed and gone to the next town before I could solicit his thoughts concerning *X. maculipennis* and the Proof-by-Design.

What I refer to as the Proof-by-Design is a venerable piece of logic, lately refurbished by the creationists. One of its earliest and most influential formulations was by John Ray, an English naturalist of the seventeenth century who did pioneering work in botany and then, in 1691, published a book called *The Wisdom of God Manifested in the Works of the Creation.* Ray's argument in this book was (as the title declaims) that the elaborate design of the natural world—the matching of form to function within living creatures, the harmonious intermeshing of creatures with each other—proved the necessary existence of an omnipotent, benevolent Creator. A century later Linnaeus himself (often thought of as the first hardheaded taxonomic biologist) voiced the same idea. Right up to the time of Darwin, this view of nature was cited by both naturalists and theologians as cogent evidence for the sort of avuncular, dependable God we could all love and admire. According to one version: "This perfect Unity, Order, Wisdom, and Design, by which every Individual is necessarily related to, and made a dependent Part of the Whole, necessarily supposes and implies a universal, designing Mind, an all-powerful Agent, who has contrived, adjusted, and disposed the Whole into such Order, Uniformity, concordant Beauty and Harmony, and who continues to support, govern, and direct the

Whole." Clearly the cheerful sport who wrote that sentence had never heard of *Xylocaris maculipennis.*

Now the same Proof-by-Design is back in fashion among creationists, brought up to date for a new post-Darwinian purpose. These days the argument is used to prove, not merely that God does exist, but also that evolution doesn't.

Consider the cleaner wrasse, for instance. This little fish is the hero of an article titled "Nature's Challenges to Evolutionary Theory," published by Duane T. Gish's own outfit, the Institute for Creation Research. As any marine biologist knows, a cleaner wrasse makes its living by swimming into the opened mouths of much larger, predaceous fish and picking away parasites that have infested the soft mouth tissues. The bigger fish not only permit this to happen; they come to the stations where these little wrasses have set up shop and literally wait in line to be serviced. When the cleaning is done, the little fish is allowed, gratefully, to swim safely back out of the jaws of death. In the view of the ICR, this symbiotic interaction is too complex and too improbable to have arisen by evolution. "The case for creation will be evident in certain special ecological relationships like cleaning symbiosis," we are told. "The Christian recognizes that such processes reflect the continuing care by which God faithfully upholds His creation."

Another big favorite is the bombardier beetle. Duane T. Gish himself has been known to cite this manifestation of God's hands-on involvement in the designing of nature. The bombardier beetle is a small coleopteran of the genus *Brachinus* that carries a fancy system of chemical self-defense. Inside its abdomen are two chambers, one holding certain enzymes, the other containing a gumbo of hydrogen compounds. When threatened the beetle internally mixes these two fluids, producing a hot caustic potion of benzoquinones that explodes forth, at over two hundred degrees F., from a pair of anal spigots. The spigots can be rotated voluntarily, enabling the beetle to aim its vapor blast straight into the eyes of a hungry frog. Make my day, frog. To Duane T. Gish this stalwart little insect represents nothing less than the wisdom of God manifested—directly—in the works of nature and refutes that farfetched evolutionary alternative. Dr. Gish has even publicly challenged an eminent coleopterist to explain "how an ordinary beetle could evolve into a bombardier beetle. I want to know how natural selection has done that." The coleopterist has responded, in plausible detail, but Dr. Gish doesn't seem to have been listening. And last year the ICR publishing house produced a children's book titled *Bomby, the Bombardier Beetle,* devoted to showing that Bomby's physiology, too clever for evolution, can only be the product of an individual act of creative ingenuity by You Know Who.

At this point I can't help remembering a quote from the evolutionist and philosopher Yogi Berra. Jim Piersall, before stepping into the batter's box, scratched out a talismanic cross on the dirt near home plate. Yogi said: "Why don't you just let Him watch the game?"

Enough frivolity. Let's talk about bedbugs.

It can be reasonably argued that *all* bedbugs are disreputable. These are sly little wingless insects, with flattened bodies that allow them to hide in tiny crevices, mouthparts suited to puncturing and sucking, and a taste for protein-rich meals of blood. They are fast on their feet and sneaky; they stay out of sight during daylight. Two related families, equally unsavory in character, are together generally known by the "bedbug" label, though only a few species actually lurk among funky mattresses to stage their blood raids against humans. Other species either parasitize bats, birds, or various larger mammals, or else prey upon mites and small insects. The association with bats is especially strong, and some scientists speculate that it's because the bedbug group developed from cave-dwelling ancestors, vermin that prowled the guano piles hunting for insect prey and then eventually transferred their attentions to the red-blooded mammals dangling above. *Cimex lectularius* is the most famous species, the common bedbug that has been fervently hated by mankind for hundreds of years. Back in eighteenth-century England, *C. lectularius* provided work for what may have been the first professional exterminators, including a family named Tiffin whose slogan was "May the Destroyers of Peace be destroyed by us, Tiffin and Son, Bug Destroyers to Her Majesty and the Royal Family." An interesting beast with a noble history, *C. lectularius,* but the most remarkable thing about it is its method of copulation. This kinky procedure is known in the euphemistic scientific jargon as *traumatic insemination.* In language more vivid but no less precise, it's a combination of stabbing and rape.

The male of *C. lectularius* is armed with a long sharp penis. Instead of linking genitals with the female, though, he uses this organ to puncture her in the abdomen. He then ejaculates into her body cavity, and the sperm travels through her bloodstream to special receptacles, where she can store it until her time of ovulation. The puncture wound heals over, and all is fine. To you and me this may sound like the worst sort of S&M, but to bedbugs it's just a reproductive strategy that has proven successful over many generations.

Why should traumatic insemination be necessary? The answer to that, evidently, is something called the *mating plug,* another bizarre reproductive strategy seen among some insects, worms, reptiles, and even a few species of mammal. By means of a mating plug, composed of glutinous secretions from his own body, the male of certain species manages, after having mated with a female, to literally glue her genital tract closed. This prevents her from mating with other males, and thereby increases his own relative reproductive success. Males of some roundworm species glue the females shut, after mating, in exactly this way. So do males among ground squirrels and moles. The traumatic insemination practiced by *C. lectularius,* biologists guess, arose as a way of circumventing that sort of mating plug.

But hang on, it goes further. Now we come to the variant practiced by *Xylocaris maculipennis.* This libertine creature (for news of which I am indebted to a fascinating new book called *A Natural History of Sex* by the Canadian biologist Adrian Forsyth) is a close relative to the common bedbug, but its own special fame derives from taking traumatic insemination one step beyond. Instead of just stabbing-rape, *X. maculipennis* practices homosexual stabbing-rape. The males puncture and inseminate other males. In fact a male of *X. maculipennis* may be thus assaulted even *while* he is copulating with a female.

No, I am not inventing this stuff from my own depraved imagination—but if you don't believe me and Adrian Forsyth, you can consult a monograph in the journal *Science,* which adds the interesting information: "After homosexual rape in the anthocorid bug *Xylocaris maculipennis,* the sperm of the rapist enters the vas deferens of the victim and is used by the victim during copulation." The punctured male serves as a proxy, in other words, a genetic courier, delivering the sperm of his attacker on to the next female with whom he himself mates.

To an evolutionist, that bit of genetic advantage for the rapist might explain why such behavior exists. To a creationist, though, the whole subject must be inconvenient. Unlike the world's bombardier beetles and cleaner wrasses, *X. maculipennis* would seem to lend itself poorly to the Proof-by-Design.

The same ICR publishing house that brought us *Bomby* has served (by one account) as distributor of a tract titled "God's Plan for Insects"—and for that matter another called "Unhappy Gays"—but I strongly doubt that either of those comes to grips with the phenomenon of homosexual rape among bedbugs. If *X. maculipennis* is another instance of God's wisdom made manifest in the works of creation, I suspect that the sort of god manifested is not the one Duane T. Gish wants.

My own instinct is to agree with Yogi Berra. If God does exist, He or She is probably patient enough to take the long view.

STALKING THE
GENTLE PIRANHA

*An Intimate Link Between
Amazon Fishes and Trees*

To get there you follow the Rio Aguarico downstream out of the
Andes, past a petroleum boom town called Lago Agrio where the
vultures congregate by hundreds over the municipal dump, and
when the last cruising vulture disappears from view behind forest
canopy at a bend in the river, you will find yourself surrounded
by unspoiled Amazon jungle. The oil companies and the timber
cutters and the would-be cattle barons haven't gotten quite this
far, quite yet. In the treetops will be toucans and monkeys; on a
snag near the bank you might, with luck, see a basking anaconda.
To go where you are headed you will be traveling, of necessity, by
dugout canoe. If it happens to be a long sturdy log of a boat with
a 55-horse Evinrude mounted on the rear, the downriver leg of
the journey will take only a couple of days. The Rio Aguarico is a
broad shallow river that flows caramel-brown with suspended
sediment—same color and consistency as the upper Missouri
during spring runoff—but the Zabalo, its tributary, is narrow and
deep and black. The blackness signals dissolved acids, steeped
from rotting vegetation or leached from soils in the swampy lowland forest that the Zabalo, so slowly, drains. The mouth of the
Zabalo is where your real adventure begins. You turn there and
ease off on the Evinrude, heading upstream through a winding

jungle tunnel like Marlow in search of Kurtz. Except that you yourself are merely in search of a fish dinner.

The idea is that the diner will be you and the role of entree will fall to the fish, though the reverse is also a possibility. This little blackwater stream, the Zabalo, is full of eager piranha.

Your guide, if he is a good one, will inform you that the Zabalo is no place for a noontime swim. Better to wait until you are back on the Aguarico, where the worst to expect is that you might step on a stingray in the shallows. For that matter, today on the Zabalo you'll want to refrain from so much as dangling a hand overboard.

Our own guide for the trip was a young man named Randy Borman, and he was a very good one. The son of missionary parents from the U.S., he had been raised in a small Cofan Indian village just downriver from Lago Agrio, where he blossomed into the Huckleberry Finn of the upper Amazon. He was fluent in the Cofan language, adept in their traditional skills of jungle subsistence, and pragmatically grateful for that Evinrude at the back of his forty-foot dugout. He had just enough American hellion in him to drive the canoe like it was a souped-up '59 Dodge. As the Zabalo narrowed down tighter, and our passage upstream seemed blocked by fallen trees that lay floating across the channel, Randy would merely back the canoe off to a distance, then crank up his outboard to full throttle and charge ahead, planing out, vaulting the boat and a dozen white-knuckled passengers over each log like it was a water-ski jump at Coral Gables. He made it look easy, he even made it look sensible—but if Randy hadn't lifted his propeller clear at just the right moment, we would have been paddling home with palm branches.

Finally came a log barrier too high for even the most reckless canoe jockey, so we made a lunch camp there on the bank. Hand lines were brought out, as well as a couple of fishhooks roughly the same size and gauge as the bend on a coat hanger. Randy balanced his way barefoot out on the barrier log to a spot in midstream, two feet above the blackwater surface of the Zabalo. He was joined there by his compadre Lorenzo, a shy Cofan man who wore a red feather through his nasal septum on formal occasions and a baseball cap reading "Oklahoma Sooners" when he was in mufti. Lorenzo was chief petty officer on this voyage, and a master of Amazon hand-line fishing. Then those two were joined on the balance-beam log by me, an incurable fool for angling of any sort.

The bait of choice was large chunks of hard salami. It released savory oils into the water and if you gave it a bit of action—some twitches and jerks, like the spasms of a small wounded fish—all the better. The first piranha to strike bit the hook in half.

So far this was not much like casting a dry fly to snooty trout on a Montana spring creek. My own touch was slow and inept. In truth, I was preoccupied with keeping my balance on that log —to set the hook on a fish and then somersault backward into the Zabalo would have seemed a hollow triumph. Lorenzo and Randy knew their craft, though, and before long they had hauled in three lunker piranha, each one as large as a flattened football, each one snapping its jaws maniacally at every finger or toe that came near. After three fish like that in ten minutes, I tiptoed carefully back to dry land.

That evening, along with our stewed caiman, we ate roast piranha. They were bony but delicious. I saved the lower jaw from one of those fish, and it sits here on the desk before me now. The teeth are pyramidal, each with a sharp point and a razor-like cutting edge. Perfect for clipping away mouthfuls of flesh from the side of a fish or a mammal—and perhaps, as we'll see, surprisingly well suited to another function too.

I tell this whole story because several matters of science underlie it—the least interesting of which is that piranha, as advertised, can be dangerous little creatures with an eclectic palate for meat. I knew that before seeing it so vividly demonstrated, and you know it too. More fascinating, and more significant, is the network of ecological relations connecting four separate elements of this vignette. That network of improbable connections has only lately been discovered by science. The four elements are: certain piranha species found in blackwater rivers like the Zabalo, subsistence fishermen like Lorenzo, certain tree species of the lowland jungle, and floodplain development projects like the one at Lago Agrio.

The forest and the fishes turn out to be more intimately related, in parts of Amazonia, than biologists had realized.

For a long period each year the lowland forest throughout much of the Amazon basin is covered by floodwater, in some places up to forty feet deep. Depending upon the area, the water may remain there from two to ten months. This cycle of drastic but regular flooding is the result of geologic and meteorological conditions that are not duplicated on any other continent. The ecological consequences of that flood cycle, which has repeated itself annually over millions of years, seem also to be unique on the planet.

To begin with, a large portion of the Amazon basin is extremely flat. From the Peruvian border to the Atlantic, the river drops only about 250 feet. (In the northern Rockies, for comparison, a whitewater river might drop as far within four miles.) There are exceptions to that overall Amazon flatness, of course— most notably the Andes. North of the main trunk of the river rises another formation, a modestly elevated area known as the Guianan Shield, and to the south is a similar uplift called the Brazilian Shield. Lying in among these three zones of high ground is the great Amazon floodplain. Rainfall is prodigious throughout the entire drainage, ranging between about sixty and one hundred and twenty inches per year. In consequence, the Amazon river system contains one fifth of the total amount of river water on Earth. So much water in a rush to the sea, so much flatness, and the ineluctable result is flooding. Every year, during the wet season, roughly 30,000 square miles of the Brazilian Amazon are covered with standing water.

This land is known to ecologists as the flooded forest, and to rural Brazilians as *igapó*. Brazilian fishermen, in particular, have good reason to be familiar with *igapó*.

Over the epochs the plant species of the flooded forest have had to adapt themselves to this regularly recurrent inundation. They now live semiaquatic lives. Seedlings, saplings, and shrubs must—and do—survive being totally submerged for months of every year. Full-grown trees resist drowning despite having their roots and lower trunks covered; some species have developed special respiratory roots that top out above the flood level, like cypress knees in a Georgia swamp. But coping with floodwater itself is not the only problem those trees face. They must also cope with seed-eating fish.

During every wet season fish in great number and variety invade the flooded forest, searching for food. They come chiefly from nutrient-poor blackwater rivers, like the Zabalo, and from other streams so impoverished of minerals and small aquatic organisms that no real food chain can be supported; they come, hungry and desperate, to feed on the seeds and fruit that fall from those *igapó* trees. Feasting voraciously, they build up fat reserves to help carry them through the rest of the year. In some fish species the seeds and fruit taken during flood time may account for almost their total annual sustenance. And of course these fish, like the trees, have in the passing of time adapted themselves especially to this way of life. A delicate and mutually satisfactory balance seems to have developed.

An ecologist named Michael Goulding, after two years of field-work along the Rio Madeira, a major Amazon tributary in western Brazil, has produced the first broad study (*The Fishes and the Forest: Explorations in Amazonian Natural History*) of this interrelationship in the flooded forest. The featured players in Goulding's study are a group of fish known as the characins, a highly diversified and successful clan that numbers up to a thousand species in Amazon waters. Included among the seed-eating characins is a species called the *tambaqui,* one of the largest fish found in the Amazon and possibly the single most important source of protein for the region's human population. Also included, unexpectedly, are some of the piranhas.

Tambaqui are seed predators of huge appetite. They migrate into the flooded forest and gather in crowds beneath their favorite food-furnishing species, the rubber tree *Hevea spruceana.* Like most tree species in the Amazon, *H. spruceana* grows not in clusters or groves but as widely separated individuals, surrounded by other tree species yet with a large distance between each *spruceana.* Consequently, a whole gang of tambaqui may simultaneously address themselves to a single *spruceana* tree. They could conceivably eat every seed that it drops. To crush the hard nut walls of those seeds, tambaqui have evolved large jaws and strong, broad, molar-like teeth. They crunch up the *spruceana* seeds (which are about as tough as Brazil nuts) and swallow the nut shells as well as the seed tissue—though only the seed tissue gives them any nutrition. A single gorged tambaqui, weighing thirty pounds, might carry two pounds of ground-up seeds in its stomach. That's like you or I tucking away twelve pounds of peanuts, shells and all, in the course of an afternoon ball game.

The seed-eating piranhas are a bit more fastidious, and it seems to be precisely those pointed, razor-edge teeth that make such fastidiousness possible.

Even the most notorious flesh-eating piranhas—for instance, that large species commonly known as the black piranha—evidently move up into the flooded forest on a seasonal search for food. They aren't necessarily there for the seeds. In the *igapó* these flesh-eaters continue to function as secondary consumers, preying upon other fish, insects, occasionally a bird or a mammal or any other animal that might inhabit the forest waters or be so unlucky as to fall in. Black piranha do seem to be omnivorous rather than strictly carnivorous, opportunistic enough to make seeds and fruit a small fraction of their diet when those foods are easily available. But the piranhas that specialize in seed-eating, though closely related, are distinct.

Michael Goulding has identified at least two species of piranha —*Serrasalmus serrulatus* and *Serrasalmus striolatus*—that live mainly on a diet of seeds. Each of these species retains jaw and tooth structures almost identical to those seen in its infamous, flesh-eating cousins. *Serrulatus* and *striolatus* merely put those structures to different use. According to Goulding: "Piranhas shell the nuts they eat and ingest only the soft seed contents. . . . After the nut wall is broken, the endosperm contents are removed and the shell is discarded. By doing this the piranha does not fill its stomach and intestines with material that cannot be digested but that will take up space. The sharp teeth of piranhas allow them to masticate the soft seed contents into small bits that are usually of nearly equal size." By slicing through the nut wall and rejecting it, eating only the seed tissue itself (and ignoring also the fleshy fruits in which some *igapó* trees wrap their seeds), the piranha maximize their nutritional benefit from each belly-load of food. It is a delicacy of appetite that, during the lean times when no seeds are falling, when the fish must live off stored fat, could make the difference for survival.

Take away those floodplain trees, though, and survival becomes far more problematic.

Timbering, slash-and-burn agriculture, clearing away floodplain forests with the notion of pasturing cattle or planting rice or for other development projects intended to make the jungle "productive" or "habitable" by our civilized standards—all these represent attacks not only on the lowland tree communities but also on the fish species that feed among them. And by Michael

Goulding's estimate, those seed- and fruit-eating species account for something like seventy-five percent of all the fish sold at markets in Manaus and other cities of the basin. Since fish are the primary source of animal protein for the human population there —not just for canny fishermen like Lorenzo, not just for tribes like the Cofan, but throughout both backcountry and urban Amazonia—this whole chain of interdependence is crucial by any standard.

Remove the trees, and you can expect the fish to disappear. Kill off the fish, and likewise some of those tree species (the ones that depend on fish for dispersing their seeds) may not survive. Contrary to common misconception, the soils from which grow the Amazon jungle are very poor, and the rivers draining those soils are also therefore infertile. So the fish that spend half their lives in those rivers depend utterly on the manna that falls in the forest, and on the floods that carry them to it.

It's just another demonstration of what we already know. The great jungle ecosystems of Amazonia are not a *symptom* of the region's richness. They *are* that richness. Wreck them, and you wreck everything.

SEE NO EVIL

*The Fragile Truce
Between Man and Scorpion*

Allow me to confess an invidious personal bias: I don't trust any
animal with more than six legs and more than two eyes. No
rational explanation for this, it's just a cringe reflex from the
murkiest subconscious, but there you are. Six and two. I go
queasy with terror and disgust whenever confronted with a beast
who flouts those magic limits. Six and two. Octopuses are suspect
but acceptable. Insects, however bizarre, are fine. Snakes are
among my favorite living things—beautiful, sleek, unadorned,
binocular. A dizzying wave of repulsion passes over me, on the
other hand, at the mere glimpse of a color photograph of a tarantula. One, two, three, four, five, six, seven, gack, eight—and *then*
the legs. Am I alone or does anyone else experience this neurosis?
Have you ever looked a black widow spider in the face? Poison
isn't the problem; a rattlesnake has poison, yet a rattlesnake is
merely handsome and dangerous. Hideousness is the problem. I
know it's subjective, I know it's unfair. But a creature with that
many legs and eyes, Judas, you just never know what it might be
getting ready to do. One on one, it already has you outnumbered.
Spiders are bad enough. Consider, though, the scorpion.

My own heartfelt conviction is that scorpions are perhaps the
most drastically, irredeemably repulsive group of animals on the

face of the Earth, even including toy poodles. Maybe that's part of what makes them so interesting.

Scorpions violate the six-and-two rule flagrantly: four pairs of walking legs, one pair of pincers, one pair of leg-like appendages modified to serve as jaws, another pair that are hidden beneath the abdomen like landing gear and perform some still-mysterious sensory function—which makes fourteen limbs altogether—plus anywhere from zero to twelve eyes, yipe, in most species eight, arranged in three widely spaced clusters like Cinerama cameras. The mere listing makes me sweat. And as if that weren't enough, they also carry a nasty hypodermic stinger hanging overhead on the end of a long tail. Scorpions are more cluttered with obnoxiously useful hardware than a Swiss Army knife.

They travel under cover of darkness. They prey on insects and spiders, as well as the occasional small lizard or mouse. They kill people too—surprisingly many in some countries—though only while defending themselves, or by mistake. A scorpion drops from the thatched roof of a house into a baby's crib, a young child runs barefoot through a garden, an adult carelessly picks up a piece of firewood, and whammo. In Mexico, at least until recently, more than a thousand humans died each year from scorpion stings. Most of those victims were kids. Another 69,000 Mexicans annually survive a sting that is at least bad enough to report. In Brazil the death rate for young children stung by scorpions is almost one in five, and a single Brazilian city recorded a hundred fatalities in a year. Algeria is another zone of high jeopardy, as are Egypt, Jordan, Turkey, and Trinidad. Scorpions can be found nearly everywhere in the warm latitudes, jungle and mountain terrain as well as desert, but among different species there is wide variation in the potency of the venom.

Some venoms merely cause local swelling and pain. Others attack the nervous system, resulting in high pulse rate, irregular breathing, feelings of fright or excitement, impaired vision, vomiting, and a range of other symptoms of which the final, if it comes to that, is complete respiratory failure. Death by suffocation, out there under the clear equatorial sky.

J. L. Cloudsley-Thompson, a British zoologist who spent part of his career as a museum keeper in the Sudan, described the whole baleful sequence: "First, a feeling of tightness develops in the throat so that the victim tries to clear his throat of an imaginary phlegm. The tongue develops a feeling of thickness and speech becomes difficult. The victim next becomes restless and there may be slight, involuntary twitching of the muscles. Small children at this stage will not be still: Some attempt to climb up the wall or the sides of their cot. A series of sneezing spasms is accompanied by a continuous flow of fluid from nose and mouth which may form a copious froth. Occasionally the rate of heartbeat is considerably increased. Convulsions follow, the arms are flailed about and the extremities become quite blue before death occurs." This progression of symptoms, he says, closely resembles poisoning with strychnine.

Cloudsley-Thompson might be talking about a sting from *Androtonus australis,* the fearsome North African species said to have venom as toxic as a cobra's—but he isn't. He's talking about an American scorpion called *Centruroides sculpturatus.* Most infamous of the forty species found in the southern United States, *C. sculpturatus* is familiarly known as the bark scorpion, from its habit of hiding beneath loose and fallen pieces of tree bark. During one twenty-year period it accounted for sixty-four deaths in just the state of Arizona.

The Cloudsley-Thompson scenario and that last statistic, though, may both be unduly alarming. *C. sculpturatus* is quite common in Arizona, and many people are stung by it without suffering any harrowing effects. One of those victims, Steve Prchal of the Arizona-Sonora Desert Museum near Tucson, describes the experience this way: "Take a sharp needle and jab it into your hand. Hold a match or a lighter to it for a couple hours. Then add the needles-and-pins sensation you have when a foot falls asleep. That's what a bark scorpion sting feels like." Evidently the reaction can range anywhere from modest discomfort to horribleawful death, depending upon the body size and general health of the person stung, as well as other obscure factors, including luck. Best to steer clear of scorpion habitat, then, when you feel especially frail or unlucky.

Steve Prchal got his sting during a family camping trip, five minutes after having warned the other family members to be careful of scorpions. He reached for a boat cushion that had been drying on top of a bush. Whammo. That pattern seems to be typical. But considering both the number of scorpions and the number of people at large in the state of Arizona, sting incidents don't happen nearly so often as they might. What makes scorpions a threat to humanity is no special bellicosity on the part of the scorpions but the fact that, because of their shy inconspicuousness, you don't see them until it's too late.

They hide during the day, under bark or in rocky crevices or burrowed down into the sand, emerging nocturnally to hunt. They are discreet. If you have ever lain down in a sleeping bag on the warm Arizona earth, you have probably had a closer encounter with these creatures than you realized. Still, on visual evidence you might well conclude that they aren't really there. Vivid remedy for any such happy illusion can be derived, it turns out, from another strange scorpion attribute: Under ultraviolet illumination, they glow in the dark. They fluoresce. Shine a black-light beam on them and (due to photochemical properties of the scorpion integument about which little seems to be known) they reflect back an eerie greenish-blue radiance. Like a zodiac image in garish neon except that the animal, and the sting, are quite real.

Steve Prchal designed the live-scorpion exhibits at the Desert Museum. He tells of going out on collecting trips, sometimes to a hilly area cut by a certain gorgeous little hidden canyon, down near the Mexican border west of Nogales. Like many collectors, he went at night and used an ultraviolet flashlight, shining his invisible beam along the steep walls of a wash. "It was like stars," Prchal says. "It would scare the hell out of you to see how many you'd be sleeping with if you camped there." He didn't camp there, because he was too smart. I wasn't, when I lived in those parts, so I did. Saw not a single scorpion. Carried no ultraviolet flashlight. Padded around on the gravel after dark in my stocking feet. Got an excellent night's sleep. I believe that the phrase Thurber used, in a similar application, was "living in a fool's paradise."

Curious about how others have fared among those great scorpion multitudes of the Arizona outback, I decided to consult a couple of postdoctoral desert rats. First I called one Doug Peacock, an eminent monkey-wrench environmentalist and authority on the wild behavior of grizzly bears and humans. Peacock, in his many years of crashing around the desert outback, has collected three scorpion stings, and he remembers them all rather vividly. The first time was the worst. He was tucked into his sleeping bag, somewhere out on the Cabeza Prieta wildlife refuge, and in the middle of the night he chanced to roll over, flopping his arm out blindly onto the sand. Whammo. This one may or may not have been *C. sculpturatus*—he didn't get a look at the perpetrator— but the localized pain was ferocious and he went through a few hours of bad headache, nausea, and fever. The third time, out scouting for billboards to chain-saw or bridges to dynamite, he sat down in a clearing and laid his hand back for support—right on a scorpion, which went off like a mousetrap. Either because it was a less toxic species, or because by now Doug was growing immunized, or for some other unplumbable reason, in this case the effects were no worse than those from a bee sting. The second time was perhaps the most interesting. Again on a solo ramble across the Cabeza Prieta, he was sitting up late to read *Moby Dick* by the light of his campfire. He set the book down, tossed a few sticks on the fire, watched the sparks rise into black eternity, picked the book up, leaned back comfortably on an elbow, and whammo. In his annoyance he pummeled this one to death—in fact, past all chance of taxonomic identification—but a reasonable bet makes it *C. sculpturatus.*

I also talked with Ed Abbey, whose credentials to speak in any matter of deserts or ornery critters are unequaled. Amazingly, Abbey has only been scorpion-stung once, and that time while sitting quietly on a couch in a trailer house, late one night about a dozen years ago. He was barefoot. He was reading *Gravity's Rainbow.* He didn't notice the scorpion that had come crawling peacefully up. He lifted one foot and set it down again, whammo, but Ed was so engrossed in Pynchon's novel that all he recalls is tromping the scorpion to death with his stung foot, then quickly fetching a bucket of ice water, jamming the foot into it, and continuing to read. Yes, his assailant seemed to have been that species they call the bark scorpion. Yes, he had some sharp pain at the site, definitely, but nothing much more. On the whole, says Ed, it wasn't nearly so traumatic as the time a tiny insect, species unidentified, crawled deep into his ear and refused to come out.

There are several morals to be drawn. First and most obviously, heavy reading causes scorpion sting. Second, a person is safer while remaining stationary than in making even the most innocent movement—and safer still if the person remains stationary somewhere outside the borders of Arizona. And a third point to note is that the obliviousness seems to be mutual: They don't see a human hand or foot coming, those bumbling scorpions, until it's too late. Otherwise they would surely, like us, prefer to avoid the whole experience.

They don't see us coming because they don't see much of anything. Ironically, despite their superabundance of eyes, most scorpions seem to be almost hopelessly blind. Scientists who study scorpion biology generally mention this handicap ("The eyes are too crude to be of much assistance. . . . The eyesight seems to be of secondary importance. . . . Scorpions have poor eyesight"), which is so pronounced, evidently, that it has been a mystery how scorpions could ever find their way to a meal. Stumbling around blindly out there in the desert, bumping into rocks and each other and Doug Peacock, the poor things should have long since starved to death and lapsed into extinction. Just lately, though, the mystery seems to have been solved.

In a recent issue of *Scientific American,* Philip H. Brownell has presented impressive experimental evidence for a new theory of how scorpions perceive the presence of food or danger.

They see with their feet.

More precisely, they rely on pressure-sensing organs near the ends of each of their eight walking legs to detect subtle shock waves that propagate outward, even through sand, when another creature passes by on the desert floor. According to Brownell, the scorpion orients itself toward the focus of any such disturbance by gauging the minuscule differences in the times at which the shock wave reaches each of its eight spraddled legs. Spaced apart, those legs serve as stereoscopic receptors. Take away the sensory input from one or two pairs of legs, or from all four legs along one side of the body, and the scorpion becomes confused. Disoriented. Like a human with only one good ear, and therefore no sense of auditory direction—or with only one good eye, and therefore no sense of depth. Take away all the input from those leg organs, and the scorpion is functionally blind.

They see with their feet. No wonder they need all eight. Okay, this I can accept. But I'm still uneasy about all those sparkling eyes, which seem to serve no purpose except sheer decorative vanity. They don't walk with them. They don't depend upon them for vision. Couldn't they be satisfied with just five or six?

TURNABOUT

The Well-Kept Secret
of Carnivorous Plants

Plants that eat animals are looked at, by us animals, askance.

They are perceived as grotesque, menacing, unnatural, horrific —or sometimes just delightfully sinister, in the campy spirit of Vincent Price. Above all, they are seen as aggressive beyond their proper station in life. Their presumptuousness seems Promethean, with us for once on the side of the gods. Nature knows them in 450 different species, and the human imagination has been compelled to invent more. Those imaginary varieties grow to huge elephant-ear sizes and flourish in dense Hollywood jungles, feigning innocence among the other foliage, waiting to clamp closed on a cockatoo or a chimp. Minor-key organ chord while the chimp preens, oblivious, and the big ugly plant drools its caustic juices. Most recently we have Audrey II, the ravenous cabbage of *The Little Shop of Horrors.* But even Audrey is the epigone of an older model: On the island of Madagascar, according to legend, there lived a man-eating tree.

Some of the genuine botanical realities can be made to seem, on their own modest scale, almost as chilling. The American pitcher plants feed not just on insects but also on small lizards and frogs. A large pitcher plant called *Nepenthes,* native to Borneo, has been caught in the act of digesting mice. The biggest of the sundews, an Australian species named *Drosera gigantea,* grows into a three-foot-high bush of sticky, grabby paws. Then there's the gaping red maw of the Venus's flytrap, armed along each lip with a row of needle-like spines that were once thought to be capable of impaling victims. My own favorite bit of lore, though, involves the collective accomplishment of a whole field full of common British sundews.

On August 4, 1911, in the county of Norfolk on the east coast of England, a scientist named F. W. Oliver came across a two-acre meadow carpeted solid with sundews. These pretty little plants consist of a rosette of club-shaped leaves radiating from a central stem, each leaf covered with small tentacles at the end of which is a knobby gland, each gland wrapped in a drop of glistening mucilage. In the meadow when Oliver found it, every individual plant had recently captured between four and seven specimens of *Pieris rapae,* a small white butterfly. Evidently the butterflies were a migrating flock that had flown across from the Continent, settling on this flowery field for a rest and a snack. They had chosen badly, and the flock would be going no farther. The sundews were in the act of digesting them.

By Oliver's estimate, that field of plants had just eaten six million butterflies.

Now the *Pieris rapae* butterfly, in its larval stage, is itself a notoriously voracious plant-eater. For six million of them to gobble away two acres of vegetables would be a routine agricultural annoyance. So why should it seem more macabre when the tables are turned?

Evolutionary biologists have been intrigued by the varieties of flesh-eating flora ever since Charles Darwin, who wrote an entire book titled *Insectivorous Plants.* Darwin himself had gotten interested during the summer of 1860, just after publication of *The Origin of Species,* when (on a heath in Sussex) he stumbled across a large insect-kill like the one later described by Oliver. The perpetrator in Darwin's case was also the common sundew, *Drosera rotundifolia,* and because that species was locally plentiful and could be cultivated at his home for use in experiments, *D. rotundifolia* became the main focus of Darwin's book. "I care more about *Drosera* than [about] the origin of all the species in the world," he confessed intemperately in one letter. He also harbored a special fond fascination for the Venus's flytrap, which is a purely American species that Darwin had never seen in the wild, and which he called "the most wonderful plant in the world." Darwin begged samples of the flytrap from his American colleagues, tried to raise the species in his own greenhouse, and had to lament that "I cannot make the little creature grow well."

He needn't have been hard on himself about that, because the Venus's flytrap is drastically finicky about its habitat. There is only one species, and that species confines itself to only one native range: a narrow strip of coastal plain in the Carolinas. The flytrap is so sensitive to its own habitat requirements that, even within such a small range, it can survive only in very particular types of terrain. More about this choosiness in a minute.

Despite its rarity, the Venus's flytrap is the most famous of carnivorous plants, and we are all roughly familiar (we think) with its general anatomy and behavior. Each leaf is modified to the shape of a leg-hold trap, two semicircular lobes on a hinge, cocked open invitingly but ready to slam shut the instant a trigger is tripped. Right? Along the rim of each lobe protrude those needle-like spines. Maybe they can't stab an escaping fly, as once thought, but they certainly add to the aura of implacable malice. Right? The inner surfaces of the lobes are cobbled with tiny liquid-filled glands, some of which show a mysterious red coloring, some of which exude a clear nectar. An insect is attracted by the color and smell, lands on or crawls into the open trap, and then —the heart-sinking snap. The insect's demise is ugly, remorseless, and sudden. Right?

Well, yes and no. The reality is more complicated and more interesting.

The flytrap's anatomy includes a few ingenious features that allow it to *measure* and *taste* its potential prey before committing itself to the meal. This plant is no heedless glutton. On the contrary, its behavior is forbearing and judiciously economical.

First the question of taste. Those reddish glands crowded onto the flytrap's palate secrete a digestive fluid, a mixture containing weak acid and an enzyme called proteinase, which dismantles animal protein. Once the animal protein has been broken down into soluble fragments, that nutritious solution can be reabsorbed by the plant. But unlike the pitcher plants (which hold a permanent reservoir of digestive fluid, into which victims fall), the flytrap remains dry-mouthed until a morsel of prey has been caught. Furthermore, it isn't to be fooled by poor substitutes. It responds only to real food. The lobes close on a cricket or a fly—and the proteinaceous saliva begins flowing. The lobes close on a small gobbet of raw beef—here also the saliva begins flowing. The lobes close in reaction to the touch of a glass rod, or the tip of a pencil, or the weight of a pebble fed to it just like the beef—and nothing at all happens. The plant does not waste its time or its juices.

It isn't receiving the right signals of chemical feedback. In other words, the pebble tastes wrong. Still dry-mouthed, the flytrap opens its lobes again as soon as possible, resuming the wait for a genuine meal.

After a false alarm, the plant is ready again in less than twenty-four hours. If the chemical signals are positive and the chamber floods with digestive fluid, on the other hand, five to ten days will pass before the flytrap can reopen. That difference in the expenditure of resources (time and digestive fluid) seems to be why the plant also *measures* its prospective victims, and proceeds or refrains accordingly. It simply refuses to bother with insects that are too small to be worthwhile.

The measuring is done in two ways. One is inherent in the structure of the triggering mechanism. On the inner surface of each lobe, among the digestive glands, are three sensitive hairs that serve as trip wires for the trap. Merely touching one hair, though, is not sufficient to spring the trap. At least two distinct touches (upon the same hair or different ones) are required, and those touches must occur no less than about one second nor more than about twenty seconds apart. The hairs themselves are spaced just far enough from each other—as well as from the nectar glands that attract an insect's attention—that a small insect cannot bump any two in close succession.

The second method of measuring was discovered by Charles Darwin himself. He had noticed an odd fact about how the fly-trap closes: that the closing movement occurs in two discrete phases. Upon triggering, the lobes swing together quickly (in less than half a second) to a position where the long spines have crossed but the lobe edges haven't quite met, leaving a row of narrow, short gaps like the spaces between bars in a jail window. For the lobes to close completely, sealing off that row of gaps, takes another half hour. Why the hesitation? wondered Darwin.

He guessed that the Venus's flytrap was saving itself the trouble of digesting insignificant meals. "Now it would manifestly be a great disadvantage to the plant," he wrote in *Insectivorous Plants,* "to waste many days in remaining clasped over a minute insect, and several additional days or weeks in afterwards recovering its sensitivity; inasmuch as a minute insect would afford but little nutriment. It would be far better for the plant to wait for a time until a moderately large insect was captured, and to allow all the little ones to escape; and this advantage is secured by the slowly intercrossing marginal spikes, which act like the large meshes of a fishing-net, allowing the small and useless fry to escape." So the Venus's flytrap, terror of large insects, is benignly indifferent to little ones.

The most basic question remains: Why do they eat meat?

Not only the Venus's flytrap but also the sundews, the pitcher plants, and a still more elaborate genus of animal-trapping plants called the bladderworts—why do these species share a hunger for fresh flesh? Why must they feast on animal protein while other species of plant are content with sunshine, water, air, and a bit of decent soil? It seems not only presumptuous but greedy.

The truth is exactly opposite. Carnivorous plants have been driven to this extremity not by boldness and gluttony, but by shyness and starvation.

In the matter of habitat, evolution has awarded them hind tit. But like a determined runt that will grow into a proud hog, they make the best of it. They have developed strategies for collecting animal protein because, in the nutrient-poor habitats to which they are exiled, on soils so inhospitable that few other plants deign to invade, without some dietary supplement they could scarcely survive.

The floating islands of peat in the Okefenokee Swamp are a representative outpost, supporting carnivorous plants of three different genera (sundews, bladderworts, pitcher plants) within little more than a canoe's length of one another. The Pine Barrens of New Jersey can claim the same distinction. What these spots have in common with that soggy meadow in Norfolk, where F. W. Oliver saw a million well-fed sundews, is a critical shortage of the basic soil nutrients (like nitrogen and phosphorus) that most flowering plants require. One study has shown that the average patch of bog inhabited by sundews has twenty-seven times less nitrogen than the average patch of pine forest. Around the world, habitats of carnivorous species tend to fit the same pattern—plenty of water, plenty of sun, terrible soil. These are unpromising corners of real estate where, if sundews or pitcher plants weren't growing, almost nothing else would be.

Look at it this way: Meat-eating is the last resort of the shy, uncompetitive plant. Those carnivorous species have removed themselves evolutionarily from the ruthless competition of the thicket, the forest, from all those fecund and clamorous places where plants flourish in wild vigor and variety, battling each other upon nutritious substrata for position and water and sunlight. The Venus's flytrap and those few others have taken a more gentle path.

In that sense they belong in company with certain other retiring creatures that go to great lengths to avoid gratuitous violence. I'm thinking especially of the rattlesnake and the black widow spider.

THE SELFHOOD
OF A SPOON WORM

Sex Determination
as a Mid-Life Experience

The study of biology is such a fine antidote to rigid, normative thinking that perhaps all our televised preachers and tin-whistle moralists should be required occasionally to take a dose of it. The experience couldn't help but be broadening. No general truth emerges more clearly, from even a browser's tour of the intricacies of the natural world, than this: Chances are, there is more than one right way to do it.

Flying is a good example. Birds and reptiles and insects and bats and seeds have all mastered that feat, at different times and in their utterly different ways. The arrangement of anatomical support is another. Who is to say that a skeleton should be worn *inside* the body (as by us vertebrates), when lobsters and other arthropods do so well with their skeletons on the *outside,* and jellyfish get by with none whatsoever? For a further instance, consider the matter of how gender is determined among those creatures showing two distinct sexes. Boy or girl, cow or bull, colt or mare, goose or gander: The interesting question, biologically, is not *which* but *why.* What dictates that a particular individual should turn out to be male or female?

In mammals the point is decided genetically at the moment of conception. That's the most familiar sort of sex determination, and we humans are likely to think of it as the norm; but such genetic sex determination (GSD) is just a contingent fact, not a logical or biological necessity. Among certain other animals, known as "sequential hermaphrodites," sexual identity can change as a stage of growth, as routinely as a human might pass through puberty or menopause. These sequential hermaphrodites, including a number of fish species, begin life in one sexual form (say, as males) and function reproductively in that role for a time; then as they grow older and bigger, they transform at some point to the opposite sex (female), in which role their large size may be more advantageous. If physical magnitude happens to be a more crucial advantage for males than for females, in any such species, then the sequence of sexual identities will be reversed, each individual making its transition from small female to big male.

There is also a third option for sex-differentiated species, one which has not gotten much scientific attention until the last few years. This option is called "environmental sex determination," or ESD. The term means, simply, that in certain species the sex of the offspring is determined at a point sometime after conception, by some environmental influence acting upon those unhatched eggs or those sexless young. That environmental influence might be a matter of chemistry or sunlight or temperature or something else. Theoretical ecologists are still struggling to explain just how ESD might have evolved, and just why it might be useful, but in the meantime field and lab studies have shown that the phenomenon is more common than we might expect.

This ESD business was probably first recognized in a beast named *Bonellia viridis,* a benignly grotesque sea animal belonging to the phylum Echiurida, a group casually known as the "spoon worms" and not remotely related to anything you've ever heard of. *Bonellia* itself looks like some sort of bad party joke made out of latex. The adult female of the species consists of a bulbous body roughly the size of an avocado and with a similar dappled surface, from which extends a long tube-like proboscis ending in a pair of leafy lobes. It lives amid rocks on the bottom of the Mediterranean Sea, where the soft body can find safety by anchoring itself in a hole or a crevice, and the lobed proboscis can be extruded out, three feet or more, to grope for passing morsels of food. But the proboscis of *Bonellia* collects more than nourishment; it also collects mates.

When a tiny sexless larva of the same species comes into contact with this proboscis, the larva attaches itself there on the tube and (apparently in response to chemical signals) begins the process of turning into a dwarf *Bonellia* male. Eventually the mature male, still no larger than a caraway seed, will make his way up the proboscis and into the female's gut, claiming a permanent home within the uterus. There he will live off her as a parasite, a feckless but useful gigolo, conveniently on hand to fertilize her eggs.

In finding its female host, the *Bonellia* larva has found also its own sexual identity, its own selfhood. If the same larva had *not* blundered upon a female proboscis, it would (in most cases, though there are exceptions) eventually have settled down in a rocky cleft and grown into a large bulb-and-tube female itself. The presence or absence of a female proboscis is the crucial environmental fact, in the life of each young *Bonellia,* that settles the matter of sex.

This is ESD at its most vivid, and back as early as 1920 *Bonellia* had already become quietly famous among zoologists as the leading exemplum of the phenomenon. But environmental sex determination seemed then just an oddity, an aberration, the kind of garish and mildly repugnant trick that one would expect from an obscure group of marine invertebrates like the spoon worms. Today we know better. ESD has been discovered also among orchids, nematode worms, crustaceans, lizards, at least one species of fish, four or five species of turtle, and the American alligator.

In the case of the alligator, an elaborate set of experiments and field observations has recently proved that sex determination for this species involves little or no genetic component. Instead, the sex ratio in a litter of hatchling alligators seems to be completely dependent upon the temperature at which those eggs were incubated. An alligator nest maintained at eighty-six degrees F. or cooler will produce nothing but females. The same batch of eggs, if kept at ninety-three degrees or warmer, will hatch out as all males. Alligator eggs have an incubation period of about sixty-five days, but sex determination seems to occur during just the second and third weeks. At temperatures between the range of eighty-six and ninety-three degrees, the nest will yield a mix of males and females.

Still, the interesting issue is *why*. Why has the alligator come to depend upon thermal signals, rather than genetic coding, to set the sexual identities of its offspring? Why has *Bonellia* evolved a system using social contact (or the lack of it) for the same purpose?

And from that pair of questions derives another, even more puzzling: What could *Bonellia* and the American alligator have in common?

Writing in the journal *Nature,* Eric Charnov and James Bull have offered a conceptual model that might make evolutionary sense of the whole range of ESD cases. "We propose that labile sex determination (not fixed at conception) is favoured by natural selection when an individual's fitness (as a male or female) is strongly influenced by environmental conditions and where the individual has little control over which environment it will experience." *Control* is the key word. If an organism can't completely control where it's going (like a *Bonellia* larva, riding helplessly on the sea currents), then maybe there is compensatory value in retaining control over what sort of being (male or female) it will be when it gets there.

This might sound like something from *Alice in Wonderland,* but in truth there is nothing illogical about it. The apparent reversal of logic merely goes against our preconceptions. We think of sexual identity as virtually a prerequisite to existence. Under the Charnov-Bull model, by contrast, sex determination is just an intermediate step on the long path toward what might be called (in California, anyway) self-actualization.

"To illustrate," say Charnov and Bull, "if an individual finds itself in an environment where it can become a below average female or an above average male, selection will favor its becoming male because it can pass on more of its genes than if it were female." And vice versa. "Selection may therefore favour 'environmental sex determination' (ESD) because of the control it allows an individual." Fine, that seems reasonable—but several complicated assumptions lie behind this simple statement.

One assumption is that the evolutionary fitness of an individual (as tallied, always, by how many offspring survive) is measured relative to other individuals of the same species *and the same sex.* In other words, a male alligator competes only against other male alligators for the right to leave a large share of descendants. Another assumption made by Charnov and Bull is that the environment in question is patchy, with some patches conferring heightened advantage on females, other patches conferring heightened advantage on males.

From these two givens, Charnov and Bull argue that natural selection "should most strongly favour ESD when 1) the offspring enters an environment, away from the parent, which has a large effect on its lifetime fitness . . . and 2) the offspring and the parent have little control (or predictive ability) over which patch type the offspring enters. These conditions make it unfavourable to determine sex at conception because of the possibility that a male will enter a patch that is much more favourable for a female, or the reverse." So ESD allows an individual to match its own sexual identity with the particular patch of environment that will heighten its prospect under that identity—not by choosing the patch, but instead by choosing the sexual identity.

Among alligators the patch differences seem to be a matter of temperature at which the eggs are incubated. Nests built on dry levee (according to that elaborate field study, done in Louisiana) tend to stay warmer than ninety-three degrees F. and to yield males. Nests built on wet marsh tend to stay cooler than eighty-six degrees and to yield females. In either case the environment during incubation may have a large effect on lifetime fitness, because that temperature difference translates to size of the individual at hatching, which in turn affects how soon the individual will reach breeding size. Females have a greater need than males do to reach breeding size quickly, because their allotted span of breeding years is much shorter. (That part applies also to humans, providing an evolutionary rationale for why prepubescent fifth-grade boys should find themselves mystified by their classmates' burgeoning breasts.) The consequence of all this is that cool nest temperatures—which turn out *larger* baby alligators—give most females a head start toward breeding size. So if an individual alligator is relatively small at the time of hatching, it will fare better in the lifelong Darwinian competition as an average male than as a below average female. And, fortunately, ESD will have already matched its sex to its best prospects.

But what about those ridiculous *Bonellia*? They seem to be covered equally well by the Charnov-Bull model. In this case the patchiness of the environment is a matter of presence or absence of female *Bonellia*. The larvae can't control where they travel, and the adult females are sessile, traveling nowhere at all. When any one larva encounters a female, that fact has great effect on its lifetime fitness, because it means that the little devil will have an opportunity to mate. Otherwise he would be forced to take his own chances as a female, with some jeopardy of permanent spin-sterhood. ESD again is the matchmaker. ESD lets him be all he can be.

The moral: Identity is such a crucial affair that one shouldn't rush into it.

No doubt that seems perfectly natural to a spoon worm. Some of us "higher animals," on the other hand, don't have the luxury of such a convenient biological postponement. And probably our *Bonellia* would be horrified, or silenced in pity, if he (or she, depending) could see the desperate, bizarre ways by which we humans must try to cope with the intractable dilemma of self.

II
WILD NOTIONS

THE DESCENT
OF THE DOG

*A Tempered View
of Canine Evolution*

Let's begin slowly, with a relatively safe statement: Not all dogs
are bad.

We Americans live today amid a plague of domestic dogs, a
ridiculous and outrageous proliferation of the species, true, but
not every one of those animals is damnable beyond redemption.
Not every one has had its soul twisted by misery and neglect,
spending long days chained or fenced within a tiny yard and
taking its revenge by barking at the neighbors. Not every one is
ill-trained, intermittently hysterical, half insane from sensory
deprivation. Not every one is indulged to prowl free, defecating
on other folks' lawns and reorganizing other folks' garbage, play-
fully snapping the necks of other folks' cats. A few dogs, worthy
beasts, help blind people to cross streets. Several reportedly perform ranch chores. Dozens of canines in the U.S. alone fulfill a
useful service as the quiet, well-behaved pets of old people and
shut-ins. The rest, unfortunately, are as we know them. But dogs
are a sensitive subject; some dog owners, like some tobacco
smokers and most members of the Ku Klux Klan, tend to be
passionately defensive about what they are pleased to think of as
their own rights. Consequently you find two diametrically opposed and equally extremist points of view: on the one hand, that

all dogs are irredeemably noxious and should be banished, at least from our cities and suburbs, by enlightened legislation; and on the other hand, that some dogs are okay, at least some of the time. My own view is a moderate one that falls about halfway between these two.

Brothers and sisters, as the Lord is my witness: We got too many dogs.

A reliable estimate puts the total U.S. dog population at about sixty million, and that figure has risen by ten million over the past decade. Roughly five million are unclaimed strays held in animal shelters, awaiting adoption or execution, but meanwhile pet dogs are still breeding away. As I write this sentence there are six lunatic barkers within earshot (and one charming old mongrel with sad friendly eyes, next door, who maintains a monk-like silence). That's just too many. The situation is crazy. The dogs of America are—individually and demographically—out of control.

Of course we also have too many cats. Let no smug feliphile deny that. But there are a couple of important differences. First, cats are generally far quieter and less intrusive. They just don't have the vocal equipment, the heft, or the territorial instincts to assert themselves as conspicuously as dogs do. Second, when a human society has too many cats, it is mainly the cats who suffer. People drown them. Set them on fire for kicks. Hang them, in cute little nooses. Club them to death and toss the carcasses into the trash. Thereby achieving some sort of sorry equilibrium. It's less trouble that way, evidently, than exercising a modicum of foresight to get the females spayed and the males neutered. When a society has too many dogs, however, people and dogs both suffer. The extras (aside from those strays who end up in animal shelters) are not killed, but instead are given away or sold cheaply to persons who have no idea what a dog needs in terms of training and attention and sheer physical space, and who are not in a position to supply those things if they did know. Result:

miserable, desperate dogs who share out that misery generously to the humans all around them.

It wasn't always this bad. Dogs come from a noble lineage, a lineage full of intelligence and good character—they are closely related to wolves, after all. Many paleontologists even think that domestic dogs are directly derived from a small Asian subspecies known as *Canis lupes pallipes,* the Indian wolf. But the descent of the species *Canis familiaris* (to which all domestic breeds belong) is like a parable on the subject of bad company. They began losing their dignity about 10,000 years ago, when they first cozied up to humanity—the greased chute to degradation. We adopted them, we tamed them, we began breeding them selectively to our own sick tastes and mad purposes; we gave them squashed faces and curly tails and sawed-off legs, brain damage and hip dysplasia and hemophilia, permanent psychological infantilism; we generally brought out the worst in them. Among other particulars, we perfected the bark.

How did such sadomasochism ever start? Some people cherish a romantic belief that, in its earliest form, the dog-and-man association was a hunting partnership. According to this notion, our hunter-gatherer ancestors of the middle Stone Age reached an implicit understanding with certain canines to cooperate in the chase: The dogs were faster and better armed, the humans were smarter and more devious, both groups were social communicators, and the meat could be shared. But it's a fairy tale. No basis whatsoever in evidence. Reputable archaeologists guess, instead, that the dog's first role in civilization was to eat garbage.

Wild dogs were welcomed as scavengers, it seems, to the fringes of those nomad camps. The dogs cleaned up what would otherwise stink and draw flies. When a camp was moved they tagged along as walking garbage Disposalls. Tolerated, at a distance. Eventually they became familiar and permanent. Hunting and shepherding and sled-pulling and being coddled as pets all came later—not to mention their role as watchdogs.

For this last function they were outfitted with a new sort of voice. It was a voice lacking all modulation and felicity, but which carried and penetrated exceptionally well, with its sharp pulses of energy confined within an unwavering range of frequencies, its cough-like bursts of pure graceless noise—a voice offering the same musical quality as the sound of a pouting child whacking away at a cinder block with a cheap meat cleaver. The canine bark: one of mankind's first acts of genetic planning, and an enduring monument to our own fearful territoriality. Like the spear and the loin cloth, it might well have been useful in its day.

But some people claim even today that their yappy little curs function as watchdogs—though it's a mystery to me why anyone would be foolish enough to rely on a warning system that delivers twenty false alarms every day. My own theory is that those "watchdog" people value their poodles and their scotties not for warning but as personal surrogates, less inhibited and more articulate than themselves, and take vicarious emotional satisfaction as the dogs deliver that shrill and mindlessly angry message to the outside world.

Wolves generally don't bark. Wolves howl melodically. Coyotes seldom bark. They yodel and yelp. From the Congo jungle comes an ancient domestic dog breed known as the basenji that also, bless its very soul, almost never barks. Basenjis were highly valued for their discretion by the Pygmies, who used them for hunting antelope in the Ituri forest. So quiet were these basenjis, in fact, that sometimes the human handler fitted one with a collar from which hung a gourd rattle, just so he could keep track of where the dog was. No one knows why basenjis originally fell silent, or retained the ancestral barklessness, but one very plausible reason would be that they were terrier-sized animals living among leopards, and therefore learned quickly the value of inconspicuousness. All honor to the good sense of the basenji. Unfortunately, most dog breeds did not evolve in the presence of leopards.

They evolved in the presence of humans, who are selectively deaf. It is a scientifically demonstrable fact that many people do not even hear the noise of their own dog. Generally that's because they tie the dog up in a backyard and go off to work downtown, leaving their pet to bark tirelessly at passing children and other dogs and the free-lance writer across the alley.

Why does a dog bark at all? One scientist who has spent the past twenty years studying dog behavior and origins, Michael W. Fox, says that "dogs may bark during greeting, play-soliciting, threat, defense, care-soliciting, distress, contact-seeking, or during group vocalizations. Barks may be simple or complex, e.g., growl-barks, repeated barks with howl-like endings and yelp-barks. This contextual variety indicates that the sound itself may not always convey specific information but rather attracts the attention of their receiver." In other words, they bark for every damn reason you can imagine, and sometimes for no reason, other than boredom. (And boredom is liable to be a large factor in the life of even a modestly bright animal left captive in a yard.) As far as attracting the attention of the receiver—there is no doubting the bark's effectiveness for that. I can vividly recall one occasion, for instance, when a pair of toy terriers had solicited my attention with such success that at 3 A.M. I got up, put on pants and shoes, walked down two flights of stairs, and crossed a street in order to throw three garbage cans over a fence at them. Like the dogs, I was seeking contact.

But of course fairness (and, even more so, my desire for continued matrimonial amity) requires me to note that not all breeds of domestic dog are equally loathsome. Golden retrievers seem to have a fair measure of charm and mental health. Toy poodles are at the other extreme, obviously. Malamutes and Siberian huskies are wonderfully handsome and tend to have a fine quiet poise about them, probably in direct correlation with the closeness of their relationship to the original wolf. Basenjis, as we've seen, should be a role model for all. And cocker spaniels are paragons of hysteria: According to one set of studies, cockers started barking with less provocation, and continued barking with more persistence, than all other breeds tested. Take a cocker spaniel at eleven weeks old, lock it behind chain link on a small patch of grass, and you have a barking machine unequaled throughout nature. One cocker in those studies set a record of infamy by barking 907 times in a ten-minute period. Interestingly, the same researcher also found from autopsy data a trend among cocker spaniels for hydrocephaly. All of which may or may not be consequent from mankind's having bred cockers toward a steeply angled forehead.

Why do dogs bark so much more—and so much more randomly, stupidly—than their wolfish ancestors? Michael Fox says: "The outstanding feature of the domestic dog—barking—may be attributed to artificial selection." We humans are responsible. But that still leaves open the question of whether we produced this excessive barkishness by liberating a trait that was suppressed in wild canines, or by accentuating a trait that was otherwise barely present—by protecting the domestic dog from those leopards, or by choosing the mouthiest dogs of each generation as our favored breeders. And that question can't be settled in isolation from the matter, also still in doubt, of the domestic dog's direct ancestry. Fox tells us: "The origin(s) of the dog therefore still remains an enigma although one might conclude on the basis of this study that if the wolf were the sole progenitor of the dog, then dogs would howl more and bark much less than they do."

So maybe it wasn't the Indian wolf after all. Maybe that immediate ancestor to our domestic dogs was the jackal (with those elegantly wolf-like huskies and Malamutes reflecting some later cross-breeding back with real wolves). Maybe it was an earlier version of the Australian dingo. Maybe it was a missing link between dingo and jackal. Or possibly (and I offer this only as an hypothesis, understand) it was a cross between the hyena and the duck.

Hyenas have a certain dog-like majesty. The duck and the poodle have a similar sort of gait. And ducks are known to eat garbage. Furthermore, come to think of it, the quack is not so different from the bark. And don't I vaguely recall an etymological tie, in the old Anglo-Saxon, between the very words for the two animals: a common origin in the form *dok*? It's just a thought.

Anyway, from wherever they come, here they are. Sixty million *Canis familiaris*: as many dogs, now, as we once had bison. That's a very sobering little gauge, in itself, of the degradation of America. Man's best friend, don't you know—at least so we are endlessly told. *The dog is man's best woof woof woof.* But with friends like that, says I, who needs enemies? Bah, humbug.

STREET TREES

The Hard, Noble Life
of a Stranger in a Strange Land

I have been trying to imagine what life is like for an urban tree. This is especially difficult—not just the life, but the imagining of it—during winter, when that life itself seems to be absent and the poor creatures just stand around, leafless and woebegone, looking dead as bleached Hereford skulls in the desert. Of course they aren't dead—but do they have reason to wish they were? That's the question. In response comes a wooden silence. I've just gotten back from a walk through the snow-packed and tree-lined streets of the town where I live, during which I took care to scrutinize in their sphinx-like stolidity a selection of naked cottonwoods, ashes, dogwoods, weeping birches, maples, and two very grand old elms towering over the sidewalk in front of the house next door. Every one of them, with the season, looking desolate and mute. I hoped for a hint of empathic inspiration, a murmur or a squeak, but they weren't obliging. No comment. Winter dormancy, that sort of stupor is called. By the time you read this, those same trees will have long since come a-flush with new greenery and I will be harboring a suspicion that they had only been gone on out-of-body experiences in the tropics. Even in summer, though, the life of a city tree can't be easy.

Landscape architects make a distinction between the "natural" or "romantic" aggregations of foliage in a rolling urban oasis like Central Park and, on the other hand, the "street trees" that serve simply to border or punctuate lanes and boulevards. There is a large literature these days on the theory of urban park design and landscape planning. The romantic style is still in favor. Better yet is the new notion of preserving patches of "urban woodland," indigenous, ragged, unmanaged. Street trees meanwhile tend to be the forgotten souls.

They grow up through that miserly gap of hard-packed dirt between sidewalk and curb, roots smothered, solitary, regimented like telephone poles, invisible as wallpaper. They get precious little attention and what they do get is often the cruelest sort. Occasionally someone will staple a poster into their bark. A dog stops to lift his leg. A drunk in a Chevrolet tries to park himself up in their branches. But no one puts a hose to their roots on a dry day in July, or gives them a fertilizer treatment in springtime, or sprawls out on a picnic blanket beneath to stare up and admire their canopy. Park trees, yes; lawn trees, yes; not street trees. Then, when they die, the city sends out a crew to fell them and grind them to chips. Otherwise they are ignored.

These are the trees that make me curious. The uncelebrated heroes of the urban environment. They not only add their small touch of shade and beauty to the starkest troughs of the city; they also cut winds, absorb noise, reduce glare, mitigate the extremes of temperature, and help appreciably to filter the city air. But how do they themselves fare? What sort of existence is it, living sealed off from the recycling flow of every soil nutrient, robbed of direct sunlight by skyscrapers, poisoned with road salt and poodle piss, deprived each autumn of even their own leaf mulch, choking on those various elaborate toxins of automobile exhaust? Is a tree such an amazingly stoic organism that such abuse doesn't matter? Or are their lives nasty, brutish, and short?

Does the mortification of having to stand stupidly in straight rows show itself in a lowered life expectancy? Does smoke stunt their growth? Does their sap flow bitter?

I wondered especially about a single small tree that grows out of a pit in the sidewalk in midtown Manhattan, on Forty-fourth Street between Fifth Avenue and Sixth. This particular tree is barely more than a sapling—slender, sparse of crown, lonely and incongruous, with the Pan Am Building looming about a half mile above in the eastern sky. Last time I saw it, though, against even those odds, the thing was alive. I happen to be aware of this tree only because, down there in the canyon of Forty-fourth Street, it graces the entrance to the once reputable hotel where I stay when I'm in New York. Actually this tree is one of a pair, both of them small but spunky, both growing right out of that sidewalk on the south side of Forty-fourth, scarcely more than a bus length between; mine is the more westerly of the two. But I use the word "mine" undeservedly, confessing that I've never so much as noticed what species it is. I have no idea how it survives. Like everyone else, I have taken that tree for granted. So I decided to call the man responsible for worrying about the creatures no one else worries about, the street trees of New York City.

His name is Adrian Benepe. His title is Director of Natural Resources for the New York Department of Parks and Recreation. He seems to be a relaxed and sensitive fellow, and it was clear that I had the right guy (after some wrong tries) when he did not judge me a lunatic or a bothersome crank for stating that I'd phoned from Montana to inquire about the condition of this particular sapling I know on West Forty-fourth.

Adrian Benepe told me: "It's not easy being green in New York."

Street trees have an improbable history. Up through the Middle Ages, in Europe, they didn't exist. The defensive walls that surrounded a medieval city were drawn about tightly, intended to protect the inhabitants and their property from raiding enemies, and trees were a superfluity that could damn well take their chances outside. Back in the imperial days of Egypt and Rome, some spectacular palace gardens had been cultivated within urban boundaries, but those gardens were emphatically private, reserved for the enjoyment of the ruling classes. Street trees, on the other hand, are by definition public and populist. So it's ironic that their most influential precursor may have been Louis XIV's spread at Versailles.

Versailles was designed between 1661 and 1674 by a fellow named André Le Nôtre, now considered the first of the great landscape architects. The term itself—*landscape architect*—suggests something of the revolution that Le Nôtre brought to urban planting; his own father, under whom he apprenticed, is referred to, in contrast, as having been the king's *master gardener.* Le Nôtre the son studied painting as well as horticulture, and was evidently affected by what he learned of drafting and perspective. He grew into a gardener with an architectonic eye. His work is marked by the use of trees—planted in straight rows or in large blocks with crisp linear borders—to create grandiose vistas along which a grandiose monarch could survey his property. The Champs-Élysées, in Paris, one of the world's most famous tree-lined boulevards, was an earlier example of Le Nôtre's style. Then at Versailles in particular, on what had been a swampy hunting preserve, he created an exotically formalized environment, mixing nature with a regal sense of order, and drew the lines and the angles with trees.

During the following century and a half Le Nôtre's design concept was converted to public uses, showing up in the street plans of London, Berlin, Washington, and again his own city of Paris. In London the early trend, beginning around 1800, was to plant trees in the large open spaces that were being set aside as civic parks. The avenue in Berlin known as Unter den Linden, graced with rows of linden trees and leading up to the Brandenburg Gate, became (with the Champs-Élysées) another of the world's best-known beautiful streets. Paris was extensively redesigned during the mid-nineteenth century by Baron George Eugène Haussmann, a city planner who favored broad boulevards and bands of vegetation for a mixture of reasons. The tree-lined avenues, according to Haussmann, would serve to "disencumber the larger buildings, palaces, and barracks in such a way as to make them more pleasing to the eye, afford easier access on days of celebration, and a simplified defense on days of riot." The margins of greenery, by Haussmann's cunning aristocratic calculation, would preserve public order by allowing "the circulation of air and light but also troops." And in Washington, as early as 1791, the job of creating a planned city was given to a Frenchman named L'Enfant, who devised a webwork of radial boulevards and tree-lined vistas in much the same flavor as Le Nôtre's Versailles.

From Paris and Washington, then, the trend spread to Chicago, San Francisco, Minneapolis, St. Louis, and other U.S. cities. A law passed in 1807 decreed that Detroit, in the territory of Michigan, should have a row of trees on each side of its larger avenues. And of course the landscaping impulse came also to New York City, arriving there in both of its antipodal forms. Central Park, designed in the 1850s by Frederick Law Olmsted and his partner, became America's preeminent urban park, a great paradoxical rectangle of rolling and irregular forest, representing the romantic tradition that derived mainly from England. The legacy of Le Nôtre and Louis XIV appeared too—as humble and soldierly street trees, some in rows, some alone, standing their ground in places like West Forty-fourth between Fifth and Sixth.

According to Adrian Benepe, there are more than 600,000 street trees (and another two million park trees) in New York City. Each year the Department of Transportation plants about

10,000 trees, replacing other trees that have been injured or removed in the course of road construction. Mr. Benepe's own department, Parks and Recreation, plants another 10,000 trees. No tree is cut down unless it is dead, terminally ill and potentially infectious, or in the path of the Transportation Department, and yet those 20,000 annual plantings are barely enough to keep up with attrition. Some sources even say that attrition is running ahead of the replanting, and that New York is moving slowly, sadly, toward treelessness.

What drives the attrition? Most of New York's street trees suffer from too little water and too much heat. During respiration (yes, trees do breathe) they absorb sulfur dioxide, hydrogen cyanide, hydrogen fluoride, peroxyacetyl nitrates, ethylene, and other noxious gases that can inhibit photosynthesis, disrupt their enzyme activity, and damage their foliage. City dust also tends to clog leaf pores, which further reduces photosynthesis and respiration and can literally cause a tree to suffocate. Weakened by such forms of stress, a city tree is all the more vulnerable to parasitic insects or some microbial malady like anthracnose, Dutch elm disease, canker, oak wilt. Even these problems, according to Benepe, are not the worst of it. "I once saw a tree that died quickly after an exterminator poured his exterminating liquid on its roots." And then again there's the poisonous insult of dog urine, contributed to the environment of New York's streets at the rate of roughly 22,000 gallons a day. Small wonder that the life expectancy of a tree in Manhattan is only seven years. It's not easy being green in that place.

"But trees *are* highly loved and respected by most people in New York," Benepe told me. "I think there's a tremendous sense that trees in New York make the city livable."

Impelled by that conviction, Benepe's department back in 1984 performed an interesting and, I think, very admirable exercise. The people of New York were asked to nominate individual trees that held special meaning, special value, in their own lives. The nominations were culled by a panel, and in 1985 a book titled *The Great Trees of New York City* appeared. Here was well-merited recognition, at last, for a certain old ginkgo at the corner of 211th and Broadway; for a certain elm at St. Nicholas Avenue and 163rd; for another elm, five feet in diameter and maybe a century old, casting its shade over Washington Square Park.

No mention was made, though, of the westernmost of two saplings on Forty-fourth Street between Fifth and Sixth. That tree (probably either a Callery pear or a locust, Adrian Benepe told me) is still in its adolescence. With great luck, against the odds, it might live to adulthood. And if we both manage to survive another thirty or forty years, I look forward to nominating it for a later edition.

THE ONTOLOGICAL
GIRAFFE

Wherein Norwegian Leo
Talks Straight and True, Mostly

Norwegian Leo called recently, out of the wild blue, long-distance from San Jose this time, with a zoological stumper question. As always, it was delightful and confusing to hear from him.

"Dave, listen." He sounded breathless and exigent, and as always the conversation began in the middle. "What's the largest mammal you've never heard of?"

I thought about that for a moment. Norwegian Leo is a mechanical engineer by profession, a precise and intelligent man of far-ranging but focused enthusiasms, a man who writes letters containing better English prose than most of what I read in magazines, who loves crisp language and German cameras and improbable living creatures, who is accustomed by disposition as well as by training to checking his facts down to the fourth decimal place. I knew he had said exactly what he intended to say. I thought passingly about several largish animals of the mammalian persuasion. And then I couldn't help thinking also about St. Anselm, an eleventh-century Italian monk with a smart-aleck streak who made a name for himself in the history of philosophy by inventing an infuriatingly clever piece of logic called the ontological argument. The ontological argument claims to be a proof for the existence of God, a proof that relies only on pure rational deduction, and believe me it's as air-tight as a can of Spanish peanuts. I had all but forgotten about St. Anselm since the week he gave me a king-size headache during one college term back in 1968, but as I held the receiver to my ear now I dimly recalled that his ontological argument works from a premise not too unlike asking *What's the largest mammal you've never heard of?* I still didn't know the answer, but since Norwegian Leo (unlike St. Anselm and, for that matter, God) is such a down-to-earth and persuasive presence, even over the telephone, I did not doubt for an instant that an answer must exist.

"It's not a cetacean, of course," Leo added. The cetaceans are the marine mammals, including whales. "Obviously you've heard of them."

"Extinct?"

"Living," said Leo. "Alive and well in the jungles of central Africa. Okay. That was your one hint."

"Duh. I was thinking, I guess, about mastodons."

"Don't be silly, Dave. You've *heard* of them."

"Duh."

"Obviously not the capybara."

"No. I've heard of them."

"And besides, they're too small," said Leo.

"What's the largest mammal I've never heard of."

"Correct," said Leo. "A straight question. Perfectly fair."

"I've heard of manatees."

"Of course. Obviously therefore not a manatee."

"I've heard of aardwolves. Civets. Those type guys."

"Right. So forget about the aardwolf."

"This is a hard one, Leo," I said. "This is a good one. I know I'll hate myself."

"The *OKAPI!*" His glee was of the gentle sort, eager to be shared, not the faintest bit smug; he announced this animal's name the way you would yodel the word *SURPRISE* from be-

hind a sofa to a person just turning six. "Found only in Zaire.
Shy and retiring. Looks like a cross between a zebra and a moose.
But actually it's a kind of giraffe."

"You were right," I said. "Spell it. I warn you, I'm taking
notes."

The okapi is still largely a zoological cipher. Isolated in its
small range within the central African rainforests, it had been
utterly unknown to science until the turn of this century, as it
was utterly unknown to me until Leo's call. The only humans
aware of it were a few Pygmy tribes in what was then the Belgian
Congo (now Zaire) who had long since been hunting okapi using
elaborate pitfall traps. When the explorer Henry Stanley went
into the Congo interior in 1890, the Pygmies he met took one
look at his horses, labeled them with the word *okhapi,* and explained that they had similar animals in their own dense forests.
But Stanley himself never got a glimpse. And the Pygmies' claim
was ecologically puzzling, because horses and horse-like animals
such as the zebra and the quagga were known to be open-land
species, adapted to life on savanna and steppe. What manner of
horse could survive in this tangled Congo jungle, threaded
through with only the thinnest network of narrow, tunnel-like
game trails?

In 1901 a complete skeleton and two skulls reached London,
evidence enough for zoologists there to conclude that this creature was no horse at all. Nor was it a relative of the donkey, the
ox, or the various species of antelope. In fact, it seemed to have
no family resemblance to any other living mammal. But then
those scientists noticed uncanny similarities between the okapi
remains and the fossils of a certain extinct beast named *Helladotherium,* a short-necked giraffe that had disappeared from
Europe and Asia ten million years earlier. Further comparisons
showed that the okapi was anatomically similar—aside from the
drastic difference in length of neck—to the living African giraffe.

The giraffe itself, though, is also a range animal, with that tall gangly shape suited to loping across savanna and browsing leaves off the high branches of a few scattered acacias. The okapi, on the other hand, has remained closer to the original ancestral pattern and in that sense is more primitive: smaller and short-necked, shaped for feeding and quick escape in those thick forests. Its main enemies seem to be leopards and humans—but that's just a calculated guess. Even today scientists know almost nothing about the ecology and behavior of okapis in the wild.

The strange pattern of coloration, for instance, is still a mystery. In silhouette the okapi might be said to resemble a horse, but when its colors and markings are filled in it becomes a patchwork, chimerical beast—like a mule painted up for Mardi Gras. The face is mostly light, with dark shadowing down the muzzle and around the eyes. The neck and the body are a solid glossy dark hue that is variously described as deep gray, rich chocolate brown, or maroon. The forelegs from the knee down are dark on their forward surfaces and white in back, as though the animal were wearing chaps. The rear legs and hindquarters are decorated with loud dark-and-white horizontal stripes, the startling white stripes radiating outward from a midpoint below the tail. Seen from directly behind, the effect is like a fireworks explosion originating from the vicinity of the okapi's genitalia—bright spears shooting away centrifugally against a blackened sky. Viewing the okapi from in front, you see an entirely different sort of animal.

The zoologists are still wondering whether this garish starburst pattern across the hind end might serve some kind of intraspecific triggering function, perhaps helping male okapis focus their attention on the prospect of sexual activity, or telling okapi young where to direct themselves for suckling. Alternatively, it may be a form of camouflage against predators, the streaks blending with blades of sunlight that penetrate the jungle canopy, the patchwork quality serving to break the animal's outline into seemingly disconnected parts. Whatever the evolutionary logic behind this coloring, no one yet knows where it came from or how it works.

There are other uncertainties. Should the okapi be considered a threatened species, or are the forests of Zaire still relatively full of them? Not known. In the wild, is their main cause of mortality those same intestinal parasites that kill them so remorselessly in zoos—or is it predation? Not known. And then the matter of their supposedly shy behavior. One authority describes them as "extremely wary and secretive, dashing through the forest at the least suggestion of danger." Another offers testimony from a missionary, one of the few non-Pygmy humans ever to have seen a wild okapi, who told of "stopping to watch an okapi in the headlights of his car; the animal walked up to the front of the vehicle quite calmly and turning round kicked through the car's radiator." The question here is the same as that posed by the visual pattern: Are we dealing with one animal or several?

Personally, I have never seen an okapi, not even in a zoo. My modest research has led me to published descriptions and anecdotes (most of those second- and thirdhand), to a few grainy photographs, and (more often, for some reason) to paintings and drawings. After three days of this, it occurred to me that the okapi might not exist.

Where is the proof, ontological or otherwise? I certainly haven't seen any. For all I know the okapi might be just a droll hoax, like the jackalope. The name itself, maybe, an anagram. *Koipa? O pika? I koap?* To the Pygmies it may stand for a month's worth of meat on the hoof, to the missionaries it may represent a road hazard, to the zookeepers it may be a precious curio, but to the rest of us (at least so it's tempting to conclude) the okapi seems less a real living animal than a riddle.

Something that Norwegian Leo understood, perhaps, from the beginning.

* * *

Now, Norwegian Leo is widely noted for his candor. His spontaneous, refreshing, and uncompromising directness. Some would say, his breathtaking bluntness. Once in a bar in Butte, Montana, for example, I witnessed an exchange between Leo and Whisperin' Jack, the famous medical researcher and bon vivant (who figured in a previous volume of these essays). Whisperin' Jack was describing the difficult fact that he himself longed to forsake Connecticut for Montana, while his wife wanted to move to New York City. Leo listened as though sympathetic until Jack was finished, at which point he said, "Then you'll just have to get rid of her." On another occasion, just after I had been laid off from a job where he and I shared an office wall, Leo (fortified by his boundless sense of loyalty and a fifth of whiskey) phoned the director of the institute for which we both worked, an impeccably pin-striped man whose ghost writer I had been and who was Leo's own boss's boss's boss. Calling at 2 A.M. on a Wednesday, Leo gave the director a short, trenchant discourse to the effect that firing Quammen had been an act of surpassing stupidity. Then, after identifying himself clearly by name, Leo hung up. He was a skilled engineer; he could always find a new job.

Because of a hundred moments like that, my affection for Leo is as unstinting as his candor. So naturally I flinched just a little when I came upon the evidence, finally, that Leo had suckered me on this whole okapi deal.

Yes, I suspect that the okapi does exist. That's not the issue. There was this other bit of data, tucked in among all the bizarre and less bizarre facts I had been combing through in my sources. One phrase: ". . . and the weight is about 250 kilograms." Another authority, more conservative, makes that 200 to 250 kilograms. In other words, roughly 500 pounds. This great moose-like, horse-shaped, zebra-striped, short-necked giraffe, which I had envisioned bashing its way crazily through the Zairian bush, kicking out radiators and tumbling thunderously into pitfalls, turns out to be about the same size as an elk. A smallish female.

Not even so hefty as a gnu. Barely bulkier than a tapir. In the same order of magnitude, actually, as a pangolin.

Leo had led me astray. Such a delicate creature couldn't possibly be the largest mammal I'd never heard of. That distinction must still belong to the dugong.

THE LONESOME APE

Out on a Limb
in the Human Family Tree

The orang-utan is a remote sort of beast. By geography, by behavior, and by the currently prevailing view of its place within primate evolution, this species of ape known as *Pongo pygmaeus* stands apart. Consider: It survives today only on the islands of Sumatra and Borneo; it lives solitarily, not in elaborate social groups like the gorilla or the chimpanzee; it associates with its own kind for mating and infant-rearing but otherwise travels the rainforest treetops alone. And if that's not enough, a zoological encyclopedia will tell you with blustering self-assurance: "Of all the great apes, the orang-utan is the most distantly related to man."

Pongo's remoteness is not illusory, but that last statement might be. By the prevailing view, mankind and the chimpanzee are closely related, with the gorilla slightly more distant from us and the orang-utan a far-removed cousin. But the word "orang-utan" itself comes from Malayan linguistic roots meaning "forest man," and a new theory suggests that the label might carry a resonance more factual than poetic. The prevailing view, as Charles Darwin labored to prove, is not *always* the right one.

*　*　*

First, though, the matters of geography and behavior.

The geographic isolation of *Pongo pygmaeus* is easy enough to explain. About two million years ago orang-utans (or orang-utan ancestors) existed not just on Borneo and Sumatra but all across southern Asia. They seem to have been related (though perhaps not by direct descent) to an earlier and more ambiguous primate, an ape-like animal known now from fossil fragments as *Sivapithecus,* dating back about ten million years. The earliest *Sivapithecus* specimen was just part of a left upper jaw, with the teeth in place, discovered a century ago in the Siwalik Hills of India; since then more bits and nuggets of *Sivapithecus* have come out of the same general area—most recently the entire left side of a face, found by David Pilbeam and his colleagues in 1980. As manifest in the various specimens, the *Sivapithecus* creature had spade-like incisors and flat molars with thick enamel, suggesting that it might have fed mainly on fruit, like modern orang-utans. On the other hand, certain aspects of the teeth and the jaws seemed also to hint toward the human line. As early as 1915 scientists were arguing in print about whether these Siwalik fossils should be assigned to the human branch of the family tree or to the orang-utan's. *Sivapithecus* itself disappeared from the fossil record about eight million years ago, leaving no immediate descendants that have been discovered so far. What followed after it, what followed *from* it, remains a mystery.

Roughly six million years later came the prehistoric orang-utans, larger than the modern species and possibly more terrestrial, bold enough to descend from the trees and undertake some ambitious travel. Their distribution stretched up into China. During a period of cold climate and lowered sea level they must also have made a peninsular, dry-land crossing from the Asian mainland to what are now the islands of Java, Sumatra, and Borneo. Then around a million years ago primitive humans (in the form of *Homo erectus*) arrived in Southeast Asia, with their primitive but effective methods of hunting. They even reached

Java—as the term "Java Man," one of many for *Homo erectus,* commemorates. The orang-utans of the mainland and Java were extinguished. But on Sumatra and Borneo—now protected beyond water gaps, safe from *Homo* and other predators—they remained. They adapted to a totally arboreal life. And so they survived to the present day.

Modern orang-utans almost never come down to the ground. They are too large to be as acrobatic as monkeys and gibbons, so they make their way slowly and carefully from limb to limb, tree to tree, gripping with both hands and feet, methodical in their progress, taking no reckless leaps. Despite their great bulk and the energy spent on all that hard climbing, they live almost entirely on fruit. The behavioral solitude of the species, so different from the sociability of other big apes, seems to be a natural requirement of this unique orang-utan ecology.

A British zoologist named John MacKinnon has explained it beautifully, based on his two years of field study in the jungles of Borneo and Sumatra. According to MacKinnon, the orang-utan's unsociable behavior is not instinctive but learned. His observations (reported in a long article in the journal *Animal Behavior,* and in several popular books) revealed that juveniles of the species *do* have an inborn interest in playmates of their own kind. Their mothers, though, enforce a strict separation of family groups, dragging youngsters away from each other. Adult males also keep their distance from each other and (except at mating) from the individual females. "But why are adult orang-utans so solitary?" MacKinnon asks. "The answer lies in the distribution of fruit foods in the Asian rainforest."

The jungles of Borneo contain perhaps three thousand species of tree. Within the range of a single orang-utan there might be 250 species that occasionally bear fruit or some other edible part. This might sound like bountiful pickings for a vegetarian, but the corollary to such breadth of variety is that no species of fruit tree grows in a concentrated clump; the members of any species are scattered widely through the forest, each one as solitary as the big lonesome ape. "Thus there are large distances between trees that are in fruit at the same time, but the orang-utan is slow-moving and able to search only a small area each day," writes MacKinnon. A large family or a tribe of orang-utans, traveling slowly as they do, would find no more food in one day than a single orang-utan can, but would have to divide that food among many more mouths. On Borneo especially the orang-utan has few natural predators (except, nowadays, man) from which an alert social group might offer protection, and the task of finding and gathering food requires no cooperative effort. So the animals operate as loners.

There's another fascinating dimension to this outwardly simple life. Full-grown orang-utans can't afford to lumber along randomly through the trees, hoping to blunder upon food; they need to conserve time and energy by systematically visiting one fruiting tree after another. This isn't easy. Some of the rainforest trees bear fruit every few months, some on annual or biannual or multiple-year cycles, and so the pattern of available fruit in a given stretch of jungle is complicated across space and time, by botanical rhythms and signals of readiness and the matter of what species of tree is located where. Orang-utans are faced with learning that pattern, then playing it like a game of Concentration. And they play like winners. Despite covering less area than its smaller and faster competitor, the gibbon, an orang-utan manages to find more fruit. "The orang-utan shows a simply uncanny ability to locate fruit," writes John MacKinnon, "and his secret is superior brainpower."

MacKinnon goes further. He rejects the idea that primate intelligence has evolved in direct relation to social complexity, as supposedly reflected in chimp and gorilla societies. MacKinnon's alternative? "The truth is that ape intelligence was evolved in response to the difficulty of locating fruit in tropical rainforests."

*   *   *

If this seems mildly provocative, an even bolder bit of orang-utan heterodoxy comes now from a scientist named Jeffrey H. Schwartz. Schwartz is a physical anthropologist at the University of Pittsburgh, and unlike MacKinnon he has not devoted years of his life ("constantly being drained by biting flies, ticks and blood-sucking leeches, clinging mud and tearing thorns, oppressive heat and humidity, the growing weight of [one's] pack, regular drenching by tropical downpours, loneliness, hunger, thirst, and despondency," as MacKinnon reminisces cheerfully) to stalking orang-utans in the wild. Schwartz is a theorist. He does his research in museum collections and libraries. He has focused on primate anatomy, not primate behavior—and in particular on the comparative anatomy of the orang-utan and of that ambiguous fossil ape, *Sivapithecus*. Based on a modest but tantalizing cluster of evidence, he proposes that the orang-utan is our own closest living relative.

It's the chimpanzee and the gorilla, according to Schwartz, that are remote from us *Pongo* and *Homo* types.

A few years ago Schwartz first advanced this theory with an article in the journal *Nature*. Then in 1987 he published a book titled *The Red Ape: Orang-utans and Human Origins,* which presents the idea at much greater (sometimes tedious) length. Schwartz's evidence and his logic are far too complex to be done justice here, in a brief essay. Let it suffice to say that the whole question of primate relationships involves (among other sorts of evidence) anatomical resemblances and molecular resemblances; and that the molecular resemblances *do* seem to link us with chimps, but the anatomical record (especially as manifested in teeth, jaws, and skulls) is another matter. Schwartz argues that the molecular evidence is inconclusive, but that anatomical analysis shows a special kinship between the orang-utan and the human. *"Homo* and *Pongo* are set apart by their low-cusped cheek-teeth and thick molar enamel," he writes, "as well as by the restriction of the double incisive foramina to a single opening palatally," and that's only the start. Never mind what a double incisive foramen is, or why it might pinch down to a single opening through the palate—the crucial point is that humans and orang-utans both have one, and that it does thus pinch down to one opening.

Sivapithecus had a double incisive foramen too; and it also pinched down to one opening.

As the science of human origins rocks back and forth on its foamy seas, buffeted by each new fossil discovery, yawing now toward Olduvai Gorge, then pitching toward the Siwalik Hills, *Sivapithecus* is the cannon that's loose on the deck. Keep your eye on this *Sivapithecus*. *Sivapithecus,* in coming years, is liable to enter the vernacular. The indisputable contribution of Jeffrey Schwartz (or so it seems to me, a confessed ignoramus in this field) has been in recognizing and highlighting that fact.

The rest of his contribution, by contrast, is intensely disputable. It is also fresh, imaginative, tortuous in its logic, abundantly researched, turgidly expressed *(The Red Ape* can't be recommended, alas, as bedtime reading), admirably provocative, downright interesting. And if you happen to like orang-utans, or solitude, or both, it has a certain appeal to vanity.

For seventy years the experts have been arguing over two diametric interpretations of those puzzling *Sivapithecus* fossils. Some have said: *Obviously these creatures were close human relatives!* Others have said: *No, obviously they belong with the orangutan!* Dignified and intelligent scientists have anguished over that choice, had their minds changed by new specimens, recanted in print. Now Jeffrey Schwartz simply says: *Why not both?*

STRANGER THAN TRUTH

Cryptozoology and the
Romantic Imagination

Reality isn't everything. Truth and certainty are fine, as far as they go, but truth and certainty don't supply all the nourishment that the soul of our species seems to require. We also have a need for marvels, for facts that are stranger than truth. We yearn to believe in (or at least to suspect) the existence of paranormalities, patterns and forces beyond rational fathoming, beings that are greater and wilder than anything we have ever seen. This restless instinct is part of what Voltaire had in mind, I think, when he said, "If God did not exist, it would be necessary to invent him." It's the same instinct that makes *The Twilight Zone* a perennial success in reruns, and has put Erich von Däniken's ragged books on the best-seller list. Probably it has also helped nurture that ineradicable notion of an elaborate dark conspiracy of which Lee Harvey Oswald was the dupe. And it goes far, this hunger for marvels, toward explaining the International Society for Cryptozoology.

Cryptozoology is loosely defined by its practitioners as "the science of hidden animals." There is some latitude in the interpretation of what constitutes a "hidden" animal (and some controversy over whether the whole business can really qualify as a "science"), but it's generally accurate to say that cryptozoologists concern themselves with creatures that have been rumored to exist in shapes, in places, in sizes, or in time periods whereby they somehow violate what is expected. Sasquatch and the Loch Ness monster are classic examples. Sea serpents are another favorite topic for cryptozoologization. The large and mysterious species of animal that supposedly inhabits Lake Champlain, the giant octopus that may or may not attain 200-foot arm spans in the Atlantic off Florida, the mermaid-like beast known as Ri to certain islanders in Papua New Guinea, and the Buru lizard of Himalayan legend are all objects of cryptozoological attention. Even the eastern cougar is included, because it has long been considered extinct but may possibly have survived within remote enclaves of Appalachia or New England. In each case the element of anomalousness, the violation of conventional zoological expectations, is important. But the element of rumor or legend is equally essential.

Cryptozoologists work, at the earliest stage, from testimonial evidence. They are committed (by tradition and preference, they explain, in answer to the cavil that their methods seem willfully limiting) to the search for precisely those hidden animals that have been heard of indirectly through the reports of native peoples and other nonscientist witnesses. They are not interested in the five or ten million species of beetle that remain undiscovered in the Amazon. Their perspective is biased toward *large* unknown animals—not because insects and nematodes are unimportant, they say, but because large animals are the ones most likely to find a place in the legends and rumors and half-incredible reports from which cryptozoologists take their first clues. There is nothing logical about this bias, they admit. It is purely a matter of choice. Entomology for the entomologists, cryptozoology for those who prefer to sneak up on a big new beast by following the spoor of its reputation.

In a sense, then, cryptozoology is really an epistemological enterprise as much as a zoological one. It is concerned with adjudicating the conflict between two belief systems. It asks: When scientific orthodoxy and local lore contradict each other regarding the existence of a creature, how often might local lore be proven correct?

The okapi is often put forward by cryptozoologists as their best test case.

The okapi is that improbable beast mentioned earlier ("The Ontological Giraffe") in this book. It is a harlequin sort of creature, with the face of a startled young moose, the ears of a donkey, and zebra-like stripes banding its legs and decorating its rear end in a gaudy starburst pattern. By skeletal anatomy it closely resembles *Helladotherium,* a giraffid that supposedly went extinct about ten million years ago. Reports of such an animal, alive and well in the Congo jungle, began reaching Europe during the nineteenth century. Those reports caught the eye of a young English boy named Harry Johnston, who grew up to be Sir H. H. Johnston and went out in service of the empire as special commissioner for Uganda. While he was in Africa, Johnston questioned some Pygmy tribesmen from the Congo about this supposedly jungle-dwelling, giraffe-like thing. Yes indeed, said the tribesmen, it was quite real and they called it *okhapi.* Johnston pressed the search and eventually, in 1901, a complete skin and two skulls were obtained. On the basis of that evidence, the animal was scientifically classified as *Okapia johnstoni.* Not until 1919 did a live captive okapi arrive in Europe, consigned to the custody of the Antwerp zoo—where, of course, it promptly died.

Sir Harry Johnston is now a patron saint of the International Society for Cryptozoology, and the image of the okapi, this living chimera patched together from parts of giraffe and moose and zebra, adorns the organization's official seal.

The society itself was founded in 1982, by a mixed group of scientists and nonprofessional researchers who had all been cryptozoologizing independently but wanted a formalized forum through which to share information and ideas. A constitution was drawn up. A board of directors was anointed, including some distinguished paleontologists and biologists such as Leigh Van Valen of the University of Chicago. Bernard Heuvelmans, a French zoologist and writer, was elected the society's first president, based on his status as the "father" of this branch of inquiry, the man who actually coined the word *cryptozoology*, and the most widely read popularizer of the subject. Heuvelmans is famous for two books in particular, *On the Track of Unknown Animals* and *In the Wake of the Sea-Serpents*—both of which are heavily researched and encyclopedic, even in some places pedantic, but which contain leaps of credulity that leave a skeptical reader behind. Heuvelmans in fact is probably not the best spokesman for cryptozoology, because he tends to be portentous and make overstated claims. Roy Mackal, the American vice president of the society who has led expeditions to the Likouala swamps of central Africa in search of a (perhaps) surviving dinosaur called Mokele-Mbembe, offers a slightly quieter and more persuasive voice. But the best view of what cryptozoology is, and what it can be, and the range of ideas and questions and intellectual temperaments it encompasses, comes in the society's formal journal, *Cryptozoology*.

This journal began publication in 1982 and during the following four years just one issue appeared annually, but those four issues are intriguing, diverse, and mainly quite sane. The contents include field reports on the latest (inconclusive) Mokele-Mbembe expeditions, theoretical articles by Heuvelmans and others concerning the nature and methods of cryptozoology, book reviews, pieces with titles such as "The Status of Wildman Research in China" and "The Loch Ness Monster: Public Perception and the Evidence," and, most crucially, a section of comments and responses, devoted to debate and dissent over what has previously appeared in the journal. This last section is where ISC members scuffle with each other over what constitutes dubious evidence or woolly logic, struggling to enforce on themselves a standard of good sense and manifesting a healthy lack of mutual reverence. *Cryptozoology* is edited with admirable rigor and clear-mindedness by a pleasant Englishman named J. Richard Greenwell, now living in Tucson, Arizona. Greenwell is the ISC secretary, and also holds the unenviable position of treasurer. (The ISC is a private and unaffiliated body, and seems to be as impecunious as it is benign.) Greenwell explains that when the journal is late in appearing, which happens not rarely, the problem is usually related to cash flow.

Greenwell himself has accompanied Roy Mackal on one of the Mokele-Mbembe expeditions, and more recently has done fieldwork on the Ri creature out in Papua New Guinea. Trained as an anthropologist, he has thrown himself into cryptozoology because, as he told me by telephone, he is intrigued by the way zoological mysteries interplay with the human, psychological element of testimonial evidence. Then, with the more stern academic critics of cryptozoology obviously in mind, he added: "Anyway, we're not doing anyone any harm. We're not getting any government money. And it's fun. It's fun." With Richard Greenwell guiding the journal in that spirit, a subscription to *Cryptozoology* seems not such a bad investment.

Nowhere else, after all, can a person find scholarly disquisitions like "The Orang-Utan in England: An Explanation for the Use of *Yahoo* as a Name for the Australian Hairy Man" and "Anatomy and Dermatoglyphics of Three Sasquatch Footprints." Nowhere else can a curious soul read up on "Vertical Flexure in Jurassic and Cretaceous Marine Crocodilians and Its Relevance to Modern 'Sea-Serpent' Reports." At the bottom of the cover of each issue of *Cryptozoology,* aptly, appears the image of the okapi, with all its mismatched parts, looking gentle and improbable and faintly surprised to be alive.

*   *   *

Not everyone takes an indulgent view of the society and its official journal. When *Cryptozoology* made its debut in 1982, just one among many new journals (including *Ferroelectric Letters, Polymer Photochemistry,* and *The International Journal of Robotics Research*) to begin publication that year, it was the only new entry that was reviewed in *Newsweek.* The folk at *Newsweek* may have been bemused, but Robert M. May, a Princeton zoologist writing somewhat later in the august scientific weekly *Nature,* was downright dour. May suggested that the undying popular interest in bizarre, undiscovered, and perhaps undiscoverable creatures was the result of "a tendency on the part of the media —and maybe the public—to prefer meretricious marvels to real ones." Well, *meretricious* is a strong word (I looked it up, so I know), yet as a member of both the media and the public, I cannot disagree with him. Yes, once in a while we all like a cheap thrill. What of it, Dr. May?

Nevertheless, my own attitude remains divided.

On the one hand, I have no special bias in favor of using cultural lore or testimonial evidence (which can be, as we all know, quite flaky) as a tool of zoological inquiry, and I still think that the question of why there are millions of beetle species awaiting discovery in the tropical canopies is *far* more interesting than the question of whether Kenneth Wilson's 1934 photograph at Loch Ness shows a relict plesiosaur with its neck out of the water or the ass end and tail of an otter.

On the other hand, I acknowledge the legitimate human need for marvels—wild and improbable marvels, as well as the more subtle natural ones.

In his discourse on the subject of miracles, the great Scottish skeptic David Hume wrote: "We soon learn that there is nothing mysterious or supernatural in the case, but that all proceeds from the usual propensity of mankind toward the marvelous, and that, though this inclination may at intervals receive a check from sense and learning, it can never be thoroughly extirpated from human nature."

Why can't it be extirpated, not even in an age as relentlessly analytical as our own? Because the romantic imagination of mankind is itself a hidden animal, a wondrous and inextinguishable beast.

DEEP THOUGHTS

A Theory
with Some Holes in It

Holes are in the news again.

It happens that way, have you noticed? Mankind tootles along nicely for years, even decades, devoting no special attention to the subject until, suddenly, there comes an outbreak of renewed fascination with the ontology and etiology of holes. Yes, holes, like in the ground. Like the opposite of mounds and mountains. When the time comes around in this cycle, new holes begin to appear; neglected holes are discovered belatedly; old holes are reinterpreted in the light of more advanced thinking. We are in such a period now.

The big meteor crater outside of Winslow, Arizona, turns up in a movie called *Starman*. Elsewhere, scientists searching for evidence of a twin star that may orbit in tandem with our sun—bringing cataclysm and mass extinctions upon Earth every twenty-six million years—have begun surveying meteor craters for possible confirmation of such a twenty-six-million-year cycle. In Great Britain a brilliant astrophysicist announces that black holes, those boggling zones of compacted matter and inexorable gravitation, might actually *emit* particles. And the latest: a pair of hole-related stories out of the Soviet Union, long a world leader in the realm of mysterious holes.

The first of these two Soviet specimens, known as the Kola borehole, is presently the planet's deepest and most expensive (and, some would say, most inane) hole. Penetrating, at last report, 7.5 miles down through hard crystalline rock, and only as wide as a pizza, this hole has been drilled from a spot on the Kola Peninsula, an extreme northwestern nub of the Soviet Arctic. Why was it drilled? That's a good question, and one we'll address in due course. The second Soviet hole is not actually new and not actually a hole (two technicalities that need not concern us here), but it has recently gotten fresh scrutiny by those who apply themselves to the contemplation of holes, thanks to certain developments in atomic theory and astrophysics. The non-hole of which I speak is a huge impact crater that was *not* found at the epicenter of devastation left by the so-called Great Siberian Meteor. It was not found at the epicenter, where it should have been, nor anywhere else: a conspicuously and tauntingly absent hole, this one. There were eyewitness accounts of a flaming mass that fell out of the sky, an explosion equivalent to perhaps twenty megatons, 1,500 square miles of pine and birch trees knocked flat by blast wave and scorched by unearthly heat—but no crater. No hole.

Aha, you say, Siberia. The Soviet Arctic and now Siberia. Why do these holish wonders tend to site themselves in such woebegone places? Another good question. Which just goes to prove my point: With so many holes lurking around so mysteriously, so many nagging questions about them (including: *If you dig a hole in the ground and then fill it up with the same dirt, is that hole gone, or just hidden?* and *Why do bakeries sell doughnut holes but not bagel holes?* and of course *How many holes DOES it take to fill the Albert Hall?*) going unanswered, there seemed reason to hope that someone should be at work on a Unified Hole Theory. As far as I can determine, no one is.

So this week I have thrown myself at that challenge, but I tell you truly, the progress has not been encouraging. I've pedaled my bicycle back and forth repeatedly between the public library and the one at the university. I've tracked down old journal articles and I've read and I've pondered. I've sat in an aluminum lawn chair beneath a tree, scratching my feet. All to little avail. Some intriguing coincidences have revealed themselves to my modest research, but a good Unified Hole Theory still looks as unattainable as the golden fleece or the end of the rainbow or, well, uh, the Holey Grail.

The oil and gas industry drills more than 10,000 wells annually just in the U.S., but most of those holes are of no help to geologists who want to study the layers of crystalline rock in the Earth's crust. They have either been drilled in the wrong place or to the wrong depth for scientific purposes, or the information turned up is kept secret by the individual companies. Consequently, research geologists have begun promoting their own borehole projects as a means of investigating otherwise inaccessible rock.

The Kola borehole (which my wife, the scientist in the family, insists on calling "the world's deepest boring hole") was started fifteen years ago and is now deeper than any ocean trench or commercially drilled hole on the planet. The Soviets' stated goal is to continue down beyond nine miles, but according to a report last year in the journal *Science,* the going has lately become difficult. What have the Soviets learned from this project? Mainly, it seems, they have learned how to drill deep holes. They have also found some methane gas and mineralized waters at unexpected depths. If anything more has come out of the Kola hole, the Soviets are keeping it quiet. Meanwhile, a group of U.S. geologists are seeking financial support for their own borehole, to be drilled six miles down from a point in the southern Appalachians. *Science* observes soberly: "To start a national drilling program under present funding conditions, scientists must not only designate an exciting hole as first priority, but they must also put a clear price on it." The price of the Appalachian hole might be $45 million. The excitement level is anyone's guess.

Compared to these enterprises, the mystery of the Great Siberian Meteor is much more profound, although not nearly so deep.

Whatever this thing was, it came suddenly out of the sky on the morning of June 30, 1908, and crashed into the taiga along the remote headwaters of the Stony Tunguska River, 2,500 miles east of Moscow and a week's journey by reindeer (as the local people figured it) from the nearest village. One farmer in that village later recalled: "There was so much heat that I was no longer able to remain where I was—my shirt almost burned off my back. I saw a huge fireball that covered an enormous part of the sky. I only had a moment to note the size of it. Afterward it became dark, and at the same time I felt an explosion that threw me several feet from the porch."

The flash of that explosion was visible four hundred miles away, and the sound carried still farther. Seismographs halfway around the world registered the concussion. In an area of forest fifty miles across, nearly every tree had been broken off or uprooted, all of them laid flat in a neat radial pattern with the trunks pointing back toward an epicenter. No scientific investigator reached this site for years afterward, but when one finally did, he found two especially curious phenomena. First, the explosion had left a number of trees still standing upright almost exactly at, or under, its epicenter. Second, it had produced no crater. No hole.

Eighty years later, scientists are still wondering how to account for this event. The puzzling fact of the standing trees can be explained by assuming that the Tunguska explosion was an air burst, occurring not precisely at ground zero but some several thousand feet directly overhead. A blast wave spreading from that point might have only stripped branches from the trees beneath, then splashed out in all directions to flatten an area of surrounding forest.

The matter of the missing crater is more complicated. One hypothesis is that the Great Siberian Meteor was not a meteor but a comet. A comet, being a loose conglomeration of dust and ice, might have vaporized explosively as it passed through the atmosphere, leaving no trace of its own mass on the ground. Another suggestion offered quite seriously is that the explosion was nuclear, resulting from a malfunction in the engines of an extraterrestrial spaceship. This idea seems to be favored by some respectable Soviet researchers, including the professor from Tomsk who claimed recently to have found metal fragments from the ship. One pair of American physicists, A. A. Jackson and Michael Ryan, have even proposed that the devastation was caused by a black hole—a tiny one, no bigger than an atom, but containing the compressed mass of a large asteroid. According to their notion, the black hole would have come whistling in at extremely high speed, generating a shock wave by the intensity of its gravitational force. Having struck near the Tunguska River on an angled path, in a moment it would have passed through the Earth, exiting with a huge burst of spray somewhere in the North Atlantic. Check the maritime records for June 30, 1908, Jackson and Ryan suggest, for reports of some outlandish oceanic disturbance.

Obviously that last hypothesis has great attraction, especially for us Unified Hole Theorists. But one further possibility offers still more promise. Maybe the Siberian forest was hit by a gob of antimatter.

Antimatter, physicists tell us, consists of subatomic particles that are opposite but identical in character to the subatomic particles we all know and love. What they mean by "opposite but identical" could take half a book to explain, so let's just say that *one* possible form of oppositeness is an opposite electrical charge.

For instance, the antimatter equivalent to an electron is called a *positron,* having the same exact mass as an electron, plus an equal but opposite charge. Corresponding to a proton is an *antiproton,* again equal in mass, equal but opposite in charge; and so on for neutrinos, pions, the whole subatomic menagerie.

None of these antimatter particles can have a stable existence on Earth. If a proton comes in contact with an antiproton, there is a potent flash of energy as both particles disappear. That phenomenon, matter and antimatter canceling each other violently out of existence, is called *annihilation.* You can see where this is taking us, yes? Another team of scientists have proposed that perhaps the Tunguska region was hit with a piece of antimatter, a hunk of sheer negation flying in from the far end of the universe.

Now comes the part that can give a person a migraine. It seems that two main conceptual models have been put forward to describe the relation between matter and antimatter. The one devised by Richard Feynman, a brilliant and puckish American physicist, invites us to view the positron as "an electron moving backward in time." By this model, which makes better sense in the context of Einstein's space-time than it does to our intuition, the annihilation event represents, not a terminal instant for two opposite particles, but the point where a single particle reverses direction in time. (Therefore Feynman's model, whatever its value to physics, at least answers the classic conundrum: *How can you be in two places at once, if you're not anywhere at all?*) The other model, conceived by Paul Dirac, describes a positron as "an electron hole."

According to Dirac, these holes might exist everywhere throughout empty space, but generally they would not be detectable because they are *filled,* each with a complementary electron. Every electron in our world of matter must have some particular level of energy; the electrons stuck in antimatter holes are those with energy levels less than zero. So they can't get out. And when an electron falls into such a hole, that electron disappears in a burst of surrendered energy. Do you understand that much? Neither do I. So the Tunguska explosion, with its strange lack of a hole, can be explained in terms of this view of antimatter: The hole isn't there now because *the hole itself* is precisely what came flying in from space.

It wasn't very massive, that gob of antimatter, but it had vast energetic potential. When it entered the Earth's atmosphere it was annihilated—along with an equal but opposite amount of the air above central Siberia. Today the hole is invisible for the very good reason that it happens to be presently full. Like the one you might dig in the ground and then fill back up: *Is it gone, or is it just hidden?*

What does all this have to do with the Kola borehole? Another good question. I wish I could answer it. But the matrix of scientific logic connecting Tunguska to Kola, in my Unified Hole Theory, is one part of the pudding that hasn't yet set.

On the other hand, bringing in Dirac's model of antimatter *has* helped to shed light on another notable hole: the big open-pit mine that sits in downtown Butte, Montana. This hole is a mile wide and more than a thousand feet deep. In its day, it swallowed away a large portion of the east side of the city. Now the Anaconda Minerals Company has quit mining it, so the thing just remains there, stark, derelict, gaping. It was known to the company as the Berkeley Pit, but a few years ago some imaginative local folk decided that label just didn't do it justice. So they sponsored a little contest: NAME THE PIT. The winning entry was "Mount Nixon."

III

FOR WHOM
THE BELL TOLLS

ISLAND GETAWAY

Insular Biogeography
and the Scourge of Guam

Ever since young Charles Darwin first made sense of his Galápagos data, small islands have played a disproportionately large role in the thinking of evolutionary biologists.

Alfred Russel Wallace spent eight years in the Malay Archipel ago, finding patterns of evidence that led him (independently but simultaneously) to the same great idea that Darwin had been incubating. Later Wallace produced an opus called *Island Life* and became known as the father of biogeography, that branch of science concerned with the geographical distribution of plants and animals. K. W. Dammermann published a classic study of the recolonization of Krakatau after the big blast, while Hawaii, Easter Island, and the Channel Islands off southern California have also come in for especially careful investigation. More recently, Robert MacArthur and E. O. Wilson have influenced a generation of ecologists with a work called *The Theory of Island Biogeography*. And it can be no mere coincidence that Stephen Jay Gould, whose mind soars like a condor over the whole vista of biological sciences, has focused his own research efforts on land snails of the West Indies. Why all this attention to remote tropical isles? Is it simply because academic biologists like to get away from the telephone and come home from their fieldwork with a tan?

No, there's a still better reason. Speciation and extinction tend to happen more rapidly on islands. At the same time, the level of species diversity (the number of different species present in a given area of similar habitat) is almost always lower than on the continental mainlands. Therefore the complex relationships balancing life against death, stasis against change, the success of one species against the decline of another, show themselves more clearly in such places. The history of life on islands reflects—in a heightened and simplified way—the entire evolutionary process. You could think of it as the pantomime version of a Shakespearean drama. And now lately, on a remote Pacific island, one scene of that stark pantomime is being acted out again.

Something is killing the birds of Guam.

Until just a few years ago Guam had six endemic species of bird—*endemic* meaning they were found nowhere else in the world. Today the bridled white-eye is extinct. The Guam broadbill is extinct. The rufous-fronted fantail is almost certainly extinct. And the other three species are not much better off. The Guam rail seems to have disappeared from the island in early 1984, though it is still represented in zoos on the U.S. mainland. The Micronesian kingfisher is also being protected and bred over here, in captivity, with only a single forlorn and unmated male left, at last report, in the wild. The Mariana crow, most numerous of the survivors, is down to about fifty wild birds. Six other species of land bird on the island, native but not endemic, are also threatened. More birds are vanishing daily. This whole trend of decline was first noticed in 1978 and grew worse very quickly, but for a long while no one could see what was causing it.

Pesticides were suspected. Disease was suspected. Lab analyses were done on some bird specimens, though, and no Guam avian epidemic could be found. Then in 1982 a graduate student from the University of Illinois named Julie Savidge went out there to study the die-off, and she came upon one other possible answer: *Boiga irregularis.*

Boiga irregularis is a snake. It is an exotic species—not native to Guam—that seems to have arrived just after World War II. It may have stowed away on a shipment of military supplies, or it may have been introduced on purpose by some misguided individual or agency with a notion about rodent control. No one seems to know. At least no one is stepping up to claim credit. For close to forty years it was casually misidentified as the "Philippine rat snake," a mistake that allowed people to think of it tolerantly. But it turns out that *B. irregularis* is not a rat snake and is not from the Philippines. It is a bird-eating tree snake, native to New Guinea and coastal Australia. Arboreal and nocturnal and stealthy, reproductively prolific, it is also flexible enough in its habits to eat the occasional rodent or lizard if fowl isn't available. In other words, *B. irregularis* is just the sort of species that is supremely qualified for invading a strange island.

The snake is mildly venomous but not dangerous to humans, and for decades after its first appearance on Guam no one gave it much heed. It has long since grown familiar to the native Guamanians. Finally Julie Savidge began paying some bounties for these "Philippine rat snakes" and, when she cut them open, in virtually every one she found birds and eggs.

Back before the arrival of *B. irregularis,* Guam had been almost as snakeless as Ireland. The only native species of serpent was a poor little blind thing that burrowed in the soil, fed on termites, and looked more like a worm than like a snake. So the birds of Guam had evolved in the absence of snake predators, a halcyon situation that eventually cost them mortally. Better train for ill and not for good, says A. E. Housman, since "Luck's a chance, but trouble's sure." These birds hadn't trained. They were behaviorally naive. They had never been forced to learn certain hard lessons. For instance, they did not place their nests on the far ends of tiny branches or suspend them as elaborate hanging baskets; they did not carefully limit their trips to and from the nest site, so as to avoid giving away its position; they did not gather in colonies with a system of mutual warning calls. They were therefore defenseless against *B. irregularis*.

By the mid-1980s there were maybe a few hundred birds left on the island of Guam, maybe a few thousand, and an astonishing proliferation of *B. irregularis*. Rough estimates placed the snake population between one and three million—and Guam is not a big area, only ten miles by twenty. That figures out at about 10,000 *B. irregularis* to every square mile, which would be bad enough if they were mosquitoes. No one can know the real number, but the snakes have grown so common that they now cause frequent electrical outages. "I've caught snakes climbing guy wires to power poles," one biologist told me by phone from the island. "I've seen snakes hanging on power lines. I can go out here and in two hours collect more arboreal snakes than I could anywhere else in the world." *B. irregularis* has attained this astonishing abundance, we can safely guess, for three reasons: 1) the pickings have been so easy among those naive Guam birds that a bountiful food supply has enhanced reproduction; 2) the snake has left its troubles behind, escaping from all its own natural predators and competitors back in New Guinea and Australia; and 3) even if the *B. irregularis* population now suffers from overcrowding, there is nowhere it can expand to—because it too is stuck, after all, on an island.

The birds, on the other hand, are being offered a last-ditch getaway. Under a program sponsored cooperatively by the American Association of Zoological Parks and Aquariums and the Guam Division of Aquatic and Wildlife Resources, survivors of those last endemic species have been taken from the wild, before the snakes could finish them off, and airlifted to zoos on the U.S. mainland. The goal is to breed them back up to viable populations for eventual release back on Guam—that eventuality arriving only when (and if) a way has been found to control or eliminate *B. irregularis*. The airlift began in 1984, and within a year the captive breeding program yielded some young birds. The Micronesian kingfisher at that point numbered twenty-three in captivity. The Guam rail was up to about forty. Since then the breeding program has been fairly successful, producing small but steady increases in the numbers of both species. On Guam itself, though, the snake has continued its population explosion and the birds have continued to suffer. Only the Mariana crow seems to have held on in safe numbers, possibly because it is larger and less vulnerable. Meanwhile, in the Philadelphia Zoo, the Bronx Zoo, and a few other mainland zoos now reside almost the entire avian heritage of Guam. For an indefinite future those birds will endure their exile, patient and helpless, like an émigré community of Czarist Russians. Maybe someday their descendants will go home. Maybe.

What if they do? What if the snakes are successfully controlled and the birds are repatriated? From the standpoint of world ecological vigor and the conservation of the gene pool at large, will anything useful have been accomplished?

Arguably, no. One of the curious things about this emergency rescue program is that—by a coldly pragmatic standard of measure, according to prevailing ideas of island biogeography—it is evolutionarily futile.

If the snakes were allowed to eat every bird on Guam, then those six endemic species would have come to an evolutionary dead end, disappearing without trace from the main lines of bird evolution. And if the rescue succeeds, if the snake is controlled, if the rail and the kingfisher are finally returned home, then their likely eventual fate is . . . exactly the same. Resettled on a safer and more pristine Guam, what they face is the likelihood of disappearing without trace from the main lines of bird evolution.

Their native habitat—by its very nature, being a small and

remote island—is what promises them this evolutionary dead end. As natural processes take their course, the flow of species between mainland and island is almost purely a one-way movement. Small islands especially are the black holes to oblivion.

Speciation proceeds more rapidly under island conditions, it's true. Mature species arrive by all forms of dispersal, evolution progresses, and the luckiest of the pioneers adapt to their new habitats. They colonize. They specialize. They succeed. They become more sedentary than they were when they arrived—because the most restless individuals among them are constantly taking their genes elsewhere, flying off to escape or else to die trying. The others stay and stay. If they are birds or insects, very possibly they may lose the power of flight, like the dodos of Mauritius, the moas of New Zealand, the elephant birds of Madagascar. It is no coincidence that those extinct, flightless species all came to their end on islands. Hard to reach but still harder to escape, an island is generally the last stop. Once a species has landed, and settled in, and transformed itself in response to the local requirements, it has nowhere to go but extinct.

So by a coldly pragmatic standard of measure, the Guam airlift might be called futile. Nothing useful accomplished on behalf of the world's natural genetic vigor. That particular rail, that particular kingfisher—they had each, in a sense, already destined themselves to oblivion. If it wasn't the snake, it would have been a disease. If not a disease, then a fire or a climate change or an eruption. If it wasn't that, it would have been man, worst of all invaders, turning their habitat into parking lots and time-share condominiums. Face it, those two little species are doomed. They are islanders, therefore doomed. To rescue them now, temporarily, is only to say no to the inevitable.

Which is precisely why it's worth doing, of course.

A coldly pragmatic standard of measure is exactly the wrong sort, in this case as in so many others, to apply. Practicalities are not the issue. Two flickering candles of life are the issue. Dylan

Thomas would understand: Rage, rage against the dying of the light. So would Karl Wallenda and Harry Houdini and Ed Abbey. Saying no to the inevitable is one of the few precious ways our own species redeems itself from oblivion—or at least tries to. For mortal creatures, on a slow-dying planet, in the ocean of space, there's really no other option.

TALK IS CHEAP

A Personal Message
from Washoe the Chimp

In a recent book titled *Silent Partners,* a man named Eugene
Linden has raised an interesting and important question.
   Linden is a free-lance writer who has specialized in reporting
upon research into language-learning ability among primates. A
dozen years ago he published a volume called *Apes, Men, and
Language,* which is probably still the best overview of the subject. The sort of research enterprise that Linden described—
experimental efforts to teach apes, especially chimpanzees, to use
a human-designed language—was in high vogue among psychologists during the 1970s. But toward the end of the decade the
vogue faded, funding disappeared, and researchers turned their
attention elsewhere. Eugene Linden also turned his attention
elsewhere. Then he got curious and went back. Chimpanzees live
a long time, sometimes up to fifty years, and most of the animals
used in the experiments had been juveniles. Knowing this, Linden had the sensitivity to wonder about those long twilight years.
The question he shaped has a great depth of moral import and
leads the mind off in many directions—tossing up challenges to
some of the fundamental assumptions of Western culture, de-
manding new and careful thoughts on such matters as the nature
of personhood, the definition of language, the proper conduct of

relations between mankind and other species—but the essence of that question is quite simple.

Linden asked: What ever happened to Washoe the Talking Chimp?

Washoe was once a star of stage, screen, and monograph. She was perhaps the world's most famous chimpanzee who hadn't ridden a rocket. She achieved her renown with a series of performances that were not so flashy as spaceflight, but arguably just as epochal: She communicated with humans in a human language.

Washoe did not speak aloud. What she did was gesture eloquently. Her career began on a day in April of 1967, when she first used American Sign Language (the standard system of hand signals used among deaf-mutes in North America) to tell her guardians: "Gimme sweet."

The crucial thing about this gestural imperative was that it seemed to involve *cognitive* communication. Washoe had evidently matched particular signs to a particular message that she wished to convey in a particular situation. By way of contrast, Eugene Linden takes note of another class of animal speech, wherein a mynah bird at a Texaco station on a certain highway in Michigan states crisply to whomever walks by: "Up yours, you jive turkey." It isn't the same.

Washoe had been captured from the wild in Africa when she was less than a year old, and acquired by two Nevada psychologists named Allen and Beatrice Gardner. She lived in a relatively privileged human environment that included good food, freedom to ramble and climb, toys and other distractions, affectionate human attention, but no chimpanzee companionship whatsoever. It had been the Gardners' ingenious idea to try teaching American Sign Language to Washoe, because earlier research had suggested that chimps might be smart enough to learn human speech but were thwarted by their vocal anatomy. Washoe, like other chimps, could compensate with manual dexterity for what she lacked in voice control. By the time she was four years old she had a vocabulary of 85 signs. Eventually she mastered 132 signs. She could ask questions and she could use the negative. Occasionally she invented new signs, with particular referents of her own choice, and taught them to the Gardners. She even learned to swear (not so fluently as a mynah bird, but with more conviction) when she was annoyed. Some people said at the time—and a few might still say—that by crossing the language barrier Washoe had irreversibly blurred the boundary between her species and ours.

Undeniably she was special. She was something very much like a person.

After the period of her early work under the Gardners, two important changes came to Washoe's life. First, she was gradually shifted to the guardianship of a young graduate student named Roger Fouts. Second, she left Nevada (and Fouts with her) to take up residence at the Institute for Primate Studies, a research facility on wooded land outside of Norman, Oklahoma. The Institute for Primate Studies was in those days home to a raucous collection of gibbons, macaques, capuchin monkeys, and primates of various other species, including a sizable population of chimpanzees, and during the early 1970s it emerged as one of the main national centers of language-learning experimentation with chimps. At one point it housed a dozen chimps who each had some competence at sign language, plus a number of others not under instruction. Here at the institute, for the first time in her life, Washoe was put into a cage among other members of her species. She was horrified by the accommodations and disgusted by the other chimps, whom she described disdainfully, with her sign language, as "black bugs." In other words, from her acquired point of view they were not persons, like herself.

Roger Fouts helped to ease Washoe's adjustment, continuing her instruction in sign language and (at least as important) developing a heartfelt and mutual relationship with her that extended beyond the context of experimentation. They went for walks, Fouts and Washoe, hand in hand. They exchanged hugs. They argued and made up. (Chimpanzees in the wild can be quite belligerent toward each other, but are also distinguished by a great eagerness for conciliation and forgiveness after such fights.) They talked continually in sign language about simple quotidian matters.

Eventually Fouts became the most important individual in Washoe's life, and Washoe became the central subject of Fouts's career. But she was also more to him, it seems, than a scientific subject. Much later Roger Fouts wrote: "Several years ago, when Washoe was about seven or eight years old, I witnessed an event that told about Washoe as a person. . . ." He described an occasion when she had used courage and wit, dangling herself out precariously from the edge of a lake, in order to save another chimpanzee from drowning. "I was impressed with her heroism in risking her life on the slippery banks," Fouts wrote. "She cared about someone in trouble; someone she didn't even know that well." Having lived for a while among these creatures, she apparently no longer dismissed them as "black bugs."

And likewise, to Roger Fouts, Washoe herself was not just a clever test animal but an appealing and valued individual. To him she was not a beast but, in his own choice of word, a *person*—whatever that distinction may signify.

Among the other language-learning chimps in Oklahoma at this time, three besides Washoe achieved some measure of notoriety. Lucy was a captive-born female who spent her first eleven years in a pampered suburban life like Washoe's in Nevada, raised by a human couple in their home, with their young son for her companion and a pet cat of her own. Lucy learned a vocabulary of seventy-five signs and showed facility at creating her own compound words, such as "candy drink" to indicate watermelon. Sometimes she spoke to her toys in sign language. Ally was another, an especially bright male, also raised in a human household, until age four when his foster mother returned him to the institute. He took the separation hard, but then developed a new bond with a male researcher who wanted to study Ally's grasp of prepositions.

The third was named Nim Chimpsky—an irreverent allusion to the linguist Noam Chomsky. Nim was another male, born at the institute and then shipped off to Columbia University for use in an experiment that became rather famous, precisely because it was eventually declared a failure. At Columbia, Nim had sixty different teachers but apparently no close friends, no single supportive and personal relationship. After four years he was shipped back to Oklahoma, and the principal researcher at Columbia announced his conclusion that, though cleverly imitative, Nim was incapable of cognitive language use. In New York, for whatever reasons, Nim had not been a person.

What is a person? One message of the whole poignant pageant of language experimentation with chimpanzees, I think, is that this question is worth wondering about.

Aristotle, Descartes, and the entire Western philosophic tradition of spiritual-material dualism would have us believe that a person is a human being, period. A human possesses a rational soul, and in that soul inheres the essence of personhood. By contrast an animal (as these thinkers generally put it, though what they meant was "a nonhuman animal") has either a more primitive form of soul or none whatsoever, and therefore cannot be imagined as meriting personhood. John Ruskin and others have talked of the *pathetic fallacy,* a term which implies the assertion that, notwithstanding the liberties of metaphor, no storm cloud can truly be angry, no mountain can truly be haughty, and no chimpanzee can truly be heroic. All this seemed certain beyond question. For about eighteen centuries, in fact, the very idea of acknowledging personhood in a nonhuman creature was potently heretical. In some corners, it is still heretical.

Darwin is supposed to have cured us of some of this categorical smugness, but the Darwinian idea of continuity and incremental transformation throughout the spectrum of earthly life is seldom applied to the intangible aspects of what we call human nature. Darwin himself had a strong disagreement with his co-discoverer of natural selection, Alfred Russel Wallace, over the question of whether the human mind was a product of organic evolution. A half-mad South African naturalist named Eugène Marais later offered a wild and interesting notion when he argued (in a book titled *The Soul of the Ape*) that what Freud called "the unconscious" in humans had evolved directly from the conscious mentality of prehuman primates, and had merely been pushed into the psychological background by the more recent development of human consciousness. E. O. Wilson, with his concepts of sociobiology, is also working in this area. But generally the modern view closely resembles the traditional view in seeing mankind as set apart—absolutely and qualitatively—from the biological and (such as it may be) spiritual continuity of all other living creatures.

So *Homo sapiens* is supposedly unique, utterly distinct from the rest, through some miracle of cumulative neurological alchemy. Very well—then what *is* it exactly that manifests that uniqueness?

Religions all offer their own irrefutable answers, but the biological and social sciences have a little more trouble with the question. For instance, biochemical genetics suggests, not only that humans and chimpanzees are very closely related, but that the relation between chimps and us may be even closer than the one between chimps and gorillas. (Though orang-utans also have a plausible claim as our closest living relatives, as described above in "The Lonesome Ape.") Argument from behavior has turned out to be equally inconclusive. At times it has been claimed that mankind, uniquely, is the tool-using animal. Or that mankind is the weapon-using animal (as proposed so vividly in Kubrick's

2001: A Space Odyssey). But chimpanzees in the wild use both tools and weapons. It has also been claimed that mankind is the only tool-*making* animal. Wrong again: In the wild, chimps fashion tools especially for gathering one of their preferred foods, termites. And at last it was said, more conservatively, more confidently, that mankind is distinguished as the sole animal making cognitive use of language. That was until Washoe.

What is a person? Well, "person" is just a word, after all, and maybe the project of defining it is of no philosophic or scientific consequence. But in my own view it is an eloquent word, a richly connotative word, and one well suited for use in exactly that foggy no-man's-land between humanity and the rest of the biological community. I think it's a word that is wasted if judged to be merely a synonym for *Homo sapiens.* To me it seems that a person is any creature with whom you—or I, or Roger Fouts—can have a heartfelt and mutual relationship.

The great value of Eugene Linden's book, *Silent Partners,* is in telling us what became of those famous language-learning chimps in the years after the spotlight deserted them.

In 1982 Ally and Nim were sold off, along with a few other sign-using chimps from the institute, to a medical research laboratory in the state of New York. The destiny facing them at this laboratory was to be used in the testing of hepatitis vaccines.

It should be said that the laboratory maintained its chimps under relatively comfortable conditions, and that the testing program was generally nonfatal. But then CBS News ran a short piece on the matter, and that led to a brief but vociferous public outcry, which in turn led to a decision that Ally and Nim—only those two, and because of their famous names—would be spared from medical research. Nim was eventually sent to a ranch in Texas, a place run by the Fund for Animals as a refuge for abused horses, where he would receive benevolent care but where, according to Linden, he had no chimpanzee companionship. Ally was sent to a breeding farm for chimps, where his name was changed and his illustrious past was of no interest, and so he has in effect disappeared, one of several indistinguishable chimps put out to stud in that place. There is no news about whether anyone ever chats with Ally or Nim in sign language.

Lucy was luckier. Like Washoe, she had acquired a devoted and stubbornly loyal friend. She was shipped to a certain refuge in West Africa where promising work had been done on reintroducing displaced chimpanzees to the wild. But because Lucy had lived for so many years like a human in human surroundings, and had never before even seen an equatorial jungle, the adjustment to her ancestral habitat has been difficult. Her human friend, a woman named Janis Carter, who originally met Lucy in Oklahoma, had at last report spent almost eight years over there herself, in the West African bush, trying to help Lucy learn the ways of a wild chimpanzee.

And Washoe is still with Roger Fouts, now at a different research facility in a different state. Together they are still exploring (in a style of interaction that is less formalized than science generally prefers) the question of what humans and chimpanzees might be able to teach each other about thinking and talking and learning. Meanwhile they seem to have discovered something far more precious, and far more communicative, than language.

ICEBREAKER

A Brief Rapprochement
Between Whales and Russians

News dispatches arriving from the Soviet Far East in a recent year revealed surprising new evidence of intelligent life at sea. The evidence was musical. The surprise belonged to a group of whales. The intelligence belonged to a group of Soviet mariners.

On February 6, 1985, the government newspaper *Izvestia* reported that a Soviet icebreaker, the *Moskva,* had been diverted from its usual duty, keeping shipping lanes open in the Bering Sea, and was presently on its way to attempt the rescue of a thousand desperate whales. These whales were penned into a small area of open water within Senyavina Strait, just southwest of the Bering Strait, where they had gotten trapped by shifting ice floes while feeding on a shoal of fish. They were part of a great herd of migrating beluga, *Delphinapterus leucas,* the only species among all cetaceans that is a pure snowy white. The largest of the males were twenty feet long and weighed a ton and a half; the females were slightly smaller. They couldn't escape by going under the ice, they couldn't get around it, and as the open area shrank further they were doomed to begin dying of starvation or suffocation. The water of Senyavina was "boiling," according to *Izvestia,* with their frantic efforts to thrash a way out. The whales' only hope seemed to be that Soviet icebreaker.

But it was an improbable hope, since the Soviets are notorious in certain quarters for their unregenerate slaughter of whales. The U.S.S.R. is a member of the International Whaling Commission, but Soviet whaling fleets often refuse to abide by the IWC's rulings. Already that year they had flouted the kill quota for minke whales (a small species of baleen whale that became commercially attractive only when most of the larger baleens had been killed off) with their factory-ship operations near Antarctica, and had announced their intent to exceed the quota by a full thousand minkes before they stopped killing.

But those thousand belugas, in contrast, were for some reason more precious alive. This was no impulsive act of sentiment by one whale-loving sea captain; clearly a decision had been made in Moscow. Before it was all over, the icebreaker's time alone had cost $80,000, a sum that no Soviet bureaucrat would allot to seemingly quixotic purposes without confidence that those purposes had the blessing of Moscow. And whoever in Moscow made that decision, for whatever motives, that person had undeniably been visited with a moment of transcendent good sense. Maybe it was a public relations stunt. Maybe there had come a sudden new Soviet recognition of kinship with the cetaceans. But whether you take the most cynical view, or the least cynical, that $80,000 was money well spent.

The *Moskva* arrived, threw itself at the ice blockage, couldn't break through. The ice was twelve feet thick in some places, and the blockage was twelve miles across. The ship was forced to withdraw for refueling. By the time it could return, the whales had been trapped for almost a month, though there was no sign yet that they had begun dying off. The icebreaker tried again. Meanwhile, workers from the mainland were keeping that penned area clear of new ice and dropping loads of fish to the whales, in the hope of bolstering their strength—possibly also their morale. Nevertheless, about forty belugas did die, with more destined to follow soon. Then the *Moskva* broke through. It had cut a channel twelve miles long and seventy yards wide, from the open sea to the whales. Now all the whales had to do was follow the *Moskva* back out.

But they wouldn't. They wouldn't go. No doubt they were still distressed and addled from the entrapment, but they also had good grounds for a more deep-seated confusion. Experience had not prepared these animals to expect kindness from humans, in ships of Soviet registry or any other. As a species they had been butchered by virtually every tribe of mankind that sails and hunts Arctic waters—Eskimos, Greenlanders, Norwegians, Russians, and every sort of Siberian. They had been driven up onto beaches, stabbed and shot to death, strangled and drowned in gillnets and sweep nets and seines. These thousand survivors had no reason *not* to be terrified. All whales are smart, of course, but belugas are among the smartest and most wary, so they may well have wondered: *Is this another murderous trap?* They wouldn't follow the ship. Not until someone on board thought of music.

"Several melodies were tried out," said a Soviet press account, "and it turned out that classical music was to the taste of these Arctic belugas." So with classical music pouring from loudspeakers on board the *Moskva,* a thousand white whales swam behind the ship, trailing it trustingly down that channel to freedom.

Who says there's no cheerful news in the papers? Even Greenpeace sent a telegram of congratulations. And I began poking into it, in a modest way, with my own small list of unanswered questions.

Of course the most obvious was: *Which* classical music? The Moscow press sources gave no specifics, didn't name a particular piece or even a composer, and to me that seemed a tantalizing oversight. Who did those belugas like? What composition was it that so moved them? What was it that sang to them so clearly, so reassuringly, in tones of benevolent fellowhood? Was it some wild romantic sonata by Rachmaninoff? Was it "The Great Gate of

Kiev"? Was it Tchaikovsky? Stravinsky? Prokofiev? Or maybe, despite understandable chauvinist pride, was it something by a non-Russian? Possibly Pachelbel's weatherproof "Canon in D," for a parade of one thousand happy whales? Or Wagner's "Ride of the Valkyries"? Not likely that, no; not for such amiable creatures. Or maybe the choral movement from Beethoven's Ninth? The last of these was my own preferred candidate: I loved the image of that symphonic ode to joy booming out over the Bering Sea while a thousand belugas each came through the channel, spouted once to the ship in thanks, and then arched and dived, disappearing.

So I dialed the Soviet Embassy in Washington to ask. But the Russians weren't answering their phone. Again and again, all afternoon: no answer. It was strange. Nobody seemed to be home.

The second thing I wondered about was the character of the belugas themselves. What sort of a species were they? How did it happen that a thousand of them should become trapped in a single small inlet? And what did science have to say about their auditory sophistication? I knew that humpback whales are famous for those wonderful mating songs that stretch on for as long as a half hour, complex and melodious, and then are repeated with boggling exactitude as though the humpbacks were sight-reading off a printed score. But I had never heard any claims made for the special phonic capabilities of the beluga.

Only because I was very ignorant. It turns out that those capabilities are legendary. The beluga is not just the noisiest of all whales; it also produces the largest variety of noises, some of which are more musical (to a human ear) than others. One scientific source reports that the various sounds in the beluga repertoire resemble bird calls, dull groans, the bellow of a bull, the grunt of a pig, the scream of a woman, teeth being gritted, a boat motor at low idle, and "the sound of a flute, modulating warble and whistling." This source also mentions chirping, clicking, and gurgling. Another expert describes "a well-modulated bell tone which is unique amongst cetaceans." Still another speaks of "barks, squawks, jaw claps, whistles, squawls, buzzes, whinnys, and chirps." Two scientists who tracked belugas off the coast of Quebec heard "high-pitched resonant whistles and squeals, varied with ticking and clucking sounds, slightly reminiscent of a string orchestra tuning up." No wonder, then, that early whalers gave this species the nickname "sea canary."

But what is the biological explanation for all this vocal versatility? Or *is* there an explanation that is merely biological?

Though marine mammal researchers have scarcely begun to decode the beluga's vocabulary, they are confident about one thing: At least some of those sounds serve a navigational function. Hearing is the dominant sense among whales, far more important than sight or smell, for the very good reason that sound travels much better through water than do either light or chemical signals. And the toothed (as opposed to the baleen) whales, including the beluga, seem to rely heavily on echolocation. They use the echoes of their own clicks and chirps, just as a bat does, to spot food and guide themselves as they move. For the beluga species, in particular, those more elaborate bellows and grunts and whistles may be forms of communication, useful in mating, herd forming, and other types of social behavior. The simpler high-frequency sounds probably function as sonar, allowing the animal (even in dark or murky seas) to maneuver among obstacles. And again for the beluga, because of its Arctic habitat, the most familiar and most threatening obstacle is ice.

Belugas live much of their lives near the sea ice of the extreme north, and in the gaps and natural channels that stay open in that ice during the transitional seasons. They even go under the ice when there is reason, hunting or hiding—though after fifteen or twenty minutes a beluga, just like a seal, needs to surface through open water for a gasp of air. Occasionally individuals are caught beneath solid ice sheets and drown. But a beluga has one advantage that a seal does not: Carrying a ton or more of heft, with a hard area on the back of its head covered with tough skin but no cushion of fat, the beluga can bash its way up through a four-inch thickness of ice. Its complete lack of a dorsal fin, a contrast with most other cetaceans, also helps make this ice-breaking trick possible. Elsewhere on its body the beluga is padded with blubber, enough to keep it comfortable in the coldest waters, where it feeds well on crustaceans, salmon, Arctic cod, and other small fish. With these adaptations, *Delphinapterus leucas* is well suited to life in the northern ocean.

Its chief enemies are killer whales and humans, not necessarily in that order. For the beluga, hunting and hiding amid the kaleidoscope of shifting ice evidently has been—notwithstanding the incident at Senyavina—the lesser of alternative dangers.

The third on my list of unanswered questions was: Why had the Soviets performed this act of mercy?

Why send a ship to rescue belugas while leaving other Soviet ships to proceed with the slaughter of minkes? Why not be consistent, one way or the other? If the Soviets had just wanted to buff up their international image, they could have announced a decision to abide by the IWC quota—or, better still, a decision to join the complete worldwide moratorium on commercial whaling, scheduled to begin the following year, which the Soviets (as well as the Japanese and the Norwegians) had so far vowed to ignore. Either of those steps would have cost their economy more than $80,000, true enough, but not really so very much more. On the other hand, if the Soviets felt such exigence about "harvesting" whales in Antarctica, why didn't they just "harvest" those thousand trapped belugas? Nothing could have been easier than going into Senyavina with guns and tail grapples and flensing knives instead of with food and music. It wasn't simply the difference in species, because there existed a hearty tradition among Soviet coastal peoples (at least until the mid-1960s) of hunting the beluga. Its meat was processed into sausage and animal fodder and fertilizer; its skin was prized for boot leather; its oil went into soap, unguents, margarine. With that sort of market standing ready, a dead beluga could be a valuable commodity.

What had changed? Why were a thousand belugas suddenly more precious alive?

I was still dialing that Soviet Embassy number, and they were still declining to pick up the phone. I checked back with directory assistance and tried again. No answer, no answer. At this point I began imagining things. Maybe it's Lenin's birthday and they're all drunk. Maybe we've broken diplomatic relations, one of those gut-twisting international incidents, and the whole delegation has packed and left, headed back for an underground bunker in Moscow. Maybe the embassy was blown up by a crazed Azerbaijanian separatist.

I called the Tass office in New York and finally got a human voice. Hi, I'm a journalist, just wanted to ask someone a few questions about . . . But I was too slow. The man sounded somber and nervous. He couldn't help. He hung up.

Next, the Soviet Consulate in San Francisco, and the fellow I caught there clearly thought I was either perverse or out of my mind, quacking at him about a bunch of ice-bound whales.

"Izn't it being a wrung time for zuch questions?" Deep, rich nasal accent. This one too sounded somber and nervous. Wrong time? I don't know, why is it being a wrong time?

"Becuzz now our president, he iz dead. And we are—"

"Mr. Chernenko?"

"Yez. Mr. Chernenko."

"Judas, I'm sorry. I didn't know." No TV and not having seen a newspaper for three days, just up here in my Montana snowdrift with whale books stacked around, I was evidently among the last several people in America to hear about it. I hung up.

I went out to a newsstand. Gorbachev was already comfortably installed and making peaceable speeches. The disarmament talks were opening on schedule. The Soviet negotiators were in Geneva, ready to go, and they had their instructions—from Mr. Gorbachev. The *vozhd* is dead, long live the *vozhd*.

I wanted to get that consulate fellow back on the line and say: *Look here, it all seems to be settled. I can understand that you're a little nervous about your own position. You might even be a bit sad. But now it's time to talk about whales. Whales are very damn important also.*

I suspected he wouldn't agree.

It seems to me there are two ways of viewing the incident at Senyavina Strait. The first is cynical and bitter. Since fairness demands that at least one Soviet voice be given ear in this essay (and since the various official Soviet spokesmen were so preoccupied and uncommunicative that particular day), I have turned to a quote from Yevgeny Yevtushenko. In a superb poem entitled "Cemetery of Whales" he has written:

> *In the cemetery of whales*
> *by the hummocks of ice*
> *there are no sanctimonious flowers:*
> *the Eskimos have tact.*
> *Hey, Eskimo hunchback,*
> *white men have a funny custom:*
> *after planting the harpoon,*
> *they weep over the corpse.*
> *Murderers mourn like maidens,*
> *and tearfully suck tranquilizers,*
> *and parade in crêpe,*
> *and stand honor guard.*
> *The professional hunters,*
> *who would look out of place,*
> *send wreaths to the whales*

from the State Bureau of Harpoonery.
But the flowers are twisted together
with steel cables and barbs.

In applying a jaundiced view to the Soviets' seemingly benevolent but contradictory behavior at Senyavina, it should also be
noted that, back in 1970, some populations of *Delphinapterus*
were discovered to be carrying high levels of mercury in their
flesh. The Canadians abandoned commercial whaling for the species at that point. And the marketing of beluga meat was forbidden throughout the West—not on sentimental grounds, but on
toxicological ones. As the commercial value of dead belugas de-
clined, of course, it became less inconvenient to impute some
level of preciousness to their lives.

Nevertheless, the interpretation of Senyavina that I recommend is more optimistic, more forgiving, and arguably more in-
genuous. All I can say of this second viewpoint is, Let's try it on
for the meantime. It is expressed by another poet, a non-Russian
now, in a passage that has suffered even more overexposure than
Pachelbel's canon, but is equally weatherproof:

> *The quality of mercy is not strained,*
> *It droppeth as the gentle rain from heaven*
> *Upon the place beneath: it is twice blessed;*
> *It blesseth him that gives, and him that takes . . .*

The intriguing part there, the part that remains fresh, is *It bless-
eth him that gives.* Shakespeare understood that the performance
of an act of mercy can be, for the party who grants that mercy, a
transforming experience. It can alter perspectives and attitudes,
possibly. It can unite strong beings and helpless beings with a
bond like no other: by making the very life of the helpless being
into a shining emblem of the strong being's decency, wisdom,
restraint. In some cases it might even be habit-forming.

It is twice blessed. A boon for those thousand belugas, certainly. Just as certainly, the Senyavina rescue had to be good in at least some minuscule measure for the Soviet nation's collective soul—including even those bureaucrats who make decisions about icebreakers and whaling moratoriums. So by all means the best thing was to grant them congratulations, the benefit of the doubt, and a moment of pride. They deserved it. And maybe they will find that they enjoy the practice of mercy much more than anyone could have expected.

AGONY IN THE GARDEN

A Plague of Starfish Eat
Their Way Through the Pacific

It is one of the central axioms of ecology, held by most (though not all) scientists in the field, that the stability of an ecosystem is directly related to its complexity. The greater the number of species coexisting in one community, and the greater the number of relationships linking different species, so much greater will be the natural resistance to change, perturbation, catastrophe. From diversity comes strength; from variety, steadiness. So goes the axiom, anyway.

In the case of tropical rainforests, which are considered the most complex terrestrial ecosystems on Earth, the axiom seems to hold true. Tropical rainforests (in the absence of serious disruption by man, at least) tend to be paragons of ecological stability, maintaining their balance of physical and ecological conditions over many thousands of years. Arctic tundra offers a good example of the same principle at its opposite extreme, a relatively sparse and simple ecosystem that is therefore also quite fragile. But in the case of tropical coral reefs—generally judged the Earth's most complex *marine* ecosystems, the oceanic equivalent of mature rainforest—there is lately some reason for skepticism. The complexity-stability equation seems in doubt. The reason is a plague of starfish.

Acanthaster planci is the species in question, an imposing echinoderm that grows up to two feet in diameter, with as many as twenty-one arms. It moves slowly across the sea bottom in shallow Pacific waters. It feeds on live coral. Its common name is the crown-of-thorns starfish, reflecting the tangle of long sharp protective spines that protrude from the dorsal surface. Each spine is tipped with a toxic mucus. Any such two-foot-wide bush of poisonous spines is, understandably, threatened by few natural enemies. Even a human diver who handles it risks a bad sting. Consequently, *A. planci* was considered a formidable species even back when it seemed to be quite rare. Nowadays *formidable* is an understatement and rarity is a puzzling memory. Something new has begun to happen. The ecological balance has tipped.

In droves, in swarms, in startling multitudes, crown-of-thorns starfish are gobbling up the Great Barrier Reef. "There is a possibility," one scientist has written, "that we are witnessing the initial phases of extinction of madreporarian [reef-building] corals in the Pacific."

The sudden abundance of *A. planci* has raised a few interesting questions. First and most controversially: Is this plague of starfish really so bad—and so unprecedented—as it seems? Expert opinion has been divided. Second: Has the plague somehow been caused by human actions? There is evidence to support this suspicion, but the evidence is mainly circumstantial. Studies to prove or disprove the human role are continuing at present. Almost everyone agrees that if the starfish plague has been caused by humankind, then firm measures should be taken to control it.

The third question is rather more tricky, leading quickly from the solid realm of marine fieldwork and ecological evidence into the empyrean of philosophy, aesthetics, and balance-of-trade economics: If the plague has *not* been caused by humankind—if it has been an epochal but naturally triggered catastrophe, like a lightning-caused forest fire howling across Yellowstone Park—in *that* case, should anything be done to rescue those glorious coral reefs? Or should we let unsentimental nature, and the crown-of-thorns starfish, have their way?

A. planci has been infamous to marine biologists and scuba divers for more than twenty years, since the first public reports of its population explosion at a place called Green Island, just off-shore from the city of Cairns on the northeastern coast of Australia. Green Island marks the approximate center of that long chain of individual reefs known collectively as the Great Barrier Reef, the largest formation of coral ever seen on Earth. For some decades Green Island has also been a focus of tourism to the Great Barrier Reef. The island's facilities now include a pier, an underwater observatory in the midst of the coral, a gift shop, a cafeteria, a picnic area, a beach, and cheap daily boat service from Cairns. But the attractions of Green Island were abruptly threatened back in 1962, when it was discovered that unusual concentrations of crown-of-thorns starfish had begun feasting on the surrounding coral.

Coral, like starfish, are animals. They belong to the same phylum as sea anemones, and in adulthood make their living as sessile creatures, attached permanently to a hard substrate, gathered together in large colonies of a particular species, each individual waving its tiny tentacles to capture planktonic food from the seawater. Their more famous attribute is that they secrete stony skeletons of calcium carbonate (lime) to support themselves. These lime skeletons—both those that still contain living coral and those that stand derelict—form the main structural matrix of coral reefs. Every reef is built up over a vast mass of compacted limestone, but it is the thin layer of live coral that keeps the reef forever renewed as a living ecosystem. That layer is precisely what *A. planci* at Green Island had begun to devour.

From 1962 to 1964 the starfish population grew inexorably. The various species of stony corals were killed off in large swaths and patches. The starfish legions accomplished this at a slow but implacable pace, each single starfish destroying roughly a square yard of coral per month. The mode of attack was simple, and slightly grotesque. Climbing onto a coral surface, the starfish would evert its own stomach out through its mouth, pressing the stomach folds down among the hard coral branches, where its digestive fluids could dissolve the corals' soft flesh; after absorbing its fill of those digested nutrients, the starfish would then pull in its stomach and lumber on. Behind the advancing front of starfish, which shuffled along like a herd of headless porcupines, were left dead coral skeletons that remained ghostly white for a few days or weeks, then gradually took on a gangrenous film of algae. The algae penetrated the lime skeletons and eventually weakened them, until normal wave action reduced the whole edifice to rubble. By that time, of course, the reef-dwelling fishes and other members of the coral community, dependent upon that edifice of lime for their cover, were long gone. *A. planci,* grown abundant beyond proportion, was literally collapsing its own ecosystem.

The proprietors of the Green Island businesses hired divers to battle the infestation, and in little over a year the divers destroyed 27,000 crown-of-thorns starfish. The area of coral seen by most tourists was saved. But the plague hadn't been conquered. On the contrary, eighty percent of the stony coral of the Green Island reef had been killed, and the starfish was now merely moving on.

Until this outbreak at Green Island in 1962, no such episode— *A. planci* in huge numbers devastating a zone of live coral—had ever been reported in the scientific literature. Following the Green Island experience, though, marine scientists heard belatedly of a similar occurrence near Japan. A reef in the Ryukyus archipelago had suffered infestation in 1957, and more than 200,000 starfish were collected during a government-sponsored control program. Then, soon after the Green Island and Ryukyus reports, came a sequence of further outbreaks across the Pacific. Reefs were attacked at Guam, at Samoa, at the island of Molokai in Hawaii, at Palau and Fiji and Wake and New Guinea, off the coasts of Malaysia and Thailand and Okinawa. In the Guam case, during just two years in the late 1960s, ninety percent of the stony coral along twenty-four miles of coastline was destroyed. A control program was mounted there, and 44,000 starfish were killed. In Samoa, about the same time, a two-week roundup produced 14,000 starfish. Also at that time, 20,000 specimens of *A. planci* were counted on one section of reef at Molokai. Along the west coast of Okinawa, in 1972, the *A. planci* population was estimated at 210,000. All of these numbers, bear in mind, apply to an animal that was formerly considered rare.

Exactly how rare it was can't be known, in retrospect, but one team of scientists has written: "A month spent on a typical coral reef might have brought to light one or two specimens." Another biologist reports that, in the old days, when she came upon a crown-of-thorns starfish, she would tuck it safely under a coral ledge—so that tourists might not find the poor thing and kill it. Now, just a few years later, money was being spent by worried governments and businessmen to exterminate *A. planci* by the thousands.

Meanwhile, as hordes of starfish turned up in those far-flung places and new pockets of infestation appeared on the Great Barrier Reef, Green Island was left alone. The journal *Science* announced that "recovery is reported to have already begun; the island was free of starfish in 1968, and new colonies of four coral genera had become established."

See there, said the optimists. These fluctuations of *A. planci* population are merely a natural phenomenon, kept within bounds by the internal checks and balances of the reef community. One shouldn't get too excited, they said. Most of all, one shouldn't intervene in these natural cycles, on the ever-precarious basis of good intentions and incomplete knowledge. An ecosystem as complex as a coral reef, and as stable, can bloody well take care of itself.

Or so went the hopeful assertion.

But it wasn't that simple. In 1979 *A. planci* came back to Green Island.

Robert Endean, an Australian biologist who has been a leading authority on crown-of-thorns starfish for the past two decades, dived the Green Island reef that year and found that sixty percent of the coral had been killed—recently. He estimated the current *A. planci* population at 350,000. Since then, says Endean, things have gotten still worse. This time *A. planci* is not only killing the plate-coral and the branching-coral species. It is also killing the great massive brain-coral colonies, some of which are hundreds of years old.

There is a rough pattern to all those centers of starfish infestation that erupted across the Pacific during the 1960s and '70s. The pattern is that *A. planci* appears in great numbers, generally, where *Homo sapiens* has also appeared in great numbers. The earliest outbreaks of the starfish plague have been focused mainly on reefs near those coasts and islands with considerable modern human settlement. This is the circumstantial evidence that points an accusing finger at humankind.

What could the etiology be? What human actions could conceivably bring on a cataclysmic proliferation of starfish?

The most logical guess is that we humans might somehow have released *A. planci* from the pressure normally exerted upon it by predators. Those missing predators might have fed on the eggs of the starfish, or on the free-swimming larval forms, or even perhaps (improbable as it seems) on the imposing adults, two feet across and armed with poison spines. Possibly there was a constellation of predators who fed variously on all three stages, thus keeping *A. planci* trimmed down to a sparse population, a mere half dozen for every square mile of reef. Possibly. But no one knows.

How might humanity have eliminated the predators? With industrial pollution? With insecticides, running off in erosional waters from the land? By dredging and blasting operations in crucial zones of coral? All of these notions have been mentioned in the scientific debate, and none of them seems very likely. But no one knows.

Robert Endean, speaking by phone from his office in Brisbane, offers an alternative view. He suspects that the critical stage at which *A. planci* suffers predation (or in the more recent situation, the stage at which it *should* suffer predation but doesn't) is neither as eggs nor as larvae nor as full-grown adults. Instead, Endean posits that the post-larval juveniles might be the preyed-upon form. At this stage the animal has reached its adult shape but not its adult size. It is a miniature starfish, just an inch or a few inches across, a convenient morsel for a fish or a large snail, and the long potent spines have not yet developed. In the juvenile stage, Endean says, *A. planci* could be quite vulnerable to a whole constellation of predators, species such as are native to coral reefs in an undisturbed state. Among those predators would be the giant triton, *Charonia tritonis,* a snail-like gastropod that grows twenty inches long and has been seen feeding on crown-of-thorns starfish. Also included might be such fishes as the hump-headed wrasse, the spotted toado, several types of triggerfish, groupers, coral trout, and a number of other reef-dwelling species. Taken together, the pressure of predation by these animals upon *A. planci* in its juvenile and small-adult stages might be just adequate to keep the starfish at low population levels. Taken away, those animals by their absence might explain the *A. planci* plague.

And, according to Dr. Endean, precisely those animals *have* been taken away by human activities in places like Green Island. Beginning back in the 1950s, the giant triton has been collected by the tens of thousands for its beautiful shell, which was sold to tourists as a souvenir. The various predatory reef fish have been drastically reduced by spear-fishing divers and commercial fishermen. Some of those predators were probably specific, focusing on *A. planci* to the exclusion of other prey. Some were no doubt generalists, eating juvenile *A. planci* among other things. One result of their combined disappearance, suggests Endean, is a population explosion among starfish.

But what about simplicity versus complexity? What about stability versus fragility?

A tropical rainforest is undeniably complex, and presumably therefore quite stable. But stability is a relative value—relative to the magnitude of the disturbance inflicted. No ecosystem is invulnerable. And no ecosystem is immune to disturbances of the magnitude that humankind often inflicts. If you remove the canopy trees from a large area of the richest Amazon jungle, chances are that you *will* destroy the ecosystem there, for a very long time indeed, if not permanently. Likewise if you take a heavy enough toll—a subtle toll, maybe, but a critical one—on the complex community of a coral reef.

An ecologist named Ramón Margalef has written: "A strong exploitation of very mature ecosystems, like tropical forests or coral reefs, may produce a total collapse of a rich organization. In such stable biotopes, nature is not prepared for a step backward. Man has to be very careful in dealing with systems of high maturity."

Certainly the Great Barrier Reef is one of our planet's most mature ecosystems. And if it dies, under a crown of thorns, there may be no prospect of resurrection.

THE POSEIDON SHALES

One Family's Quest
Through the Strata of Time

In an inconspicuous brick building on the outskirts of the village
of Holzmaden, in southern Germany, is a large female animal
caught in the act of giving birth. The moment is frozen precisely,
rather poignantly, as though by the snap of a shutter. The image
is stark, nearly flat, black and white. This isn't a photograph. It is
a natural bas-relief executed in marine mud and bone and the
awesome pressures of time and accreting rock—in other words, a
fossil. Almost 200 million years old but preserved in all delicate
filigree, like a maple leaf pressed lovingly in a book by the hand
of a child who has long since grown old and wizened, this particular fossil is different from any other you are ever likely to see.
The anatomy is unusual. The specimen is whole, intact, and
breathtakingly vivid. The tableau contains a double share of silent drama, since in this case the moment of birth was also, evidently, the moment of death. Altogether it may be one of the
world's most eloquent fossils. The animal is called *Stenopterygius
crassicostatus*. The inconspicuous building is called Museum
Hauff.

This maternal beast is an ichthyosaur, a marine reptile from
the age of the dinosaurs. She was not herself a dinosaur; she was
something else, something other, something more than a little

oxymoronic: a fish-like reptile that breathed air but lived all her life in the sea, shaped by evolution to the same body form and the same ecological role as a dolphin, all those millions of years before dolphinhood was reinvented by the mammals. She died at sea and was buried in sea-bottom mud, very gently, with her one newborn beside her and five embryos still in her abdomen. The cause of death can't be known. Possibly it was childbirth itself. Finally in the year we call 1948 she was pried up from a shale quarry, right there at Holzmaden, and teased out of her slab by the painstaking efforts of two men, both of them named Bernhard Hauff. They were father and son, founder and first heir of a quiet dynasty that has supplied the twentieth century with ichthyosaurs.

"These ichthyosaurs were animals that evoluted very specially for water life," says Rolf Bernhard Hauff, grandson in the same line and now director of the museum and its renowned fossil-preparation workshop. The young Herr Hauff is handsome and genial, no archetype of dour fossiliferous stodginess as one might expect but a contemporary man, dressed this morning in jeans and a scarlet sweatshirt. He is conducting a tour in English for a group of American teenagers, high school kids from a nearby Air Force base, and struggling amiably toward a compromise with the attention span of his audience, the scientific complexity of his subject, and the language. His English is good but imperfect and the word he wants is *evolved.*

These ichthyosaurs had indeed evolved very specially for life in the ancient seas. The fossil is the proof. It tells of an animal twelve feet in length, weighing perhaps half a ton, with a strikingly large eye socket that suggests a creature dependent on keen sight, and a long toothy beak suited for preying upon small fish and squid. It tells of streamlining, and the transformation of legs to flippers, and a powerful shark-like tail, and more.

Herr Hauff points to the rib cage of this great gravid *Stenopterygius,* hung in its gray slab on one museum wall. Five miniature skulls, five little bodies, show clearly between the ribs. "And inside we see very small ichthyosaurs. And these ichthyosaurs, we know then, they bring forth very small babies. They give live birth. Not like an alligator or a turtle, eh?, that lays eggs on a beach. And so we know that the ichthyosaurs were *very* well adapted to life in the sea." A live-bearing sea reptile was one that *never* needed to go ashore, because its newborn could swim up to the surface for air, whereas an egg laid on the sea bottom would, literally, drown—this being an important point scientifically, if not one to draw gasps from school kids. Herr Hauff keeps his tour brisk and palatable, moving quickly across matters of evidence—captured in these extraordinary fossils—that have given the Hauff collection, and the Hauff workshop, a revered place in paleontology for the past ninety years.

He is good with this crowd of distracted, hormonal adolescents. He smiles, he looks them in the eyes, he makes jokes and quizzes them Socratically. He knows that they might hear half of what he tells them, and retain a twentieth overnight—or maybe they will retain a tenth, if he gets them involved. Maybe in a few years one or two of them will remember that once, on an escape from the classroom, they visited an astounding, tiny museum in some little town of south Germany. Herr Hauff cares about that possibility. He avowedly views his own efforts, his family's ancestral mission, as directed not just toward science but also toward the public. Ichthyosaurs, he seems to believe, are a miracle that belongs to everyone.

He leans over a smaller specimen in a tabletop case. "This is the backbone. And this black line is not painted here," he says. Flattened almost to two dimensions on its bed of gray shale, the skeleton is surrounded by a smooth coal-dark silhouette: the full outline of a body, left behind by chemical transformation of the animal's skin. That outline is a rarity, an artifact as improbable as the face in Veronica's veil, with scientific significance that a modest man like Rolf Hauff could scarcely exaggerate. It establishes that ichthyosaurs had almost precisely the same shape as dolphins, with a dorsal fin and a tall upper horn on the caudal fin that do not show up in the skeleton. "We find this only with very careful preparation. Soft-body parts preserved so good, we find only here in all the world. This takes *very* careful preparation. Almost a year to prepare one specimen."

The tradition of fine craftsmanship in the Hauff workshop is only part of what has made these fossils so useful to science, and so beautiful. The other part involves geological accident. This area of southern Germany in which Holzmaden lies—just forty kilometers east of Stuttgart, at the base of a hilly upthrust known as the Swabian Alb—once lay at the bottom of a shallow sea. During the Jurassic period of Earth history, roughly between 190 and 136 million years ago, that inland sea covered a large portion of what is now western Europe. In the Holzmaden area, which was some distance off the coast, fine-grain muddy sediments were laid down upon the sea bottom, compressing and hardening finally into rock, and in the process entombing dead marine animals wherever the bodies fell. The sea bottom here was especially stable, undisturbed by currents, poor in oxygen, so that carcasses settling into the mud were often preserved free of dismemberment or rot. Laced richly with organic material (not just ichthyosaur bodies but various marine reptiles, fish, mollusks, and an abundance of other invertebrates), the hardening layers of mud eventually became strata of oil shale. Those dark carboniferous strata are known by geologists as the Black Jurassic. The sea retreated, the Swabian Alb was uplifted by pressures along the Earth's crust, and erosion gradually stripped away other strata formed after the shale. Millions of years later, Rolf Hauff's great-grandfather came to Holzmaden as an industrial chemist, with the notion of exploiting that oil shale. But his son, the founding grandfather of the fossil operation, was more interested in the shale as a mausoleum of vanished reptiles than for its sheer bitumen content.

For hundreds of years the shale has been quarried also for decorative rock. Today that commercial quarrying continues, at a handful of sites around Holzmaden, with tools and methods nearly unchanged over the past century. Now you might see a dump truck or a power shovel helping to move shattered rock, but the delicate labor of prying up large sheets of shale, unbroken, suitable for paving the floor of a den or the wall of a fireplace, is still done by workmen using crowbars and picks. Occasionally one of those workmen will lift a slab and notice a brownish shape in the blue-gray shale—the hint of a fossil embedded there. Setting that slab aside, the workman will send a message to Herr Hauff, who will hurry out to the site. Other slabs will be pried up and inspected. The ideal is to capture a whole animal within just a few large pieces, then get those pieces back to the workshop and fit them together like a puzzle. Once that matrix is reassembled, the shale is chiseled and etched away— mainly again using hand tools, the fine finishing done with dental picks under a microscope—to liberate the fossil. For ninety years one Hauff or another has been responding to those messages from the quarries.

But the fossils have never been more than a by-product of Holzmaden quarrying. Nowadays, as in the past, it is not economically feasible to work the quarries purely for fossils. In this particular age, with humans and not reptiles dominating the Earth, raw fireplace stone carries more value than raw ichthyosaurs.

Once the Hauff craftsmen have intervened, of course, that balance tips. Museum Hauff is a private institution that supports itself largely through the sale of specimens, and a fully prepared ichthyosaur might bring $20,000. The customers are other museums (for specimens with unique scientific significance), as well as large corporations and private collectors (for decorative specimens with less scientific value), and this cottage industry allows the Hauff operation to remain independent, an old-fashioned family-run exercise in crazy devotion and pride. In this combined dedication to craftsmanship, private enterprise, and science, they seem like a cross between Harry Winston and the Leakeys.

The commercial Holzmaden stone comes from one particular layer of those Jurassic marine sediments, twenty feet below ground level and just seven inches thick. This buried seven-inch layer, which splits nicely and has an attractive surface, is what drives the quarry economy. The strata that are broken and pried out to reach that layer are cast aside as scrap—but from among that scrap, rescued from power shovel and dump truck, come the ancient reptiles. Paleontologists all over the planet know those fossil-rich Holzmaden strata as the "Middle Epsilon" division of the Black Jurassic period, and the slightly less formal label in German is "Posidonien-schiefer." To you or to me: the Poseidon Shales. A sea god's gift to posterity. Go to a good science museum in Stuttgart or Tübingen, or for that matter in Paris, Berlin, Cambridge, New York, and wherever you find ichthyosaurs you will probably also find a small plate saying, "Middle Epsilon, Black Jurassic. Holzmaden." Or perhaps only "Posidonien-schiefer." You may also see the name Hauff. Most of those specimens have passed through the family workshop.

But the Poseidon Shales are famous not only for ichthyosaurs. They have yielded a whole menagerie of marine life from the Jurassic period, and the walls of Museum Hauff display that life as a great stonework frieze, a portrait of the offshore community as it existed 160 million years before Christ. Besides ichthyosaurs there are two other seagoing reptiles, the plesiosaurs (resembling giant long-necked turtles, but without shells) and the steneosaurs (similar to the fish-eating gharials that survive in India and Nepal); there are also pterosaurs, those delicate flying reptiles, which sometimes died at sea and sunk to their graves in the underwater mud; and a selection of garish invertebrates, including the sea lilies (plant-like creatures with long stems and flowery heads, which were actually animals related to starfish) and the ammonites (a group of spiral-shelled mollusks that disappeared at the same time as the dinosaurs). All of these life forms—the giant and the small, the delicate and the robust, the predaceous and the benign—have been preserved in stunning detail by the gentle embrace of those Jurassic marine muds, and brought back to light by the methodical scraping of Hauff chisels.

One wall of the museum is filled by a huge panel of sea lilies, a parquetry of gray slabs stretching from the floor to a peaked roof fifty feet up, upon which a colony of these bizarre animals are frozen in ropey entanglement, like an orgy of giant sea worms with sunflower heads. This amazing thing turned up in a quarry back in 1908. For forty years it remained in the raw state, locked inside chunks of shale. The Hauff craftsmen began work on it, finally, in the 1950s. By then old Bernhard Hauff, the grandfather and founder, was dead. Fifteen years later, the sea lily panel was finished. Now it hangs here majestically, the largest community of fossil invertebrates exhibited anywhere in the world.

On the wall just opposite hangs an oil portrait of Bernhard Hauff. He seems, as always, to be taking the long view. Dreaming the dream of time.

This museum itself is a private dream, a heartfelt and heritable whimsy, that exists to amuse and to edify the public. It expresses one family's quixotic conviction: that the history of life on our planet is not only intriguing but beautiful, a miracle that belongs to everyone.

"So, you will find nearly nowhere on the world where you can take out information and fossils like we have it here in Holzmaden," Herr Hauff tells the American teenagers. He has not exaggerated. He smiles. The students have listened and stared at his fossils for nearly an hour, a great feat of prolonged attention, and Herr Hauff knows he dare not try to hold them five minutes longer. He pushes his hands into the pockets of his jeans, and shrugs. He is an optimist. He believes that one or two of them will remember.

THE BEAUTIFUL
AND DAMNED

*Genetics and Aesthetics
in the Life of a Dashing Animal*

Beauty is one of the lies we live by. The joys of success is another.
God knows, we have been offered enough minacious parables
over the centuries to discourage both of these stubborn delusions
—from *The Iliad* and *Oedipus Rex* to *The Picture of Dorian Gray*
and "Richard Cory"—but still they survive, eternal inverities.
Evidently we need them at least as much as we need mere truth.
The latest increment of counterevidence against that pair of sleek
cheery falsehoods came and went recently as an article in the
journal *Science,* and unless you were watching closely, you may
have missed it.

Based on the experimental work of a team led by S. J. O'Brien,
a geneticist from the National Cancer Institute, this article
presents a technical assessment of the unusually low genetic diversity within a certain species. O'Brien's study is noteworthy to
a broad audience not so much because of its results ("we found a
total absence of genetic polymorphism in forty-seven allozyme
loci and a low frequency of polymorphism in proteins") as because of the test subject in question. That species was *Acinonyx
jubatus,* the cheetah.

Every schoolchild in America knows that the cheetah is the
world's fastest mammal. Anyone who has seen and studied these

creatures in the field is liable also to argue that they are the most beautiful of all carnivores, and the most successful of all wild cats. A dozen years ago I spent one lucky hour watching four cheetahs stalk game on the East African savanna, and I still haven't begun to forget their gorgeous, prepossessing grace. But the cheetah today, despite appearances, is not well. It is genetically depauperate.

Though there may still be as many as 20,000 cheetahs at large on the plains of Africa, the gene pool of *A. jubatus* appears to be much smaller than it should be for that number—too small, perhaps, to carry the species through any sudden adversities. Insufficient genetic options equals insufficient adaptability. So far, admittedly, only one of the two remaining large populations has been investigated: the South African cheetah, not the East African. In the course of O'Brien's study, blood tests were done on fifty-five animals, some of those from the Transvaal, some from Namibia, a few that had previously been exported to zoos in the United States. This scattered group of cats turned out to have all the genetic diversity of a palace full of incestuous Romanovs.

Cheetahs are currently an endangered species. Twenty thousand is not such a large total, and the real number may be much less, possibly as low as 1,500. No one really knows, because the elusive habits of these animals make them very hard to count. Though officially protected in some of the countries where they occur, they are still occasionally threatened by fur poachers and stock-raising peoples. They are threatened even more by habitat loss. But the worst threat they face may be the genetic one. They are just dangerously short on genetic variety.

And that's one threat that we humans can't rectify. All we can do is give them time. A depleted population of animals can sometimes recover quickly. A depleted gene pool cannot. Thousands of new generations must be born and grow and achieve successful reproduction themselves, before the slow process of mutation will have restored a previous level of gene variations. Populations fall and rise again at geometric rates but, like some morbidly hurtful memory, genetic impoverishment lingers afterward.

Where did those missing cheetah genes go?

O'Brien and his coauthors are cautious about offering speculation, but their work, together with what is known of the history of this species in both the recent and the distant past, suggests a couple of sad possibilities.

The cheetah evolved independently of the other big cats and arrived at its modern form much earlier. Today it stands separate from all other living representatives of the cat family, a lonesome anomaly that in some ways shares more in common with dogs. Besides being faster, it is far more delicate, more slender, and less imposingly armed than any lion or leopard. Its teeth are shorter. Its jaws are rather weak. Other cats can voluntarily retract their claws into claw sheaths, thereby preserving the sharp points for piercing and slashing; the claws of the cheetah, in contrast, are not fully retractile and grow dull from being walked on. A cheetah's footprint, consequently, looks more like the print of a wolf than like the great soft ominous pug of a tiger. Though it may travel in small social groups (a mother with kits, a mixed trio of adults, even a pair of bachelor males), the cheetah seems most often to perform the act of killing solitarily. As slight of build as it is, as poorly equipped with lethal weapons, it would have little chance of winning a meal at all, if not for speed.

Speed it has, of course—unequaled speed—as well as a nicely matched set of anatomical adaptations that make that speed possible. The femur bone of the cheetah's leg is elongated, unusual among cats. The spine is long and flexible, and it bows dramatically with each stride, giving still greater reach to the legs. Those short, blunted claws are good for traction and quick turns. The nasal openings are especially large, as are the bronchi and the lungs, invaluable for an animal that needs huge volumes of oxygen for burning huge amounts of energy in very brief stretches of time. The heart is also large. The tail is long and held straight out, for balance, while the cheetah screams along at seventy miles per hour. Even the arteries are exceptionally muscular. *A. jubatus* is born to run.

More specifically, born to chase. The cheetah shows a few curious behavioral patterns that become comprehensible only in light of its anatomical assets and limitations, and one among these is perhaps the most intriguing: According to reliable observation, a cheetah will almost never attack a potential prey animal that does not bolt and run.

Its favored prey species are modest-sized grazers like the impala and the Thomson's gazelle, generally taken at weights less than the cheetah's own. But let an impala stand its ground (either from stupid daring or because it's paralyzed by fear) and the cheetah will pass it right by, focusing instead on one of the other herd members that has taken flight. For two or three hundred yards the cheetah will pursue at top speed, until (on a successful chase) it has pulled up beside the chosen impala's rear flank. Then it will do what is, to my mind, a charmingly roguish thing: It will swing out a paw (in mid-stride now, remember, at seventy miles per hour) and *trip* the impala.

The impala goes head-over-teakettle. The cheetah slams on its own brakes, and pounces. The actual killing is then accomplished with a throat bite—which must be held as long as it takes for the impala to strangle, since the cheetah's jaw muscles and teeth are too meager for chomping through the spine or ripping out the jugular. But what about that other brazen impala, the one left standing back at the start? Why did the cheetah choose to ignore it? No one can be sure, but the most plausible answer is that, without a high-velocity chase, without a well-timed trip, the speedy-but-weak cheetah simply has no means of knocking an impala off its feet.

The cheetah's hunting technique, with that long stealthy stalk followed by that sudden heart-shocking sprint, seems specifically designed to induce—rather than to preempt—a panicky bolt by the prey. That induced panic makes a gazelle or an impala vulnerable to the cheetah's modest killing tools in a way neither animal would otherwise be. The successive stages (spook-chase-overtake-trip-pounce-strangle) are all linked together with fine economy. The method is highly dramatic and highly successful.

It is so successful that the cheetah, lacking defensive weaponry in a fiercely competitive habitat, can afford to be (and is) frequently robbed of its own fresh-killed prey by lions and leopards and hyenas; yet the cheetah still survives quite well on the portion of kills left unstolen. And it is so dramatic that, for almost five thousand years, human potentates on three continents kept tamed cheetahs for sport hunting.

The possession of coursing cheetahs has been a self-flattering perquisite of royalty, in fact, for almost as long as the possession of gold. The Sumerian rulers used cheetahs on their hunts around 3000 B.C. The Pharaohs had captive cheetahs. So did the Assyrian kings. In the Caucasus a burial mound dated to 2300 B.C. has yielded a silver vase decorated with the figure of a cheetah—and this cheetah is wearing a collar. In Italy cheetahs were prized and collected from the fifth century onward. Russian princes hunted with them in the eleventh and twelfth centuries. Charlemagne enjoyed running cheetahs after game, as did William the Conqueror, and also Emperor Leopold I of Austria, who used his for deer hunting in the Vienna Woods.

Marco Polo reported that Kublai Khan had a stable of cheetahs, possibly as many as a thousand, at his summer palace in Karakorum. Those animals were kept hooded and subdued like falcons until the moment of being released for the chase; when a victim was taken away from them by their human handlers and they were rewarded with the viscera, they seem to have accepted that bad bargain with the same equanimity as if they had lost the whole meal to a pack of hyenas. The later Mogul emperor Akbar also had a thousand captive cheetahs, according to an account left by his son. What Akbar's son especially recalled was that, one time, a male cheetah slipped its collar and found a female to mate with, which union produced three kits who survived to adulthood. It was remarkable, said the son, because it never happened again.

Indeed: That accidental litter in Akbar's stables seems to be the only such case of captive breeding recorded from Sumerian times up to 1960. Though cheetahs can be chased to the point of exhaustion by horsemen and then lassoed, though they tame rather easily, they almost never (until recently) have been persuaded to reproduce in captivity.

All those thousands and thousands of regal pets, all those hunting cheetahs, had been taken straight from wild breeding populations. And it was a one-way trip. Their genes came out of the reproductively active gene pool, and we can safely assume that very few ever went back.

O'Brien's study reveals that those fifty-five members of the South African cheetah population are just too similar to each other, biochemically, for their own good. One startling bit of evidence was that their bodies failed to reject skin grafts traded surgically between different cheetahs—even their own immune systems couldn't distinguish among them. Another form of evidence came from electrophoresis, a technique whereby genetic differences can be deduced through the measuring of small electrical differences among enzymes and other proteins. Again, by this standard, the South African population was found to contain "10 to 100 times less genetic variation than other mammalian species." In addition, the male cheetahs had a drastically low sperm count and a drastically high proportion of abnormally shaped sperm in what they did have, two symptoms common among inbred livestock and inbred populations of lab mice. They also showed a disastrous vulnerability to disease (for instance,

when eighteen cheetahs at a wildlife park in Oregon died suddenly from a virus that seldom threatens other cats). O'Brien and
his colleagues concluded that "the catastrophic sensitivity of this
genetically uniform species does provide a graphic natural example of the protection afforded to biological species by genetic
variability." Without that protection, the same sort of epidemic
die-off that happened in Oregon could also strike the wild African populations.

And still there's the unanswered question: Where did those
missing genes go?

Possibly, alas, to the entertainment of seigneurial humans,
back in the days when coursing cheetahs were such a vogue.

The O'Brien group hypothesize what they call a *population
bottleneck* in the cheetah's recent (two hundred years) or less
recent (two thousand years) past. This bottleneck could have
been any situation where for one reason or another the number of
breeding cheetahs was dramatically reduced—to a low point
from which the population level subsequently recovered, but
from which the gene pool so far has not. The American bison
went through that kind of bottleneck during its near brush with
human-caused extinction a century ago. So did the northern elephant seal at about the same time. The elephant seal survived in
only a tiny population on one remote island off Baja, then re-
bounded prolifically when humankind stopped killing it, but today the seal still shows a severe shortage of genetic diversity. And
if the California condor survives at all, squeezing through its
present perilous bottleneck, it can look forward at best to the
same sort of lingering genetic deficiency for a thousand years.

The next big question in cheetah research, meanwhile, is
whether the East African population (of the Serengeti and the
high Kenyan plains) shares the genetic depauperacy of the South
African group.

If the East African population is genetically robust, then it will
seem that the South African cheetah's bottleneck was a recent

and localized situation, possibly attributable to killing by skin hunters and ranchers of the Boer period. But if the East African cheetah is similarly impoverished, then the problem is likely much broader and much older.

It might be as old as Xanadu and Karakorum, as old as the pyramids, as old as that silver vase from a burial mound in the Caucasus. And it might be equally the consequence of a certain implacable, greedy human impulse: the impulse, not only to admire the embodiment of beauty, but to capture and possess it.

PROVIDE, PROVIDE

The Gaia Hypothesis
and Global Evolution

An Englishman named J. E. Lovelock believes that he may have discovered the largest of all living creatures. This thing he has found is so incomprehensibly huge that almost nobody until now had even noticed it. Bigger and more advanced than the biggest dinosaur that ever slogged through Cretaceous marshes. Bigger than the biggest whale that ever came up for a gasp of air. It is not an extinct species, furthermore, but an organism that thrives today, a survivor throughout three and a half billion years. Lovelock calls this creature *Gaia*. He is talking about the Earth itself.

He suggests that our planet, floating sublimely in space like the Star Child from Kubrick's *2001,* is a single great animate being.

Lovelock has outlined the idea in various scientific papers (some of them coauthored with the distinguished biologist Lynn Margulis) published over the past dozen years, and developed it at length in a book titled *Gaia: A New Look at Life on Earth.* The name Gaia is borrowed from the ancient Greeks, who applied it to that goddess they knew also as Mother Earth. What Lovelock proposes is that "the Earth's living matter, air, oceans, and land surface form a complex system which can be seen as a single organism and which has the capacity to keep our planet a fit place for life." Of course any cold-eyed reader will note that *"can be seen* as a single organism" is a slippery formulation, and Lovelock never makes quite clear whether he means that to be a literal suggestion or just a useful metaphor. Elsewhere he calls Gaia "a vast being who in her entirety has the power to maintain our planet as a fit and comfortable habitat for life." *Being* is another vague term that never receives precise definition, but never mind. The more solid and persuasive part of Lovelock's idea—also the more significant part—is the second half. According to his Gaia hypothesis, earthly life has created its own required environment.

The biosphere has to some extent dictated the physical and chemical conditions on Earth, rather than merely vice versa, he argues. Ever since life began, it has taken active measures to keep the planet livable. The ratio of gases in the atmosphere, the degree of salinity in the oceans, the acidity level of water and soil—all of these, says Lovelock, are selfishly controlled by the collective body of living creatures. Nothing is left to chance. Fluctuations are not suffered passively. Gaia provides for her own.

If true, this is news indeed. One of the implications, as Lovelock points out, would be that the Earth has the ability to cure itself of catastrophic environmental disruptions—ozone depletion, the greenhouse effect, acid rain, even the poisonous aftermath of a nuclear war—as easily and routinely as the human body cures itself of a cold.

Some people will find great satisfaction in that idea. Others will judge it a terrifyingly dangerous bit of optimism.

The atmosphere as we know it is highly improbable. It is not the one our planet should have. Based on the overall chemical composition of Earth, certain atmospheric gases that are rare should be far more common. Certain common gases should be far more rare. The law of entropy seems to be in abeyance. The only explanation for these anomalies, says Lovelock, is that life itself has taken a guiding hand.

Carbon dioxide is one familiar example. Besides being a by-product of respiration by animals and plants, and of the burning of fossil fuels, this gas occurs naturally as a result of various nonbiological processes. By admitting and then trapping solar radiation, it plays an important role in helping the Earth hold heat. We have all heard the dire scenarios about how the increased level of carbon dioxide from all our fossil-fuel burning is raising the Earth's temperature; a program of human restraint (or, alternatively, nuclear power) seems the only way we can avoid melting the polar ice caps. What we don't usually hear about is the steadying influence of Gaia, against which our worst excesses and our noblest restraints might both be moot. Currently the concentration of CO_2 in the atmosphere is roughly three hundredths of one percent; before humankind began burning coal, it might have been two hundredths of one percent. On the very same planet without Gaia, without any life, the expected CO_2 concentration would be 98 percent.

Without Gaia, the atmosphere would consist almost completely of carbon dioxide and steam. And the temperature of that planetary greenhouse would be about 600 degrees F. Gaia prevents such an unlivable situation, says Lovelock, by extracting CO_2 from the atmosphere through biological processes. Plants and marine animals take it up in vast quantity, and a large portion of the planet's supply gets buried away harmlessly as limestone and chalk.

Oxygen concentration is also under Gaia's control, in this case a rare gas being made artificially common. On an Earth without Gaia, according to Lovelock, free oxygen would account for less than one percent of the atmosphere. That's probably how things stood three and a half billion years ago, at the dawn of organic evolution, when life seems to have first taken hold in the form of simple anaerobic creatures suited specifically to an oxygen-poor environment. But then about two billion years ago there came one of evolution's most drastic transitions, the changeover to an oxygen-burning metabolic economy, which has provided greater

supplies of chemical energy for a greater range of biological possibilities. Since that time, Gaia has worked to keep the atmosphere pumped up richly with oxygen. She does it (at least
partly) by splitting CO_2 in half during photosynthesis and burying the carbon away in forms such as peat, coal, and oil. In other
words, through the life and death of plants.

But too much oxygen would be worse than too little. If the
level stood just a few percent higher than it does now, even the
wettest rainforests would constantly be bursting into flame—because free oxygen is precisely what makes fire possible. Without
some counterbalance to oxygen production (as it proceeds at the
current rate), such a flash point would have been reached in just
50,000 years. Many millennia ago, that is, the biosphere would
have burned itself to a cinder.

Fortunately for life, there *is* a counterbalance. Free oxygen is
constantly removed from the atmosphere by reaction with methane gas.

And the methane gas is another product of Gaia. It is created
at the rate of about a billion tons each year, exactly enough to
hold oxygen at the optimal level. Just where does the methane
come from? Thirty years ago one distinguished ecologist postu-
lated that it came mainly from the farts of large animals. Well,
yes, undeniably that is methane, produced by anaerobic bacteria
performing their routine digestive function in the animals' guts—
bacteria such as the *Escherichia coli* we carry in ours. But a
billion tons annually? No, more likely we large animals account
for only a small (if noisy) fraction. The major part, Lovelock
explains, must come from free-living anaerobic bacteria at work
on plant decay in the world's seabeds and peat bogs and lakes
and marshes. Methane, remember, is the same stuff we call
"swamp gas."

The Gaia hypothesis is a very complicated idea. It would have
to be: It merely seeks to encompass all of ecology, biochemistry,

chemical oceanography, tectonic geology, and atmospheric physics. Applying bits of information from each of these disciplines,
Lovelock goes on to explain how soil and water acidity, ocean
salinity, trace-element distribution, and a number of other crucial
conditions are maintained within life-fostering ranges through
the active intervention of Gaia. He even suggests that the spawning migrations of eels and salmon, from salt water to fresh, might
be Gaia's way of recycling washed-away phosphorus.

Most evolutionary biologists would roll their eyes at that one.
And it makes me wonder what other points in Lovelock's grand
hypothesis might set the biochemists, the geologists, and the
physicists to rolling *their* eyes. Lovelock himself admits that his
presentation of the idea—if not the idea itself—is inescapably
contaminated with anthropomorphism and teleology. Personally,
I can forgive anthropomorphism and, after checking a dictio-
nary, I can even forgive teleology. But I have a different reservation about Gaia.

Lovelock's central tenet is that the Earth possesses a potent,
cybernetic, and vastly underrated capacity to keep itself healthy.
To heal itself, when its environment has been injured. To clean
and restore itself, just as a human's kidneys and liver clean and
restore the blood. He is emphatically reassuring on this point.
The worry over ozone reduction by aerosols is ridiculous, says
Lovelock. The concern over greenhouse-effect warming is unwar-
ranted, he says. All right, possibly that much is true. Possibly.
The worst industrial pollution belched forth from smokestacks,
puked forth into rivers, spilled forth onto seas is no more than a
minor discomfort to Gaia, Lovelock tells us. The most egre-
giously toxic dumping amounts to nothing, he claims. This, I
think, is rather more dubious. Lovelock even goes so far as to
state that "a nuclear war of major proportions, although no less
horrific for the participants and their allies, would not be the
global devastation so often portrayed. Certainly it would not
much disturb Gaia."

Fine for *her.*

Evidently this Gaia of Lovelock's is as cold and as Olympian a bitch as any goddess that any man ever dreamed into being. She will endure as she has endured, she will provide as she has provided, she will cure herself of whatever damage humanity may inflict. Which is good, I suppose. It's grounds for a certain stoic and hyperopic sort of satisfaction. Okay, well, whoopee. Life on Earth will continue, according to J. E. Lovelock's hypothesis, whether humankind cooperates, or the contrary.

But the question that nags me is this. When humanity's earthly misbehavior has progressed to the point where even our farts can't redeem us, won't Gaia simply cure herself of *Homo sapiens*?

THE FLIGHT
OF THE IGUANA

*Evolution and Extinction
in the Galápagos and Beyond*

Imagine a moment in the history of ideas: A young man stands
on the coast of a tropical island, many miles and many years
from his home, throwing an oversized lizard into the sea.

The lizard swims back to shore. The young man follows this
animal, corners it, catches it by its long muscular tail, and throws
it again into the sea. Again the lizard swims back to shore. Still
another repetition. Always the lizard swims straight back to that
same stretch of rocky shoreline where the young man waits to
catch it again, throw it again. The lizard is a strong swimmer but
seems stubbornly disinclined to try to escape through the water.
The young man takes careful note of that fact and, despite his
homesickness, wonders why.

"Perhaps this singular piece of apparent stupidity may be accounted for by the circumstance," the young man eventually
writes, "that this reptile has no enemy whatever on shore,
whereas at sea it must often fall a prey to the numerous sharks.
Hence, probably, urged by a fixed and hereditary instinct that the
shore is its place of safety, whatever the emergency may be, it
there takes refuge." The young man of course is Charles Darwin,
and the lizard is *Amblyrhynchus cristatus,* better known as the
Galápagos marine iguana.

The incident of the tossed iguana occurred in autumn of 1835, during Darwin's brief stopover in the Galápagos Islands toward the end of his five-year trip on board the surveying ship *Beagle.* It was recounted in his popular book *The Voyage of the* Beagle, published a decade later—which was still fourteen years before *The Origin of Species* suddenly made Darwin the most famous and controversial biologist in the world. Today we all know about *The Origin;* we all know about Darwin's great idea, that evolution has been produced by a process he called natural selection; we all know about how this idea was made vivid to him by the Galápagos finches, their different species having evolved to fit different niches on the various individual islands of the group. So we all know, or at least think we know, the biological significance of the Galápagos archipelago. These islands, volcanic nubs pushed up above the ocean surface five hundred miles west of Ecuador, constitute one of the shrines of modern science. We can tune in public television any night of the month, it seems, and find them gorgeously photographed, reverently explained. Giant tortoises, blue-footed boobies, finches with a spectrum of different beak shapes, exotic fauna and flora showing all manner of unique adaptations, Darwin's visit, presto, theory of evolution—the syllogism has been polished by repetition. The incident of the tossed iguana, though, generally passes unmentioned.

This is too bad, because that incident happens to be rather eloquent. It not only tells us about Charles Darwin the person, as he was in 1835—boundlessly curious, unsentimental about nature, doggedly systematic, groping, and yet in some measure still just a wealthy young remittance-man off on a round-the-world lark, riding horseback with the *gauchos* and throwing helpless lizards out to sea on a dull afternoon. It also hints toward a fuller understanding of the Galápagos Islands themselves.

A century and a half after Darwin, in the course of my own modest pilgrimage, I find myself seated on a rocky Galápagos shoreline. This particular island is Santa Cruz, one of the largest and ecologically most rich. The stretch of coast where I sit, in a jumble of sun-heated lava boulders and salt-tolerant vegetation, is not far from the Charles Darwin Research Station. Across the bay, prickly pear cactuses transmogrified into tree form, tall and thick as oaks, stand in weird silhouette above black lava cliffs. At close range, I am surrounded by a dozen marine iguanas.

One of these animals is a dominant male, looking resplendent with his crest of dorsal spines, his strong stubby face, his black skin mottled with orange and olive; there are also three or four adult females, and the rest juveniles. When I walked up and sat down among them, an hour ago, they paid me little attention. Four feet of distance seems to be all they require. Like most other animals on the Galápagos, the marine iguanas show an indifference toward human proximity that gets them labeled, perhaps misleadingly, with the word *tame*. Now we are all of us sunning. And I am wondering what might happen if I picked up the big male by his tail, swung him around carefully, and tossed him as far as I could into the surf.

I have just reread Chapter XVII of *The Voyage of the* Beagle, and the question intrigues me. The most probable answer is this: I would be arrested.

Today the Galápagos Islands are an Ecuadorean national park, with strict regulations protecting the native wildlife and vegetation from being tampered with by the likes of you or me. Even Darwin himself would now need a research permit, before he heaved his first marine iguana into the brine or (another of his lighthearted experiments during that visit) climbed up to ride on the back of a giant tortoise. Some tourists are prone to the self-indulgent delusion that those regulations can reasonably be bent —surely there's no harm in petting a "tame" sea lion or feeding bread crusts to a finch?—but it isn't so. The Galápagos require extraordinary, uncompromised protection from human impact. They need that extraordinary protection for four reasons: 1) because they have already, in the past three hundred years, been pillaged almost beyond rescue; 2) because they hold precious significance in both our natural and our intellectual heritage; 3) because they now endure heavy traffic as a tourist destination; and 4) simply because they are *islands*.

The first three of those reasons are, admittedly, tendentious and self-evident. The fourth is an intricate, fascinating matter of science.

Islands are different. Evolutionary biology as manifested on islands is an exaggerated and specialized subcategory. The same general principles apply—there's a competitive struggle for reproductive success, in the course of which those organisms best adapted to their environment are "selected" to perpetuate their genes—but, on an island, the application is so stark and unbuffered as to seem almost qualitatively distinct. For one thing, islands are generally poorer in species diversity than any equal area of similar habitat on a mainland. They have more than their share of unusual species, but fewer than their share of species overall. A corollary to that low diversity is that they are more fragile than the mainlands. Complexity translates to stability, for almost any ecosystem, and islands because of their isolation show biologically simplified communities.

Being islands, therefore, the Galápagos are especially vulnerable. Being islands, they are also especially instructive. Being what they are, the Galápagos are both drastically unique and at the same time quite similar to most of the planet's other islands.

That paradox is part of the insular condition: All islands tend to harbor ecosystems that are full of bizarre features (a shared pattern), but each island or group of islands is bizarre in its own eccentric way.

In the case of the Galápagos, so celebrated, so familiar, that paradox is commonly overlooked. Even a fairly eminent biographer of Darwin has declared: "The fame of the [Galápagos] islands was founded upon one thing; they were infinitely strange, unlike any other islands in the world." The statement is true, almost tautological, and it's also very misleading. The fuller truth is that *most* islands are infinitely strange, and unlike any others in the world.

The Galápagos are broadly representative for the very fact of being so strange, so unique—and that representativeness is what made them useful to Darwin. He might just as well have based his great insight upon a stop in Hawaii, or the Seychelles, or the Malay Archipelago, or Madagascar. And we might now talk about "Darwin's lemurs" or "Darwin's honeycreepers" instead of Darwin's finches. He might even have recognized natural selection from a study of South American rodents—though an island experience made his task easier, because those simplified island ecosystems display the evolutionary process in a boldface, cartoonish version. He might, he might have, he might— but as it happened, he didn't. Darwin *didn't* go to Hawaii, he didn't go to Madagascar, and he was not forced to derive his idea from the confusing patterns of faunal variation on the South American mainland. Fate and the *Beagle*'s survey itinerary brought him instead to the Galápagos.

Where he found an iguana that swam like an eel and lived on a diet of seaweed.

"It is a hideous-looking creature, of a dirty black color, stupid, and sluggish in its movements," Darwin wrote. Here I think he was a little unfair. In the morning of my second day on Santa Cruz, I am out on the black lava rocks of the shoreline again, with the marine iguanas, watching them as they gape stolidly out at the returning tide, and wondering what—if anything—is going on behind those inscrutable hooded eyes. Are these animals truly stupid and sluggish? Or are they just dignified and calm?

Amblyrhynchus cristatus is the world's only oceangoing lizard, an interesting distinction for several reasons. Like most other iguanas, it is a vegetarian, which means that it needs to feed

longer and more voluminously for the same amount of nourishment as a carnivore gets from one protein-rich meal. Also like
other iguanas, it is ectothermic (dependent on external sources of
body heat) and lacking in stamina. Since there is no better way to
sap a body of heat and stamina than by dunking it in seawater,
the marine iguana seems to have chosen a strange path. It feeds
on algae exposed at low tide or, more athletically, swims out into
the sea and dives down to graze underwater. Herpetologists who
have studied its physiology (which seems scarcely different from
the standard iguana physiology, suggesting that its marine adaptation is purely behavioral) continue to sound puzzled that *Amblyrhynchus* can live its life as it does.

The iguanas I'm watching this morning stand aloof from that
scientific conundrum. They stare at the surf, beneath which their
pastures of algae are now buried by the risen tide. They shift their
positions as the sun shifts, as their bodies warm, and seldom
otherwise move. I want to see them swim. But they don't oblige.
Occasionally the big male bobs his head, a quick series of three or
four jerky nods that seem to say: *Believe it, Jack, I'm the baddest
dude on this piece of beach.* At one point two females come face-
to-face and blow salt out their nostrils at each other. Mainly they
all bask. They are poised and opaque. They seem utterly indifferent to time's passage, boat traffic nearby, the herpetological puz-
zlement they have inspired, and the large pink creature sitting
among them again today with a ring notebook and sunburned
ears.

One hundred and eighty million years ago, while dinosaurs
were flourishing on land, the seas also were full of reptiles. Not
anymore. Nowadays there are still a few species of sea turtle and
estuarine crocodile (both of which tend to be much larger than
iguanas, one way of mitigating heat loss), and some sea snakes,
but lizards that exploit the seacoast environment, in or out of the
water, are rare. In the Philippines is a gecko that reportedly
hunts crabs; on the island of Cerralvo, off California, is an

iguana-type lizard that sometimes does too; on a Colombian island called Malpelo is a skink that preys on crustaceans in the
zone between low and high tides; and on Nosy Bé, just off Madagascar, another intertidal skink. It's no accident that these anomalies are all native to islands, where necessity and opportunity
can be so exceptional. *Amblyrhynchus cristatus* is the only lizard,
though, that clambers straight into the ocean for an underwater
meal.

After long patience, I am rewarded: I see a big male iguana
come swimming past, six feet offshore in the churning surf. He
parallels the line of the coast for a hundred yards, moving
strongly, only his dark head showing. He surges through the
water, neck craned, breasting along like a labrador in a duck
pond. Then he swings away from shore to cross a narrow channel
of open water, headed toward another part of the bay. Mesmer-
ized, I follow his progress for ten minutes.

To me this large swimming lizard seems a small miracle. But
the other iguanas ignore him, and no one else is around.

In 1866 Joseph Hooker, a botanist and a close friend of Darwin, delivered a lecture before a British scientific society on the
subject of island biology. Darwin himself had already given the
subject some attention in *The Origin of Species* (of which one
section is titled "On the Inhabitants of Oceanic Islands"), and
Alfred Russel Wallace (mainly remembered as the co-discoverer,
with Darwin, of natural selection) later published an important
book called *Island Life*. But Hooker's lecture, a less famous performance by a less famous man, is notable for having articulated
a handful of factors inherent to the biology of islands. Those
factors are still recognized as essential clues, not just for understanding evolution as it happens on islands, but for understanding how island oddities helped Darwin (and have continued to
help biologists to this day) understand evolution as it happens
everywhere.

Among the points Hooker discussed were: impoverishment, disharmony, dispersal ability, *loss* of dispersal ability, size change, and extinction.

Impoverishment was one of the factors that Darwin had already noted in *The Origin:* "The species of all kinds which inhabit oceanic islands are few in number compared with those on equal continental areas." Even a tropical rainforest on an island like New Guinea, impressively rich as it may be, will not harbor nearly the number of different species as will an equal area of rainforest in the Amazon. Likewise, a square mile of island desert will contain fewer drought- and heat-tolerant species than a physically similar square mile in Arizona. This sort of impoverishment is closely entangled with the matter of disharmony.

Disharmony means that the relative proportion of various species and groups of species—the profile of the ecosystem—will be different between an island and its most proximate continent. South America, for instance, has a glorious abundance of snakes and amphibians; but the Galápagos have only three native snake species, all from the genus *Dromicus,* and no amphibians whatsoever. South America is also full of terrestrial mammals; but until humans arrived (bringing dogs and goats and other forms of ecologic catastrophe), the Galápagos had no terrestrial mammals except a few species of rodent and bat. On the other hand, the Galápagos even today are exceptionally well endowed with different finch species. Disharmony.

Good dispersal ability is common to the lineages—both plant and animal—that occupy islands. The ancestors of insular species had to be hardy travelers, after all, or they never would have arrived. Life forms didn't just *appear* on islands (notwithstanding what the creationists want us to believe); they had to *get* there somehow, and that implies long pioneer crossings of salt water. Since salt water is inimical to the metabolism of most terrestrial and freshwater animals, since it also destroys the viability of many plant seeds, the lineages of flora and fauna that have established themselves on islands tend to be those that can fly great distances, or at least ride along in the feathers or the intestinal tract of a bird, or float passively on the air, or endure long periods of metabolic dormancy while being carried by currents to an island landfall. So on the Galápagos you find an abundance of ferns, whose spores are lighter than wind. You find frigate birds and albatrosses, capable of soaring endlessly with almost no effort. You find great tortoises, which can float clumsily but comfortably on the waves and go for months without food or drink. You find very few plants whose seeds are large and heavy. You find no freshwater fish. You find no frogs.

Loss of dispersal ability, on the other hand, is something that often happens to island lineages after arrival. Hardy travelers though their ancestors may have been, the island-dwelling descendants in some cases evolve toward being more earth-bound, sedentary, stranded. Birds lose the use of their wings, atrophied over generations into comical little flippers. Insects lose their wings entirely or (some beetles) find their outer wing cases fused shut so that the functional wings can't be unfolded. Plant seeds lose the little parachutes or the burr-like hooks that originally helped them cross oceans. The Hawaiian archipelago, for example, harbors two hundred species of flightless beetle, plus a number of other flightless insects. On the island of Tristan da Cunha in the South Atlantic is a flightless moth and a flightless fly. And on the Galápagos is *Halmenus robustus,* a flightless grasshopper. Among birds the phenomenon is just as pronounced and maybe a bit more familiar. The dodo, of course; it was one species of a group of large flightless birds, all related to pigeons, that were native to small islands in the Indian Ocean. On Madagascar were the elephant birds, and on New Zealand the moas, huge and grounded and both now extinct. But New Zealand still has its kiwis and Madagascar also still has a few smaller flightless birds. Cassowaries in New Guinea, emus in Australia, and a different group of flightless (or nearly flightless) rail on each of twenty oceanic islands, including a species in the Galápagos. More prominent among the Galápagos bird life, though, is *Nannopterum harrisi,* the world's only flightless cormorant. I could make the list longer—but what's going on here? Why has evolution in island situations transformed all these fliers to pedestrians?

Biologists suspect two possible causes. The first is absence of predation. Having left their natural enemies behind on the mainlands, island animals can *afford* to dispense with flight and devote their metabolic resources to other anatomical or behavioral needs. The second factor is that flightlessness tends to keep individual creatures (plant or animal) in the particular island's gene pool. Those seeds or birds or insects that can fly well are exactly the ones most likely to disappear, heading back out over the ocean; those that fly poorly are most likely to stay and breed. Neither of the two causes has been experimentally verified, but together they probably account for the widespread pattern.

Size change is another island phenomenon, this one especially familiar in the Galápagos context. Evolution tends to dictate that insular species be either bigger or smaller than their mainland relatives. Most species of land snails on Pacific islands are unusually small. The beetles of Hawaii are small. So are the beetles of St. Helena. Nosy Bé off Madagascar harbors a chameleon the size of an ant. By contrast, St. Helena also offers the world's largest (and therefore most disgusting) earwig, more than three inches long. Those extinct moas of New Zealand stood twelve feet tall, and the Madagascan elephant birds, not quite so tall but heftier, probably reached weights of a thousand pounds. (Sheer magnitude like that is no doubt another good reason they didn't fly.) And finally now we come to *Geochelone elephantopus,* the species that gives the Galápagos Islands their name and their famous image. "Galápagos" is the Spanish for tortoise, and no living thing represents this place so vividly as the giant tortoises.

The Galápagos tortoises are, like the Egyptian pyramids, a

marvel of which the dramatic effect can't be spoiled even by overfamiliarity. No matter how many zoo specimens you have seen, no matter how many photographs, these animals are still magically impressive in their native land. They are huge, they are gentle, and as a half dozen of them munch their way through a field of pangola grass in the highlands of Santa Cruz Island, they are astounding. What they are *not,* however, is incomparable.

Part of understanding island biology—and part of appreciating, therefore, the Galápagos—is to recognize that those Galápagos giants aren't alone. On the island of Aldabra in the Indian Ocean survives a related tortoise species called *Geochelone gigantea,* roughly the same size as the Galápagos animals and produced (insofar as biologists can guess) by the same evolutionary conditions. Having escaped mainland predators and mainland competitors, these island tortoises were free to become enormous, moving into the large-herbivore niche that elsewhere is occupied by moose, rhino, wildebeest.

Isolation and escape are what give island ecosystems their peculiarity. Isolation and escape are the preconditions that allow those other characteristic conditions (impoverishment, disharmony, the arrival of good-traveler lineages, the retention of bad-traveler offspring, changes of size) to appear. The isolation compels an inbreeding population to shape themselves, genetically, toward the new challenges of this new island habitat; and the escape from predators and competitors allows that same population a great latitude of experiment, transformation, aggrandizement. A tortoise grows huge. A finch takes on the life-style of a woodpecker. A prickly pear cactus stiffens and raises itself into a stout tree.

The exceptional becomes routine. An observer as keen as Darwin might even see an iguana fly through the air.

No sensible person travels all the way to the Galápagos just to sit on one pile of lava rock, staring at iguanas. And neither have

I. Leaving behind that stretch of coastline on Santa Cruz, I board a boat and spend seven days cruising around the archipelago.

To visit a number of these islands in brisk succession, taking note of the differences in vegetation and wildlife from one to another, the differences in relative concentration of those various species, the differences in physical terrain, is an essential part of the experience. Just as it was for Darwin: "I have not as yet [noted] by far the most remarkable feature in the natural history of this archipelago; it is, that the different islands to a considerable extent are inhabited by a different set of beings." My own week of island cruising will pass too quickly, too full of amazing sights for adequate appreciation of each, but at least I have come prepared. Despite having already destroyed my binoculars (in a maneuver so clownish as not to bear recounting), I am equipped with a field guide, a snorkel mask with prescription lenses, a packet of seasickness medicine, a silly hat, a Royal Robbins shirt that washes well in salt water, and a paperback copy of *The Voyage of the* Beagle. Most helpful of all, I am accompanied by my own personal consulting biologist, with whom I share a fondness for homely arthropods and a wedding anniversary. She is here mainly to scout for new species of fiddler crab, but consents also to show an interest in birds, plants, reptiles. After a day at sea we reach Española Island, nesting site for virtually the world's entire population (twelve thousand pairs) of the waved albatross.

In a quiet bay off another island, Santa Fe, we see spotted eagle rays, their leopard-pattern fins swirling out of the water as they frolic (or possibly mate) near the surface. On the island called South Plaza we see land iguanas, fat mustard-colored lizards that are cousins to *Amblyrhynchus cristatus* but even larger, and that sustain themselves on this arid slab with a diet of prickly pear pads. On Tower Island, far up in the northeast corner of the archipelago, we see male frigate birds with their scarlet throat pouches inflated for mating display, and red-footed boobies roosting in bushes, webbed feet wrapped clumsily over the thin branches. Just off the shore of James Island we witness a feeding frenzy of blue-footed boobies, falling out of the sky in formation to make their plunge dives—*whop, whop, whop, whop*—like a mortar attack hitting the water. On Seymour we see prickly pears that grow horizontally, resting their pads on the ground, an indulgence they can afford partly because Seymour has no tortoises to feed on them. And then already the boat tour, this dizzying pageant of exotica, is over.

After such a spectacle, almost anything would seem anticlimactic. But the biologist wants more time at the Darwin Research Station, and I want more time communing with iguanas, so we return to the bay on the south coast of Santa Cruz.

There is still that one other point from Joseph Hooker's lecture: extinction.

The drawback for any species in having evolved on an island, under conditions of isolation and escape, is that eventually the isolation is breached and the escape comes to a rude end. This fate is almost inevitable. Just as surely as "pioneers" found their way to the island once, "invaders" will find their way later. Suddenly, then, forms of anatomy and behavior that have served well for a million years may become, instead, under new conditions, disastrous. "Tameness" may prove suicidal. Flightlessness may prove fatal. Gigantism may prove to be a dire handicap. All at once there are unfamiliar predators (or competitors, or maybe just parasites or disease organisms) sharing the island, and those newcomers present a threat with which the native species are not prepared to cope. No species offers a more vivid example of this sorry truth than *Geochelone elephantopus,* the Galápagos tortoise.

For millennia their huge size and slow metabolism allowed them to endure droughts and famines that occasionally struck the islands, while their stately, trustful behavior was no disadvantage. They had a low reproductive rate, but each adult was likely to live a hundred years or more, so it didn't matter. The populations (fifteen distinct races, isolated from each other among the different islands) were stable.

Then humankind arrived.

There had been no aboriginal humans in the Galápagos. But beginning late in the seventeenth century, whalers and other forms of sea-borne human predator stopped on the islands for fresh water and plundered the tortoises for meat and oil. The tortoises were defenseless; still worse for them, their reptile metabolism allowed them to survive months of storage in the hold of a ship, making fresh meat available without refrigeration. In two centuries possibly 200,000 adult tortoises were butchered. Even Darwin helped eat them.

Meanwhile goats and pigs and dogs and rats (all brought to the islands by humans) did their share of damage also, preying on tortoise eggs and young hatchlings or competing with the adults for limited grazing resources. By gracious fortune, protective laws were enacted before *every* race of the tortoises was extinct. Eleven of the races survive. Many of those, though, are still threatened by feral mammals.

Elsewhere in the world, the dodo wasn't so lucky. The great auk wasn't so lucky. The moas and the elephant birds and the Guam broadbill weren't so et cetera—and likewise with the rest of a whole dreary litany of unluckies. Since 1680, by one estimate, 127 species or races of birds have gone extinct, of which *116* lived on islands. Most of those extinctions were caused by humankind, but not all. In truth, humanity's role in destroying island species only accelerates (grossly and cataclysmically, yes) what is otherwise in some sense inevitable. Island species come to an end, almost invariably, without ever rejoining the mainstream of evolution. They are bad travelers. They are adapted for life in a relative biological vacuum which Nature herself abhors. In the long run, therefore, they are goners.

But then in the long run we're all goners, and the Earth itself is just another doomed biological island. It's a truism that death and entropy await everybody, everything. That certainly doesn't mean *Homo sapiens* shouldn't, in the somewhat shorter run, scramble like hell to survive—or that we shouldn't do all possible to minimize our baneful impact on island species.

Back on the south coast of Santa Cruz, the iguanas seem profoundly uninterested when I reappear.

They don't flee. They glance at me and continue basking. They allow me to rejoin the group.

Most wild animals would be spooked by a human approaching so close. Not these. These singular lizards are products of isolation and escape. Evolution has forged in them the once-accurate, now-foolhardy assumption that they have no enemies on land; that the sharks cruising offshore are the only sort of beast they need fear. If I grab one by the tail, swing him around, throw him into the water, scientific precedent says he will probably swim straight back to shore and allow me to catch him again. Three hundred years' acquaintance with humanity hasn't been long enough, evidently, to teach caution. Maybe Darwin was right. Maybe they are stupid.

But I prefer to see them as recklessly, lavishly, forgivingly trustful. And I hope they can afford to stay that way a bit longer.

IV

THE MORAL
ECOLOGY OF A
DESERT

THE BEADED LIZARD

Sanctuary in Tucson: 1984

The beaded lizard is part of the landscape. Seldom is it also part of the scenery. A distinction to bear in mind. Scenery is what you look at. Landscape is where you live and die.

Most often the beaded lizard is invisible within its favored habitat, this land of dearth and stress called the Sonoran Desert —invisible even when present. It tends to be reclusive, shy, nocturnal. Also there are tricks of perspective involved, ambiguities of the optical sort, figure-and-ground confusions. In dim light, against a dark background, the animal's black beading may blend away and the paler pink and orange markings stand forward like bleached desert sticks, leaving no lizard outline whatsoever. And vice versa against a pale background. In daylight it retreats to a burrow. Feeds ploddingly on bird and reptile eggs, rodents, young rabbits. The venom is truly potent but the reputation of lurking menace is fantasy. The beaded lizard is notorious under its more common name, and scientifically familiar as *Heloderma suspectum,* but it can be blamed, unequivocally, for few if any human fatalities. Unlike a mad dog or a man, a Gila monster evidently won't bite or kill without good reason.

So it's not really very monstrous. There are tricks of perspective involved.

Scenery is an apparition in two dimensions but landscape is a matrix for destiny. And the story in question here—this particular tangled matter of exodus, murder, thorny plants, law versus policy, ideals versus betrayal of ideals, barbed wire, religious faith, and invisible venomous reptiles—that story plays itself out, by no accident, on a harsh landscape. It begins along a remote stretch of road in the desert hills of northern Mexico, when a car pulls to a sudden stop.

Seven people climb quickly out, carrying heavy day-packs loaded with water and food. Immediately the car drives away. The people clamber over a guard rail, adults hoisting the two little children, and skid down the steep hillside into a gulch, where they will be out of sight from the road above. Beneath mesquite bushes, they pause for breath. Four of these people are Salvadorans, a young family, and they are literally running for their lives. Two others are U.S. citizens, from a certain small group up in Tucson, who are about to risk jeopardy of twenty-year prison sentences under U.S. law. One of the seven is a craven but curious journalist.

That one doesn't share so much as a language with the four Salvadorans. He is not politically and morally pellucid, like the two young guides. He is merely a dilettante with a strong interest in predation, modes of survival, landscape.

For the moment, together, they are all safe. But the border is still a mile away, and much of that mile is open ground.

The children—a boy of five, a girl of at most four—show only a hint of terror behind their stolid faces. They are silent, obedient, stalwart. Possibly they don't comprehend the stakes. More likely they have already seen enough in their brief lives to make these moments of danger unexceptional. As the group begin picking their way down the gulch, boulder to boulder, mesquite to mesquite, staying low in the tangled brush to avoid exposure, the little boy takes a hard fall, slamming his tailbone down on a rock shelf. While his mother applies a gentle rub, he furrows his face to a scowl, but doesn't so much as whimper.

They move on, trying to leave no more footprints than necessary. The young Anglo man—call him Jeff—leads the way. He has hiked this particular backcountry trail before. The Anglo woman—call her Helen—walks at the rear, keeping watch behind for traffic on that stretch of road. Her large floppy straw hat gives her the look of an innocent American schoolteacher out for a day's hike in the Sonoran hills, attentive to birds and wildflowers. A veteran of these border crossings, like Jeff, she has cultivated the image. She brushes the others' footprints away with a mesquite branch—idly, as though she were doodling in gouache.

The first half mile is tense but uneventful.

They have been listening carefully for distant guttural rumbles, then taking cover each time a truck rolls by on the road behind them. Finally they make their turn from the gulch into a wider canyon, this one running due north, which leads them out of eyeshot, at last, from that Mexican road. But now a different rumble of engine comes up on them too suddenly and too near. In Spanish, Helen hisses: *"Avión!"* They dive under the thickest clumps of mesquite, smashing themselves into the dry branches, flattening down against leaf litter and gravel, cowering there, as a small plane passes low over the canyon. Border Patrol, most likely. One glimpse, a radio call to land forces nearby, and the whole enterprise will unravel in disaster.

Still, it all seems so much like a game, so much like a television melodrama, that the journalist has to remind himself consciously: *This isn't hide-and-seek. People could go to jail. People could die. Very possible. These four people here. They could be caught, and deported, and then murdered. Very possible.* He has to remind himself that the invisible menace out here today is not fantastical, and not herpetological. *This isn't a nature hike.*

While the others climb out of the brush and move on, the

journalist takes an extra moment to rip off his right boot and pull out the cactus spine that has been driven into his big toe. Then he scrambles to catch up with the family who are running for their lives, and with the two gringos who are smuggling them into Arizona.

"I first became involved on May 4 of 1981," says Jim Corbett, a mild and middle-aged Quaker with hands badly twisted by arthritis. Corbett ran a cattle ranch here in southern Arizona until the arthritis made that sort of work impossible; before the ranching, he had taken a master's degree in philosophy at Harvard. Since Jim Corbett is one of the founders of the latter-day underground railroad that moves Central Americans to sanctuary in the United States, May 4 of 1981 marks an important beginning.

On that date a friend of Corbett's, driving back up toward Tucson from the border town of Nogales, had picked up a hitchhiker who turned out to be Salvadoran. Almost immediately, Corbett's friend and the passenger came to one of the routine Border Patrol checkpoints that are common in southern Arizona. The Salvadoran had no papers; in the view of the Border Patrol, he was an illegal alien. So the Patrol agents took him, to be jailed and eventually deported back to El Salvador. "That night, when my friend came over," says Corbett, "we talked about what might happen to that refugee."

Corbett already knew something about the conditions in El Salvador, where hundreds of unarmed civilians were dying each month, most of them evidently killed by government security forces and those right-wing paramilitary groups known as *los escuadrones de la muerte*—the infamous "death squads." He knew that people were disappearing, their mangled bodies turning up on street corners; that men and women were being jailed and tortured for any hint of "subversive" sympathies, or for the crime of remaining neutral in a polarized country; that children were being murdered to eliminate witnesses. And there was more. "We had heard reports that an entire planeload of deportees had been shot down at the airport in El Salvador, in December 1980. So we were concerned about what might happen to that hitchhiker." The next morning Corbett woke up having decided, he says, that he ought to find out.

Later, Corbett described this decision in a letter: "Last spring I planned to do a study of radical reformation, the process that leads Christians to discover that they are Jewish. (Beneath the veneer of Orphic otherworldliness and Manichaean dualism is the suffering servant who opens the way toward community fulfillment of torah.) My focus was to have been the Diggers of 17th Century England, but unforeseen circumstances wrenched me into the 20th Century." This is a fair sample of Jim Corbett the thinker, the writer, the moral theorist. In person, on the other hand, he is utterly plainspoken and direct.

What Corbett learned, over the next few days and weeks, was that large numbers of Salvadorans who had fled north from the killing were being held by the U.S. Immigration and Naturalization Service (of which the Border Patrol is one enforcement arm) in jails and camps while the INS processed them for deportation back to El Salvador. He also learned about Guatemalans in the same situation, campesinos and Indians from the highlands especially, who had escaped a murderous army in their own country and were now too facing deportation. In the preconceived notion of the INS and the State Department, Corbett discovered, these terrified Central Americans had merely snuck into the U.S. looking for jobs. By this view, they represented just another small part of the great dreary deluge of poor Latinos (mainly Mexicans) flowing illegally across America's southern border, upon which the INS expends most of its effort. By this view, the Salvadorans and Guatemalans could have no valid claim to political asylum in America. They were not "refugees." They were "economic migrants." A trick of perspective was involved.

Corbett saw it differently. "So I began in June of '81," he says, "going down to Nogales, giving the people precrossing counseling. Working out ways for them to get across. Safe-house systems for them to get off the street as soon as they did get across. Ways to get them around the roadblocks and the Patrol surveillance, on into Tucson." And each time he performed one of those services, for each individual Salvadoran or Guatemalan, Jim Corbett risked a long stint in the slammer. A Quaker philosopher had become a refugee smuggler.

But running a few desperate Central Americans through the border blockade between Nogales and Tucson, in contravention of the Immigration and Nationality Act, was not Jim Corbett's ultimate goal. How many Salvadorans, after all, could he and his wife, Pat, feed and shelter at their own house? No more than twenty at a time, Corbett says. That wasn't enough. "The creation of a network of actively concerned, mutually supportive people in the U.S. and Mexico" was, instead, what he had in mind.

So it was fortunate that, in the summer of 1981, Corbett met John Fife, a lanky Presbyterian minister who had been edging up on the situation along his own separate path.

The plane doesn't return.

They follow the canyon northward over easy terrain, low rolling hillocks covered sparsely with mesquite and prickly pear and cholla. Across the driest flats, water-starved clumps of creosote bush are scattered evenly, standoffishly, with almost nothing alive in the spaces between. The young Salvadoran father walks hand in hand with his daughter. The boy dashes ahead to catch up with Jeff, then falls back to his mother. Each of the parents carries a single leather bag, which together now hold all the family's earthly possessions; one larger suitcase was abandoned back at the safe house in the last Mexican town. The wife has brought along her Spanish Bible. During pauses in the trek, she unburies it to read silently from the Psalms. The journalist can't see whether it's Psalm 23 she's consulting—"Yea, though I walk through the valley of the shadow of death, I will fear no evil"— or some other.

This is the stretch of ground for making good time. They stride out eagerly, even a little confidently, across sun-shattered rock and clay. Not yet 10 A.M., but already the day is quite hot. It will get hotter. The second week of May, in the Sonoran Desert, is too late for spring and too early for the cooling summer monsoon. Helen hoots in shock when a snake comes alert as she is stepping over it.

But it's just a gopher snake, not a rattler. This species is a heart-stopping mimic, tan-and-brown mottled much like the Massasauga rattlesnake, or the Mojave, and Helen's specimen right now is holding its head flattened out wide to give the same fierce pit viper silhouette. A harmless and terrified creature, twitching its tail in empty bluff. Mistaken identity. The journalist has seen gopher snakes murdered for less, some vainglorious yahoo blasting the animal's head off with a revolver and then mystified to find no rattle segments on the tail. Must have just shed its skin, is the normal and nonsensical explanation. Helen gasps a breath back into her lungs, laughs nervously, and moves around this worried snake. She is carrying a snakebite kit, she says, but would prefer never to have to read the instructions.

Everyone has been tense. The false jolt of the snake has discharged that tension only slightly.

Then, over the next knoll, they come to a five-foot-high barbed-wire fence.

It is strung between metal posts, taller and sturdier than the average ranch fence, but not really so very imposing. They celebrate now: a drink from the canteens. Jeff climbs over first, so he can lift the kids down on that side. The husband assists his wife.

Then he follows. Then Helen. Lastly, trying hard not to rip his pants, the journalist climbs into America.

Reverend John Fife, extraordinarily long-legged, tips himself back in a chair, chain-smoking away the restlessness. With his neatly trimmed beard, his cowboy boots, and his irreverent, self-mocking sense of humor, he is not what you expect in a Presbyterian minister. He prefers calling himself a "preacher." As a young seminarian, he went to Selma during the early civil rights battles, then quickly realized he should be back home fighting the same battles less gloriously in Pittsburgh. Fifteen years ago Fife moved down here to become pastor of a small congregation in the Hispanic section of Tucson. The matter of Central American refugees forced its way into his life only when, over the Fourth of July weekend in 1980, thirteen Salvadorans died of heat and dehydration in the desert borderland southwest of Tucson.

They had been trying to cross into the U.S. Their professional smuggler—known in the argot as a *coyote*—had abandoned them. After two days of wandering through the hills, desperate for water, they had turned to drinking their own urine. They were found by the Border Patrol. Some stronger members of the group had survived; most of the dead were women and children.

"*That* engaged my attention," John Fife says. "The fact that people were willing to risk that kind of venture, coming across our border." Fife's church was one of several that provided aid to the survivors. From them, he says, he learned "some *incredible* stories about El Salvador." With a measure of throwaway scorn for his own ignorance, Fife stresses that, in the summer of 1980, he couldn't have placed El Salvador on a map. "I had assumed that people were coming across from Central America for the same reason that people were coming across our border from Mexico. It was hard in the village, they were poor. . . . But these folk from Salvador were telling a *different* set of stories. They were talking about death squads, and about torture, and about the kind of terrorism and violence that we now know about. . . . And so I started to do my homework, after that experience."

Fife's homework led him to the conclusion that right-wing zeal and government paranoia in El Salvador were resulting in, among other things, a pattern of bloody persecution against the Church. In March of that year the Archbishop of San Salvador, Oscar Arnulfo Romero, had been assassinated in the act of saying Mass. Local priests and lay catechists were being threatened, jailed, killed. In December of the same year, three U.S. nuns and a Catholic lay worker would be murdered near the capital city. Fife resolved not to sit idle.

He and a good friend, Father Ricardo Elford, began holding a weekly prayer vigil—ecumenical, informative, and unabashedly political—each Thursday at rush hour in front of the Federal Building.* Another step was also taken, a seemingly small thing that proved far more consequential. Fife and his congregation offered their church as a physical refuge for the Salvadorans and Guatemalans that Jim Corbett was smuggling in.

Southside Presbyterian Church is a modest stucco building with a saguaro cactus out front and one chain-pull church bell hung over the front portico, and decorated inside with little more than a rough wooden cross made of railroad ties and a few cheerful cloth banners. The congregation is small, and neither affluent nor homogeneous: about 130 members, a mix of three native American tribes (Papagos, Pimas, Navajos), plus blacks, Hispanics, and Anglos. On a Sunday morning the building rattles with old-time gospel hymns in a distinctly Southern Baptist vein—there's clapping and blackstrap harmonies and a good dose of hallelujah. Preacher Fife himself admits that "the Presbyterian

---

* Those weekly vigils would continue for at least seven years, serving as a public meeting point for all stripe of Tucson citizens concerned with issues of U.S. involvement in Central America.

Church has been called 'the Republican Party of prayer,' and not for unsound reasons." But Southside Presbyterian is something quite different. Perhaps because the members possess so little themselves, they feel they can afford to offer it all.

For a few months Fife and his congregation proceeded discreetly, providing food and clothing and temporary shelter for undocumented Central Americans, helping them assimilate into the local Hispanic community or assisting with links to other generous folk in other cities. It was a quiet operation, meeting the needs of a few dozen refugees, and the government showed no inclination to interfere—probably because the government was oblivious. Eventually this lack of concern began to look like a serious problem. "The government policy wasn't going to change until we got people's attention," says Fife.

In November of 1981 there was a meeting of the small group who had been working together on this issue—Fife, Corbett, Father Elford, a few other clergy and lawyers. What to do next? "We were really in despair at that point," Fife recalls. "We had tried the legal defense thing. We had tried the underground smuggling thing. And, as far as we could see, it wasn't gonna change anything. People in *Tucson* didn't even know there were refugees here—let alone people in the rest of the United States. The government was continuing to deport people at the rate of twenty-five or thirty a day. The bloodshed and death squads were increasing down there. The persecution of the Church was just overwhelming. All of the legal defense efforts had managed to save a *few* people. The underground was saving a few more. But obviously we could keep that up for the next ten years, and save a few hundred people, and lose thousands. *Really*—we were trying to say—*what can we do?* And the idea of sanctuary emerged."

The concept of sanctuary in the sense Fife uses the word—meaning a church or other holy place into which a fugitive can retreat and be protected at least temporarily from blood enemies or civil authorities—is as old as the book of Exodus: "Then I will appoint thee a place whither he shall flee." Christian sanctuaries were first recognized in Roman law toward the end of the fourth century; eventually, medieval canon law and English common law also codified the practice. In England a person accused of a felony could take refuge in a church and be immune there for forty days, until he decided between standing trial or leaving the kingdom. Even after forty days the civil officials would not invade church property. Instead, they would begin trying to starve the person out. In America the tradition was broadened toward outright civil disobedience by the original "underground railroad." When Congress in 1850 passed the Fugitive Slave Law, making it illegal to harbor or transport a runaway slave, churches from the borderlands into New England became key points in a network of defiance.

Fife and the others discussed these precedents, as well as a negative example: During World War II, Christian churches did all too little to help Jews flee from Nazi Germany. It shouldn't happen again, Fife thought. So two hundred letters were sent to churches and religious communities around the country. The message was: "We're going to do this. Do you want to join us?"

On March 24, 1982, Southside Presbyterian Church (joined by a handful of other congregations in California, New York, and Washington, D.C.) announced, by way of a press conference and an open letter to the U.S. Attorney General, that they would henceforth be providing sanctuary for certain undocumented Central American aliens.

Fife and his congregation were deliberately escalating the stakes for themselves, and for the INS, by going public. They were challenging the U.S. government to march into the church, if it dared, and haul people away.

Duke Austin, a spokesman in Washington for the Immigration and Naturalization Service, says: "There is no such thing as sanctuary, legally, in this country. These people have no more right to harbor an illegal alien than they have to harbor a criminal." On the tactical level, though, Austin pragmatically adds: "We will not go into churches and remove illegal aliens. We've always said that we cannot change our priorities of enforcement. Our priorities are to stop aliens at the border and take them out of the workplace." Besides priorities, of course, the INS also has some sensitivity to the factor of nasty publicity.

The entire Border Patrol, Austin stresses, comprises fewer personnel than the Baltimore Police Department. Yet in 1983 the Patrol apprehended one million illegal aliens—of whom the vast majority were Mexicans. Meanwhile, as of 1984 only three hundred Central Americans (by Austin's rough estimate, which is lower than some others) successfully made the passage into sanctuary. Austin suggests (and despite some disagreement over numbers, the point is generally persuasive) that, as far as the immediate INS mission is concerned, the traffic of undocumented Central Americans represents little more than a biting mosquito on the arm of a man who is about to be trampled by a rhino. For the State Department, however—and for the White House—it is another matter.

Especially now, after the election of Napoleon Duarte as President, the Reagan Administration cannot afford to admit that El Salvador remains chaotically violent—a place from which innocent people must sometimes flee for their lives.

"Here's the spot where we saw the Gila monster last week," says Jeff. He points to a small undercut ledge in the wall of the narrow gulch. The journalist inspects it distractedly while the others catch breath.

Last week was a dry run, an innocent day hike in from the U.S. side to scout a path through these connecting canyons. This particular gulch, a water-cut gash into the desert floor, tight as a big-city alley, with a few cottonwoods gripped thirstily into the sand and stony shoulders rising on each side, seemed a good route, deep and sinuous enough to offer cover. In Arizona you call this sort of thing a "wash." It's cooler and more pleasant than the bleak open hills, though a bad place to get caught during a rainstorm. Also prime habitat for *Heloderma suspectum.* That might seem to recommend it or not, depending on your predisposition. But no, no Gila monster is cooling itself under the ledge today. A small disappointment for the journalist.

Heloderma suspectum in its native environment can go a great while without food or water. During good times it stores away fat in its long dragging sausage of a tail. With weeks or months of starvation and drought, the tail thins away and the whole animal shrinks down to a scrawny lizard shape inside the flaccid beadwork skin. Reduced to that minimal existence, not eating, not moving, unseen, it still tends to be a survivor. Seems to have no natural enemies except the coyote, various raptors, and of course the cruel and acquisitive *Homo sapiens.* Not much traffic by any of those three taxa, through a woebegone drywash like this.

Humans in particular are poorly engineered for the terrain. As the morning wears on, the Salvadoran woman is moving a little more slowly. She needs help climbing up and down these rocky shoulders. Advance word to Helen and Jeff said that the Salvadoran husband and the children should be capable of an arduous hike, the woman perhaps less so; but no one was sure whether to credit that warning or to dismiss it as a sexist assumption.

Now it turns out that the woman is suffering from mumps. She knows the symptoms, because she is a nurse.

John Fife says, "The whole function of public sanctuary is to encourage as many churches—and people—as possible to have to deal with this moral, legal problem. To make a decision and then communicate it to the legislative bodies."

In some measure, it seems to be working. With surprising speed, the sanctuary idea has taken hold in other consciences, other congregations, other cities, and become a national movement.

Immediately after the Southside declaration, Fife and his compatriots began getting calls from religious people of every denomination all over the country. What could they do to help? How could they take the same step? There were also calls from Salvadorans and Guatemalans who had themselves escaped to the U.S. but who had relatives still in danger. Could those relatives be rescued by the underground railroad? The Tucson people were swamped beneath a huge volume of inquiries; at the same time they were still also trying to move refugees northward, and to cope with those people's immediate physical needs. At last came a call from a group called the Chicago Religious Task Force on Central America, a confederation of forty religious organizations in the Chicago area, who asked for information that they could pass on to their members—and as a result of that contact, Tucson gratefully turned over its central communications role to the Chicago Task Force.

Today* about 140 congregations and religious communities in over sixty cities have officially declared sanctuary, in defiance of U.S. law as interpreted by the INS. More are adding themselves each week. The variety is striking: a Mennonite church in Illinois, a Presbyterian church in Minneapolis, a Friends' Meeting in Cincinnati, a Lutheran church in Palo Alto, a Unitarian Universalist in upstate New York, a temple in Wisconsin, a Catholic parish in Louisville, a Brethren Discipleship group in Indiana, a Sisters of St. Joseph community in Concordia, Kansas, a monastery in Vermont. The total membership of those sanctuary support groups runs close to 50,000 people, and each responsible member who has partaken of the decision faces the prospect of prison, if the Justice Department should choose to prosecute.

But sanctuary, in the sense of these declarations, is not just a church building, not just a place; it is not even *mainly* a place. What the declaration of sanctuary really represents is a pledge of

* As of May 1984. All the numbers have continued to grow.

a community of support: shelter, food, medical care, if possible a job, concealment, legal help, and, as the last resort, a readiness on the part of many of these churchgoing Americans to accept a jail sentence for their trouble. The actual church or synagogue is for the most part just a symbol of that pledge.

In the three years since Jim Corbett began smuggling refugees, by Corbett's own estimate, roughly a thousand Central Americans have come across the Arizona border and passed through Tucson, to be relayed surreptitiously onward to their host congregations in Kansas or Vermont or wherever. Meanwhile, other conscience-driven smugglers have been assisting other crossings into California, New Mexico, and Texas. From the city of first refuge, a car relay for one typical family to their ultimate destination might involve two hundred U.S. citizens, members of that underground network of concerned citizens that Corbett had hoped for early on. A young mother with kids might drive the refugees for a one-day stretch in her own car. An elderly Quaker couple might give them lodging in a guest room that night. Next day, a nun might drive another leg of the trip in a minibus registered to the bishop. Lodging that night at, say, the home of a female psychology professor who is active in her synagogue. Next day, a smiling long-haired young man with a camper-back pickup truck, or a balding retiree in a porkpie hat driving a Chevy wagon, or maybe a Unitarian matron with a Volvo. That night, the spare room of an affluent yuppie couple or a cot in the church basement at a Lutheran congregation. And so on, to the final sanctuary. Each of those helping acts have been, by the government's view, felonious.

Eliott Abrams is the Assistant Secretary of State for Human Rights and Humanitarian Affairs,* head of that branch which effectively determines who is or is not accepted as a refugee.

---

* Abrams later became Assistant Secretary for Inter-American Affairs, and eventually achieved somewhat wider renown in the Iran-Contra hearings.

Abrams says: "My sense is that from the Caribbean and Central America, the majority of people emigrating to the United States are *not* refugees. They are people seeking to build a better life for themselves by finding better employment." Abrams admits having heard reports of torture, murder, and mutilation committed against Salvadorans deported back from the U.S. (and calls those reports, dismissively, "horror stories"), but he adds that "the fact remains that not everybody in El Salvador has the right to live in America [merely] because that [El Salvador] is not a nice country. It is *not* a nice country right now. It is one of a *hundred* not-nice countries—and not everybody has the right to live here."

Then again, we are a self-proclaimed nation of immigrants, with an ideal of welcoming the beleaguered refugee. Certain words have been carved at the base of the Statue of Liberty, after all. But there are ambiguities of the optical sort: One person's political refugee is another's brown wetback.

A rabbi in Tucson says: "My own father was an illegal alien. A stowaway. Consequently I have strong feelings on the subject. I believe in the Biblical principle *Thou shalt not oppress a stranger; for ye know the heart of a stranger, seeing ye were strangers in the land of Egypt.* It's the highest expression of Judaism to help people who are legitimately refugees. And the government claim that these people are 'economic migrants' is hogwash."

At a point heartbreakingly near what should be the end of their crossing, the hikers stumble into a serious problem.

They are within two hundred yards of the junction where this wash pays out into another wide canyon, a remote but accessible bit of country along which runs a gravel road. At that junction they are supposed to meet their American-side pickup. But Jeff has walked ahead down the wash to see whether the way is clear, and he returns with bad news: Between here and the junction, parked, temporarily abandoned, is a Jeep. It may or may not be the Border Patrol.

Helen leads the group to a hiding place just up the west hillside, beneath a mesquite thicket, where they will be invisible both from the wash bed and from the high open ridges above. Jeff goes back down toward the Jeep, nosing his way tentatively in search of a little more information. If it is a Border Patrol vehicle, the hikers are already in trouble and might need to make a desperate retreat up the wash. If it belongs to picnickers or rock hounds or local cowboys, which is more likely, they need only wait and be very careful.

For an hour, huddled in the brush, they wait. They share water and oranges and a bag of bologna sandwiches. They also talk. The journalist wants to know more about this family—about why specifically they left El Salvador.

The wife—call her Lupe—has been a nurse for twelve years. She worked at a children's hospital in the capital city, San Salvador. Because of the war and the murders, thousands of newly orphaned children are living street lives in San Salvador, she says. Sick and starving children. Even in the hospital, she saw many of them die for lack of medicine.

Her husband—call him Roberto—is a poet of some reputation. His poems have been published in Brazil and Peru, and a book of them will appear soon from a press in Belgium. Yes, he says, his poetry tends to be political. This was part of the reason for his troubles.

Roberto was also a high school teacher in San Salvador. Literature and history were his subjects. In June of 1983, apparently because he was already suspected for his ideas, men from the National Guard came to search his house. They found certain books (books any teacher of history and literature might own, says Roberto: one novel by a Cuban author, a volume entitled *The Fight of the Campesinos,* others by the Brazilian author Paolo Freire) that were considered "subversive." Roberto was taken away.

For a week, says Roberto, he was held in solitary confinement, kept blindfolded, repeatedly beaten and interrogated. "What group are you in?" the Guardia demanded. "Who are your comrades?" No group, Roberto told them. No comrades. He was simply a schoolteacher.

After that week he was transferred to Mariona Prison (the main men's prison in El Salvador) and evidently forgotten about by his captors. He remained in Mariona, in what was called "the political section," for seven months. He talked with many of the other prisoners. Professors, arrested for their "subversive" ideas. Doctors, arrested for helping the poor. Also a large number of illiterate campesinos. Roberto began teaching some of these campesinos to read.

Meanwhile Lupe, who knew that Roberto was still alive and had even been allowed to visit him, got legal help. Roberto had never been charged with a crime. His case went to the Salvadoran Supreme Court, says Roberto, and in January the judges ordered his release. But that court decision did not mean he was safe— rather the contrary. "After release, often," says Roberto, "is when the death squads come."

Taking the son, he left immediately for Mexico City. Lupe and their daughter followed as soon as Roberto had found a safe haven there. The haven was only a temporary one, because Mexico deports Salvadorans even more stringently (if that's possible) than does the United States. It was in Mexico City, late this spring, that the family made contact with a branch of the sanctuary movement.

Most of this information passes through Helen, as translator, because the journalist is ignorant of Spanish.

Jeff doesn't reappear. As the waiting drags on, they all grow gradually quieter. Midday in early summer in the Sonoran Desert, and the heat is audible in the thin shrill buzz of cicadas.

Finally the people beneath the bush are limiting themselves to an infrequent, elliptical whisper. Otherwise they listen. The two children are silent. Their eyes are wide.

Then the arrests began.

On February 17, 1984, a car was stopped by the Border Patrol just north of McAllen, Texas, a border town in the lower Rio Grande valley. The car was registered to the Catholic diocese of Brownsville, which also sponsors an institution called Casa Oscar Romero (after the murdered archbishop) that provides emergency shelter and other assistance to Central American refugees. Inside the car were a nun, another woman named Stacey Merkt, a reporter, and three undocumented Salvadorans. Four weeks later a federal grand jury issued indictments against the nun and Stacey Merkt. They were charged with transporting and conspiracy to transport illegal aliens.

On March 7 another car was stopped, on a mountain road east of Nogales, Arizona. The Border Patrol detained temporarily, then released, a pair of Tucson residents named Phil Conger and Katherine Flaherty. The four undocumented Salvadorans who had been with them were held, charged with entry into the U.S. without inspection, and eventually bonded out. Phil Conger is an employee of the Tucson Ecumenical Council (a federation of local churches), whose task force on Central America he directs. He is fluent in Spanish and has been active in what church people call "the refugee ministry" for three years. He works out of a tiny cluttered office across the hall from John Fife's tiny cluttered office at the rear of Southside Presbyterian Church.

In Tucson—with a community of sanctuary activists much larger and more visible than the one in the Rio Grande valley— the U.S. Attorney's Office dropped charges against the Salvadorans (though deportation proceedings were still in motion) and filed none against Flaherty, who had only been a passenger in the car. Phil Conger on the other hand had been driving; also, he was known to be a principal figure in the local efforts to house and feed Central Americans. Still, it can be assumed that the U.S. Attorney's Office did not approach this prosecution blithely. There would be media attention, an airing of the broader issues, political fallout. It was "just a routine smuggling case," according to Don Reno, the special assistant U.S. Attorney in Phoenix who handled the Conger case. According to scuttlebutt, though, a deal was offered. Federal officials proposed not to prosecute Conger—says a source who asks not to be identified—if he would promise to cease assisting illegal aliens.

Conger refused to make any such promise. On May 17 he was indicted on four counts of transporting.

Meanwhile, back in Texas, Stacey Merkt pleaded innocent to transporting illegal aliens (though she made no denial of transporting *refugees*) and was convicted. The nun pleaded guilty and agreed to cooperate with the prosecution; she was given a year's probation. And then another Texas man—Jack Elder, who is Conger's equivalent at the Casa Oscar Romero—was indicted too.

Unlike Conger, unlike Stacey Merkt, unlike anyone else so far, Jack Elder was not apprehended with undocumented aliens in a routine stop at a Border Patrol checkpoint. He was accused before a grand jury first, on the basis of testimonial evidence; then federal officers came onto church property and arrested him.

Some people suspect that this is the start of a general and coordinated roll-up* of the sanctuary movement by the Justice Department. Others believe that the government is still groping its way warily, reactively. No one wants to go to prison. But, says Jim Corbett, "If the government gets tough, they're going to have a lot of people under arrest—and I suppose, ultimately, in jail.

---

* Later news of sanctuary indictments and prosecutions appears in "The Desert Is a Mnemonic Device."

But I think that, in terms of what we're doing, it's going to go on and grow. Because the need is there."

At last Jeff comes back. He brings the unsettling news that two cowboys, apparently the same men who parked the Jeep, are at this moment just a hundred yards above on the west hillside, stringing fence. They seem to be working their way down, inadvertently, toward the hiding place; and in the meantime they command an open view of that last crucial stretch of the wash. Since there is every reason to fear that a pair of local cowboys would report any border crossers to the Border Patrol, it is time to move again. Quickly and quietly and invisibly. Staying hidden behind foliage and boulders, all seven people scutter back upstream along the wash.

Rounding two or three bends, past the Gila monster's cranny, they retrace their route back toward the border fence, to a point where the cowboys are safely eclipsed. The pace is faster this time, a little panicky, and when they pause for rest the canteen water begins to seem finite. But at least the cowboys showed no sign of having noticed. Now the problem is: How else to get out?

Jeff and Helen confer. The gravel road on the American side is just *not* very far away. But there is no other branch to this wash, no other shielded path between here and there.

So they all leave the wash, scaling the east shoulder on a steep traverse across desert scree that crumbles and slides beneath each footstep. They come up out of the cover of the cottonwoods, slowly ascending, exposing themselves on a bare hillside upholstered only in shin-daggers and prickly pear and the wiry, frazzled tufts of a few ocotillo. Under this midday heat, it would be a hard climb for anyone. Lupe pulls herself along haltingly, looking unwell, lagging behind the others. The boy falls again and comes up with a palm full of cactus spines, which he dolefully but mutely presents to his mother for plucking. Jeff picks an unpromising line, hikes a long way up and ahead until he finds himself again within view of the cowboys, then doubles back to rejoin the group and follow a still more roundabout traverse. Halfway up the hill, Helen stops. She is drastically red in the face. The journalist is alarmed but it's just hypoglycemia, says Helen, a chronic thing for her; and in a few minutes she is ready to go on. The canteens are passed around after every hundred steps.

They reach the ridge top. Under a last solitary mesquite (by now it's a matter of shade, not concealment), they all rest again. The water is gone. At this point they can see—and be seen from —miles away. Nothing to be done about that. Helen and Jeff are quite deliberate about stretching out this final rest. No sense in stumbling on hastily. Nevertheless, Roberto is restless and anxious; so is the journalist.

They cross the ridge top. Steering their downward traverse away from a ranch building visible to the east, they come slowly and very gratefully down to a stream running clear water beside a gravel road.

Within a few minutes the Salvadoran family is hidden among a crowd of respectable Anglo faces, in two separate vehicles, everyone headed toward Tucson.

To an outsider viewing the sanctuary movement with even a morsel of dispassion, three points stand out.

First, this is not a political phenomenon, most essentially, but a religious one. That is fact, not rhetoric. Religious people are performing these acts—smuggling and harboring refugees, transporting them across America, facing jeopardy of federal indictment—for religious reasons. The proportion of secular humanists, agnostic liberals, political radicals of the Old or New Left variety is startlingly low. What you find are nuns, priests, ministers, devout Quakers, rabbis, serious Unitarians, church assistants, church volunteers, and all other sorts of churchly people, most of whom sound quite convincing when they explain that abandoning the refugees would be equivalent to abandoning their own faith.

A second point: Notwithstanding the prominence of Fife and Corbett and Conger, this movement is dominantly populated by women. Stacey Merkt has been only the most heroically visible of many. Other unknown but resolute souls like Helen seem to account for an overwhelming female majority among those doing the smuggling, transporting, harboring. Ironically, the fact that males have played a disproportionately large role as the conspicuous spokesmen probably reflects less the real dynamics of this movement than the traditional balance of gender and power within organized Christianity and Judaism, carried over as an artifact into sanctuary.

The third intriguing point is that this movement—like so many other religious upheavals throughout history—came out of the desert.

Tucson and Nogales. Calexico and El Centro in California. San Benito and McAllen in Texas. The first battles were fought, the first commitments were made, the first wave of prosecutions have been coped with in these hot, red-rock places. One reason for that geographical pattern is obvious: To Central Americans arriving in dusty buses and on the tailgates of trucks, those desert borderlands are the doorway to America. But another factor, equally crucial, is not so obvious.

The Sonoran Desert of southern Arizona, the Chihuahuan Desert of south Texas, are lands of extremity and denial. Too hot, too rugged, not enough rain, not enough fuel, not enough food. When rain does come, there is no carpet of thick vegetation to hold back the flood. Erosion is unmitigated. The earth itself constantly cracks, falls, washes and blows away. Competition for resources is grim. Death is always a vivid possibility. Like *Heloderma suspectum,* most of the animals and even the plants carry weaponry. The environment offers no respite, no margin of error. The physical ecology is merciless. The moral ecology must therefore compensate, or a species so ill adapted as humanity couldn't survive.

Desert tribes like the Papago understand that. Desert transplants like Jim Corbett and John Fife have absorbed the same truth.

After homemade tamales and grape Kool-Aid at another safe house, now on the Arizona side, the border party continues driving. An elaborate set of procedures (involving a prearranged route and clockwork communications by telephone) serve to evade the Border Patrol cruisers and checkpoints. The journalist has not yet relaxed. He carries notes, he is implicated, and, not being so morally pellucid as the others, he has no desire to face the test of a subpoena.

If Helen can masquerade as a bird-watcher, then our journalist would have anyone understand that he is just along for the reptiles.

Luck is good, though. Today there are no arrests.

The two vehicles reach Tucson just as an operatic reddish-orange sunset is silhouetting the hills west of town. Everyone gapes and coos. But to a family of foot-weary Salvadorans, and likewise to their Anglo friends, this panorama of ragged ridges and playas and back-lit saguaros that makes southern Arizona gorgeous, and terrible, is not merely scenery. It is landscape, the theater of mortality.

DRINKING THE DESERT JUICES

Diet and Survival
in the Land of the Papago

And behold, in those days the children of Israel had taken their journey into the desert, and they were hungry and they were thirsty and they were sorely vexed, and so they murmured against Moses, saying, What *is* this nonsense? Moses, we are fixing to die out here and shrivel away like dried chilies if you don't do something, they said. So Moses cried unto the Lord and the Lord showed him a sweet spring where it flowed out of the rock. Fine, but what about some food? said the children of Israel. So the Lord sent overnight a great host of scale insects of the species *Trabutina mannipara* and *Najacoccus serpentinus*, this is true fact, and these insects fed upon the desert tamarisk bushes and then they shat upon the ground; a fine white layer of nutritious excrement, tiny granules that lay over the ground like hoar frost, did they shit. And when the children of Israel saw this stuff, they called it manna, and they did nourish themselves upon it for forty years. But they had nothing on the Papago tribe of southwestern Arizona, who have themselves known the secret of desert provenance for centuries.

Here is the secret, as those Papago have known it: The desert is dry but not barren.

The desert is harsh and intemperate and sometimes forbidding, but not without its moments of sudden bounteousness. The desert (in particular the Sonoran Desert, North America's driest yet ecologically most complex arid zone, which encompasses that corner of southern Arizona where the Papago Reservation lies) is a landscape of extremity and denial, yes, but you can indeed find things to eat and drink out there—improbable things, tasty things, highly salubrious things—if you happen to know what you are looking for.

The Papago lived by that secret for hundreds and maybe thousands of years, until the cruel magic of civilization and humidland agriculture descended upon them. Now the old ways are largely gone, and the Papago have arrived in a strange sort of Canaan, a promised land of modernity that includes refrigerators, pickup trucks, supermarket food, and an epidemic of obesity and diabetes.

The Papago tribe is just one branch of a larger group of Indian peoples known as the Pimans, all sharing a common linguistic base and all adapted culturally to life in their respective parts of the Sonoran Desert. In addition to the Papago of southwestern Arizona and adjacent Mexican borderlands, this group includes the Pima Bajo, the Salt River Pima, and a distinct population called the Sand Papago, native to an especially harsh environment at the north end of the Sea of Cortez. Besides sharing language and ancestors, the Piman tribes now share the particular health problems related to their transition away from desert foods.

In their own language, the Arizona and borderland Papago know themselves as *Tohono O'odham,* translated as "The Desert People." The name Papago itself was hung on them by Spanish colonialists, derived evidently from a garbling of several other words that roughly meant "the Bean Eaters." Both appellations were accurate, the Spanish version no less so for its tone of snide condescension. These folk did choose to inhabit some of the most unforgiving terrain of the Sonoran Desert, and they did depend heavily, through at least part of the year, on their bean crops.

The beans in question were teparies, a desert-hardy species of legume that had long been domesticated and treasured among the Papago. These tepary crops were grown each summer from strains of seed lovingly passed down between human generations. Tepary beans were ideally adapted for Papago floodwater cultivation, wherein a field (laid out at the mouth of an arroyo, with a brush dam to spread the runoff) might get only one or two summer soakings and then be left baking dry for three months. The tepary plants grew quickly after a single soaking, sent roots deep, tolerated excessive heat, and reacted well to late-season drought, taking that dryness as merely a signal to shift their metabolic efforts more concertedly toward seed production. Like a camel, tepary plants could gorge on water during a brief period when water was available, then continue to function robustly when it was not. The desert's feast-and-famine regimen suited them fine. But tepary beans were only one Papago crop among several, and the planted crops raised by means of flood irrigation were only one aspect (a minor one, though important) of how these Desert People made their living.

Through a larger part of the year they were not farmers but hunter-gatherers. In autumn after the crop harvest, they left their lowland villages for camps in the mountains, where they could find permanent water and wild game. They carried only simple possessions, plus a few baskets of dried beans and other staples, the small surplus from their farming. For the balance of the year they fed on the flesh of deer and bighorn sheep (when they were lucky), doves, rabbits, lizards, and on the fruit, seeds, and other edible parts of more than forty wild Sonoran plants, each coming to ripeness at its own time in its own sort of desert habitat. The Papago traveled their region, mainly on foot, collecting and processing. They ground mesquite pods into flour. They stained their chins with the juice of the saguaro. They had recipes for cholla buds, prickly pear pads, palo verde beans, amaranth greens. They fermented saguaro syrup into wine and agave leaves into mescal. They held ceremonial binges. They feasted, glutting themselves during each season of plenty and giving food away generously to neighbors and relatives. Then the season would change again, and they would go hungry. Sometimes they starved.

The desert provided bounty but not regularity. This was the nature of the place, and that irregularity was inherent to the deal that the Papago had made with their surroundings.

The Sonoran landscape is characterized by all manner of drastic vacillations—sweltering days followed by cold nights, long months of drought followed by storms and floods, lush springtime followed by stark roasting summer—and among edible wild plants the cycle from dearth to abundance, then back again to dearth, shows the same abruptness. Peaks of ripening and availability come and go. Gaps occur. In a bad year, some wild crops may fail entirely to materialize. And storage of most of these foods, through months of desert heat, using only traditional methods, is impossible. Consequently the Papago, like the tepary bean, were compelled over the course of time to adapt themselves to a cycle of feast and famine. They evolved a culture that placed great value on mutual generosity, and honored an ethical code among which the first tenets were: "Be hunger enduring, cold enduring, thirst enduring." Biologically, Papago individuals got by as they could during lean times, and during bounteous times stored what they could in the fatty tissues of their own bodies.

Today there exists an invidious stereotype of the Papago as a tribe of fat people—great round bodies of sun-browned flesh, male and female, driving pickups or weaving baskets or patiently, ploddingly walking the desert highways. The image is cruel (and also misleading, since many Papago today are still quite thin) but it has grown from a kernel of truth. Obesity *is* common among the tribe. Such a large number of the Papago, though, were not *always* overweight—or at least such a number were not always permanently and excessively overweight. The high incidence of obesity, and of its related health problems, seems rather to be an affliction that has come on them with the relinquishment of their desert-forged traditions.

Probably no Anglo has done more to revere and reevaluate those traditions than a young Arizona botanist named Gary Nabhan. Nabhan has studied the Papago language, done research on the uses and the biology of tepary beans, and helped establish a seed bank for desert-adapted crops, crops which have in recent decades become rare and neglected. He has also written two elegant books. The first was *The Desert Smells Like Rain*, an anecdotal portrait of Papago country from the viewpoint of a naturalist. More recently he published *Gathering the Desert*, a celebration of the ethnobotany of Sonoran Desert peoples, which won the Burroughs Medal for natural history writing. In that book Nabhan quotes a Sand Papago elder who remembers the lost self-reliance:

Long time ago, this was our way of life. We did not buy food. We worked hard to gather our food. We never even knew what coffee was until the white people came. We drank the desert fruit juices in harvest time. The desert food is meant for Indians to eat. The reason so many Indians die young is because they don't eat their desert food. I worry about what will happen to this new generation of Indians who have become accustomed to present food they buy at the markets.

That was the wisdom of the heart. But some sad medical statistics lend concrete support to the man's worry.

According to the Indian Health Service, more than half the adult population of Piman Indians, including the Papago, now suffer from diabetes.

The levels of gall-bladder disease and hypertension are also startlingly high. These diseases were not common to traditional Piman life. Until after World War II, in fact, they were virtually unknown. Something has changed.

Civilization has visited itself upon the desert tribes. They have been rescued from their hard and primitive ways into a more advanced, more comfortable state of ruined health.

In southwestern Arizona this process began as far back as 1917, when the Papago Reservation was founded and its inhabitants first came before the crosshairs of federal beneficence. A school, a hospital, and an extension service were established. A few wells were dug. "The first problem of all seemed to be the sterility of the land," in the words of one anthropologist who lived with the Papago long enough that she might have known better, and that common but crucial misconception accounts for much of what followed. During the 1930s more federal money was put toward wells, pumps, reservoirs. Those seasonal migrations to the mountains, for water and wild food, were no longer necessary. Irrigated farming of non-native, humid-land crops was encouraged. So was cattle ranching. Papago men also went off to do wage labor—in New Deal programs, then in the wartime military, later in the mines and on the big cotton farms of southern Arizona—whereby the reservation was shifted toward a cash economy. Refrigerators and freezers arrived. The cycle of gorging and starving faded into memory. By 1950 more than half the food used by the Papago people was store-bought. At the end of the same decade the U.S. government started giving them surplus commodity food as a form of welfare. Federal food surpluses, of course, did not run to cholla buds and mesquite-pod flour.

Many of the Papago, thus blessed, became fat and sick.

Was the destruction of their health a consequence of heredity or of environment? This question is a point of fierce disagreement. Have the Papago been victimized by an unhealthy diet of plasticized and sugary modern glop? Or have they been victimized by their own genetic predisposition to a cluster of related afflictions, especially obesity and diabetes? You can find medical experts who will argue each of the two hypotheses in its extreme form. Gary Nabhan, by contrast, offers a persuasive explanation that is slightly more complicated.

Nabhan sees the Piman tribes as a group whose bodies, like their cultures, evolved over many generations to be capable of tolerating the desert cycle of feast and famine. It was an evolutionary as well as an ethical mandate: "Be hunger enduring, cold enduring, thirst enduring." Those who could gain weight quickly during seasons of plenty, and could survive on their fat reserves during seasons of dearth, did; they were the evolutionary winners. Those who could *not* do that were more likely to die young, and less likely to leave behind offspring. For centuries this culling acted upon the Piman gene pool. Attuned to their habitat, the survivors gained weight and lost it again as the seasons revolved. Then, with the transition to a regularized modern diet, that hereditary predisposition to speedy weight gain seems to have become suddenly *dis*advantageous, resulting in chronic obesity and its concomitant, diabetes.

A genetic phenomenon, to that extent. But there is more.

Nabhan stresses that the Hopi tribe, the Navajo, and the Cocopa each show a similar susceptibility, suffering from their own dramatically high incidences of obesity and diabetes. So do the aborigines of Australia. It seems more than mildly interesting that, like the Piman tribes, these are all desert peoples. Throughout hundreds of years prior to contact with European civilization and exposure to humid-land diets, they had all been feeding upon the wild bounty of their respective arid landscapes. Sometimes they feasted, sometimes they starved. One way or another, they endured. Natural selection certainly played a role in shaping the genetic profile of the surviving populations. But recent work by scientists in Australia and in this country suggests that the desert itself also *actively* helped keep them healthy.

Galactomannin, explains Gary Nabhan, is a natural plant gum found in the seed of mesquite. A number of desert plant species (prickly pear, carob, and chia, among others) contain similar gum compounds. These gums seem to accomplish two biochemical functions. In a plant, they enhance the absorption and retention of water. This might account for why evolution has vouchsafed them to arid-land plant species. In a human body, the effect of those same compounds is to slow the rate at which sugars are released into the blood—and thereby to mitigate the demand for a body's naturally produced insulin.

As they consumed the seeds of mesquite, traditional Papago received steady doses of this *galactomannin.* With other wild plants, they seem to have gotten similar therapeutic gums. Drinking those desert juices and eating those desert fruits, evidently, was more than a matter of grim necessity. It may also have been the healthiest way of life that the Papago people will ever know. "The desert food," said the old man, "is meant for Indians to eat." And sometimes biology, like the human heart, has its own forms of wisdom.

THE DESERT IS
A MNEMONIC DEVICE

Sanctuary in Tucson: 1986

The traditional Bedouin of the Arabian desert had a name for it: *dakhala.* A stranger in flight for his life could rush into the tent of another man, claim the privilege of *dakhala,* and know he would be protected by his reluctant host. This was a sacred custom among the nomadic Arabs. A man who provided *dakhala* was one who lived by the rules of honor, at whatever cost to himself. He was recognized as upholding a high law—higher than kinship, higher even than vengeance—that the desert itself had helped shape. The desert itself, yes: *Dakhala* in some measure was an answer to imperatives of landscape, a tool of wilderness survival, a culture's hedge against heat and desolation and thirst. Lonely death on the sands, or else *dakhala,* were the fugitive's prospects.

In the desert of southern Arizona, today, the equivalent word is *sanctuary.* But in Arizona, today, it is a felony.

On May 1, 1986, a federal jury in Tucson convicted eight persons of violating immigration laws. Among the defendants were two Catholic priests, a granite-jawed nun, and a lanky Presbyterian minister. They were found guilty of a variety of offenses that included shielding, concealing, aiding, abetting, and smuggling—also, conspiring to smuggle—illegal aliens. The aliens in question were Salvadorans and Guatemalans, displaced by the murderous chaos in their homelands, who had come north seeking refuge. The possible penalties for these acts of aid and conspiracy ranged up to (in the case of the nun, Sister Darlene Nicgorski, convicted of five felony counts) twenty-five years' imprisonment.

The charges had resulted from an elaborate undercover investigation lasting nine months, during which a paid informant for the Immigration and Naturalization Service (INS) had worn a concealed recorder into some of the humblest church halls in southern Arizona. But the investigation had in a real sense always been moot, since the defendants were open about their activities. Many of the group had freely admitted to journalists, and to anyone else who would listen, that they were harboring Salvadorans and Guatemalans; that these Salvadorans and Guatemalans, yes, had been obliged to enter the U.S. surreptitiously; that they themselves, the defendants, sought to conceal such people and protect them from deportation. The issue, they said, was why. The issue, they said, was whether these particular Central Americans were in fact "illegal aliens" or, alternatively, legitimate refugees. The issue, they argued, was whether U.S. laws forbade the harboring of such people, or mandated it.

But the judge in Tucson saw things very differently, and ruled that all arguments on that issue were inadmissible. The case was fought and decided narrowly. Such words as *torture* and *death squads* were, in the courtroom, taboo. No one mentioned *dakhala.*

The proceedings began on October 22, 1985, and dragged on for six months, and to the reporters who covered it, to the public who followed it, this was known as "the sanctuary trial." It wasn't actually the first such trial (two church workers in south Texas have been convicted for similar activities), it almost certainly won't be the last, but so far it has been the biggest and loudest and most dramatic. It was a bellwether prosecution directed against a small group of people, several of whom are perceived as founders and guiding figures of a potent, fast-growing (and, in the U.S. prosecutor's portrayal, misguided and pernicious) national movement. The movement is called, simply, "sanctuary." It began, five years ago, with the decision by a small Presbyterian congregation on the south side of Tucson to harbor Central American refugees. Today roughly three hundred religious groups—Quaker meetings, Protestant congregations, Catholic parishes, synagogues—have made the same pledge. More than 50,000 U.S. citizens are now involved, each of them risking felony convictions like the ones handed out in Arizona, and their avowed intent is to prevent Salvadoran and Guatemalan refugees from being deported back home to jeopardy of imprisonment, mutilation, and death. One of the Tucson defendants, a tough young priest named Tony Clark, defines sanctuary bluntly as "God's hospitality."

The refugees that he has encountered, adds Father Clark, don't even *want* to be here in the U.S. "But they're forced to. They're running."

Since 1980 a half million Salvadorans and more than 80,000 Guatemalans have fled their countries for the United States. Many of them have arrived at our southwestern border without papers and, by this or that ruseful maneuver, gotten across. The total number of these desperate people is minuscule compared with the steady flow of undocumented Mexicans, but large enough to constitute a controversial phenomenon. Why do the Central Americans come north? According to one view (the one offered axiomatically by officials of the State Department and the INS) they are "economic migrants." In other words, enterprising if impoverished job-seekers, no different from the Mexicans who now pose such a sizable socioeconomic problem. By another view (that of the sanctuary activists), many of those Salvadorans and Guatemalans are "political refugees" in a full legal sense—having escaped from the war zones of Central America, having left behind murdered relatives and their own experiences of torture and imprisonment, having brought with them physical scars and grim memories—and are therefore entitled by U.S. law (not to mention tradition, as inscribed beneath the Statue of Liberty) to at least temporary protection in this country. Specifically, the U.S. Refugee Act of 1980, often cited by sanctuary activists, defines a "refugee" as any person who "is unable or unwilling to avail himself or herself of the protection of [his or her own country] because of persecution or a well-founded fear of persecution on account of race, religion, nationality, membership in a particular social group, or political opinion. . . ." Several of those conditions do seem to fit most of the Central Americans who come north. The 1980 Refugee Act also stipulates remedies by which a refugee will be protected, one of which is political asylum.

Political asylum, though, seems for one reason or another to be almost completely unavailable to Salvadorans and Guatemalans. Statistics from a representative recent year show that asylum applications filed by Afghani and Iranian individuals were granted at a rate thirty to forty times higher (as a percentage of the total applications from each nationality) than the rate for applications from Salvadorans. Applications from Poles were granted at almost fifteen times the rate for Salvadorans. Guatemalan applicants, on the other hand, have generally fared even worse than Salvadorans. The pattern within these statistics is obvious: If you flee to the U.S. from a regime in disfavor with Washington, your chances of being officially welcomed are much better than if you flee from one of Washington's clients. Thus denied almost all chance of asylum, denied even temporary exemption (in the form of "extended voluntary departure" status) from deportation, Salvadorans and Guatemalans have no legal protection in the one country on Earth that prides itself most stentoriously as a haven for refugees.

So they must live here as fugitives, with the help of sanctuary. And in the meantime our Border Patrol tries hard to prevent them from entering the country at all. So they must get over the border by stealth.

One method of crossing is to pass through an official port of entry, bluffing fearfully with false or borrowed identity papers, masquerading as a U.S. citizen or a day-labor Mexican. Another method, more taxing physically and more risky, is to make a long hike through the desert, trekking out across those remote zones of ragged mountain and dry-wash and thorn vegetation where the international fence is unwatched. Many hundreds of bewildered Central Americans have attempted that desert hike. Such desperation itself might be considered eloquent.

Some of these hikers have been caught in the act, some have passed over safely, some have died gruesomely. The desert, which often seems beautiful and sometimes benign, can be unforgiving of inexperience and miscalculation. But it comes as a lesson of desert cultures (and not just the Bedouin's) that where physical ecology is so harsh, so implacable, moral ecology must somehow compensate. That's what happened in southern Arizona.

It was no accident that Tucson, a small borderland city surrounded by desert, became the sanctuary movement's main point of origin and focus. The movement itself has been, in great degree, and from the start, an answer to imperatives of landscape.

Of the four ecologically distinct deserts covering portions of North America—the Mohave, the Sonoran, the Great Basin, and the Chihuahuan—the Sonoran Desert is the most deceptive. It does not appear bleak. It is far from empty of life. Many sensible witnesses consider it gorgeously scenic. Despite being prodigiously dry (less than two inches of rain yearly, in some parts) and prodigiously hot (often around 120 degrees F.), it supports more different species of plants and animals than any other American desert. Most famously recognizable of those species is the giant columnar cactus, the saguaro, representing the Sonoran Desert like a trademark. Also among its natives are the Gila monster, the tarantula, an awesome profusion of black widow spiders, six species of rattlesnake, several dozen species of scorpion, and a healthy population of vultures who police up after fatalities. The Sonoran is a large desert, stretching over more than 100,000 square miles, from below Guaymas on the west coast of Mexico up to Needles, California, and from east of Tucson to the far side of the Baja peninsula. It embraces a long section of the international border. The terrain is mountainous. There are broad sandy riverbeds, usually dry, and saline basins. This is a place of extremity and denial, drought and flash floods, heat at midday that can shatter a rock, frigid nights. The sunsets, silhouetting the raw peaks and the gentler hills stubbled with saguaros, may be as majestic as any in the world. In spring the desert blooms luxuriantly, flowers and green foliage bursting out from among thorns. But springtime is brief. Later, around the middle of summer, come a succession of restorative thunderstorms, brought up from the Gulf of Mexico by the monsoon. In between, for a span of months, the Sonoran is a searing and inhospitable wilderness. That's what it was when a group of thirty Salvadoran travelers tried to cross, back in early July of 1980.

For two days the story made the front page in *The New York Times.* A headline read: "13 Aliens, Cast Off by Smugglers, Die in a Baking Desert in Arizona."

The survivors, themselves very near death, had been rescued by the Border Patrol. Along a drywash not far from a paved road, and about twenty miles north of the Mexican border town of Sonoyta, searchers found a trail of discarded clothing, half-naked corpses, and delirious, heat-sick people, some of whom had smeared their faces with toothpaste or makeup as a last desperate measure against the sun. There were few canteens amid the debris—not even empty ones. Evidently it had been a party of middle-class urban Salvadorans, women in high-heeled shoes, men carrying suitcases, misguided and drastically unprepared for an arduous desert trek. They had left El Salvador in the care of a *coyote* (a mercenary smuggler of humans) and made the long trip across Mexico by bus; just south of the U.S. border, on a bleak stretch of desert beyond the last road, they were told to start walking. Among all the other mistakes, they had failed to carry enough water. Eventually, so the *Times* reported, they had been reduced to drinking cologne, after-shave lotion, and their own urine. By one account they had each paid the *coyote* $1,200 (or at least a life's savings, whatever it came to) for the privilege of being taken north. The survivors were brought to Tucson, where several churches were asked to help them with housing and food.

One of those churches was Southside Presbyterian, a small congregation in the barrio. Southside Church is an aberration, conforming badly to the archetype of comfortable middle-class Presbyterianism; it is based in a little adobe building with a chain-pull bell and one saguaro out front, a modest place that fills up on Sunday mornings with people of many complexions, people in shirt sleeves and with work-calloused hands, and then re-sounds blessedly with jivey gospel music. It is presided over by Reverend John Fife, another aberration, a tall Anglo favoring denims and cowboy boots and a silver Papago belt buckle when not in his vestments, who came out to the desert from a mean-streets urban ministry in Ohio, never dreaming he would achieve fame as a convicted felon. Back in 1980 he was immersed in concerns of his own, mainly related to pastorhood of a poor congregation of Hispanics and blacks and Anglos and Indians, and he could not then—Fife says now—have placed El Salvador on a map. The episode of the desert deaths changed everything. "*That* engaged my attention," he has said. Fife had already been aware that some Central Americans were arriving covertly in Arizona, but until this point he had vaguely assumed that they were driven only by the same restless poverty that sent Mexicans north. He had thought of those Central Americans in the same way that the State Department today still wants to imagine them

—as "economic migrants," scrambling northward to the land of opportunity. As Fife talked with the desert survivors, though, that impression changed drastically. He was prepared to hear tales of the hard life in a peasant village, the backbreaking labor for little money, the struggle to feed children. "But these folk from Salvador were telling a *different* set of stories. They were talking about death squads, and about torture, and about the kind of terrorism and violence that we now know about."

Do we all now know? Or does anyone find Reverend Fife's reference opaque? Is it possible, in 1986, to have remained innocent of awareness of *los escuadrones de la muerte* and the other aspects of terror and violence in El Salvador and Guatemala?

True enough, the horrific reports that have been filtering out of those two countries for almost ten years now—the stories about kidnapping, torture, mutilation, and murder, practiced against innocent citizens by paramilitary death squads and the uniformed military—are affronts to the mind, gobbets of reality that strike upon any reasonably sensitive consciousness like spattered blood and gore. Fathers who disappear late at night in the custody of strange men and turn up, decapitated, on body dumps; adolescents tortured and executed for suspicion of subversive inclination; young children killed to eliminate witnesses—the accounts are reliable, shocking, then numbing, and worst of all, repetitious. They come firsthand from real people, survivors, who have themselves escaped north. Pedro, formerly a photographer for a private human-rights group in El Salvador, who tells of documenting on film the sight of a pregnant woman whose abdomen had been cut open, the fetus removed, and her husband's head set in its place. Ramón, whose three daughters were raped by soldiers, before his eyes, and then the two oldest taken away to be killed. Brenda, a paramedic who saw one of her co-workers dragged off to National Guard headquarters, there to be gang-raped and tortured and then killed with a machine gun inserted in her rectum. Pedro, Ramón, and Brenda are not fictionalized constructs; they are not composites. They are actual individuals, beneficiaries of sanctuary in the U.S. and typical of those "economic migrants" who are being feloniously shielded and abetted. Many more voices offer the same sort of testimony, forcing upon us glimpses of a deep evil vein in the human character that is scary to contemplate and almost impossible to comprehend. Even the next of kin, the widows and the brotherless sisters, the parents who have lost two or three children, the grandmothers who have outlived their whole family, even these witnesses are weary of telling their stories, weary of the pain of remembering.

But the stories do nevertheless need to be told, and told again, and remembered.

John Fife heard such stories, from those desert survivors back in 1980, and he was moved to act. Others in Tucson began to act too. At first their efforts were modest and quiet: providing food and shelter to those refugees who managed to reach Tucson, helping them pass northward to other cities along a sort of underground railroad, raising money to bond out those who had been caught by the INS, assisting with asylum applications, conducting a weekly prayer vigil. The prayer vigil was held each Thursday at rush hour outside the Federal Building—partly as a protest against the wholesale rejection of asylum petitions from Salvadorans and Guatemalans and, worse, the forcible deportations. Deportation was especially terrifying to anyone who had already fled the death squads. The very act of having gone north could be counted a sign of subversive inclination, or at least of disloyalty, and any deportee arriving back at the San Salvador airport was marked and vulnerable. While the asylum-application process was being pursued almost futilely in Tucson and elsewhere in the U.S., some of the deportees (Santana Chirino Amaya, Walter Garcia Ortiz, and others) had shown up, dead and mangled, on the body dumps. So Reverend Fife and his religious colleagues decided that more drastic action was required.

They had already tried legal-defense efforts. They had tried underground smuggling. But these meliorist tactics could help only a small fraction of the refugees who were arriving, and had no impact on U.S. asylum policy. Terrified people were still being deported by the dozens and hundreds. The American populace, meanwhile, was almost totally oblivious to the whole situation. So Fife and his colleagues decided that they would need to do something dramatic, resonant, and public. They hit on the idea of sanctuary.

Within Judeo-Christian tradition the general concept of sanctuary dates back at least to that record of a tribe of desert-dwelling nomads, the book of Exodus. It came forward through Roman and English law and eventually turned up, slightly transmogrified, in the form of the original underground railroad, helping fugitive slaves escape northward from Dixie. When the U.S. Congress passed a Fugitive Slave Act in 1850, making it criminal to shield or abet runaway blacks, many churches in the North played a role in the nexus of humanitarian defiance. As reinvented in latter-day Tucson, the notion of sanctuary differs from that American precedent chiefly in being more determinedly *public.* Reverend Fife and his congregation not only decided to harbor Central American refugees; they decided to do it openly.

On March 24, 1982, John Fife announced at a press conference that Southside Presbyterian Church (joined by a handful of congregations in other cities) would henceforth be providing sanctuary to certain undocumented Central American aliens. They were pledging themselves to support and defend the refugees, and daring the Justice Department to make arrests.

Most of America remained oblivious to these events in Tucson, but the Justice Department did respond. Within less than three years Reverend Fife and a dozen co-workers had been indicted.

During the same course of time, though, that early commitment by Southside Presbyterian Church had dovetailed with similar actions by other American congregations and grown into a national movement, now including those hundreds of churches and synagogues and Quaker meetings, all united in a new nexus of humanitarian defiance.

Of course none of this—not the indictments, not the growth of the movement, not even the prolonged *need* for such a movement —had been foreseeable in 1980. Back then, during the year that followed the desert deaths and on into summer and autumn of 1981, it was all just an extemporized effort, informal and local, conducted by a few well-meaning church folk and lawyers. But the larger need was already apparent then, as deportations continued, and as more and more refugees arrived in Tucson. Many of these were brought up through the desert by a man named Jim Corbett.

Jim Corbett would later be a co-defendant with John Fife in the Tucson trial. He was acquitted, thanks to an almost accidental absence of evidence against him. Because Corbett performed his own role rather solitarily, the prosecution's star witness (a middle-aged Mexican named Jesus Cruz, who had infiltrated the movement and worn a tape recorder to sanctuary meetings) had little to say about him. Corbett for his own part has talked openly about smuggling refugees but, like Fife and the other defendants, maintains that his acts are in compliance with U.S. law.

Jim Corbett is an arthritic Quaker with a degree in philosophy from Harvard and the backcountry stamina of a red wolf. Having ranched cattle for years in southern Arizona, he knows the Sonoran Desert like a cab driver knows the back roads to the airport. Beginning in 1981 and continuing until his face became infamous to the INS, Corbett's chosen role was to guide refugees across the border. Sometimes he cadged identity cards and took the people through a port of entry, the route that was precarious but physically undemanding. More often, if the particular individuals seemed hardy, they walked the desert. Corbett was familiar with the terrain and capable of using it to advantage, traveling the washes under cover of vegetation, dodging the Border Patrol planes and eluding the agents in cruisers and on horseback, laying up at night without a fire, crossing the fence, following the natural warps of the land, then getting up to a road and out of the area inconspicuously. By one estimate, he has personally brought in seven hundred souls.

Like Reverend Fife, but in very different ways, Jim Corbett is an anomaly. He is firmly (if politely) antiliturgical, a real Quaker to his soul, suspicious of organized churches and certainly not born to found a popular religious movement. He is also an intellectual, a complex thinker and a prolific writer, who has chosen to avoid academia while spending much of his life at the hard physical labor of ranching cattle and sheep. For five years he has been one of the most visible exemplars of the sanctuary movement, making a huge contribution directly and exerting a far-flung influence, yet the path that brought him to this work has been very peculiarly his own. Most other representatives of the movement trace their concept of sanctuary to a European historical basis in Roman law, medieval canon law, and English common law, and to a theological basis in Exodus, Numbers, and Isaiah. Jim Corbett is aware of those sources but he talks more personally about Buddhist ideas of stillness, the Taoist philosopher Chuang Tzu, the anthropology of pastoral nomads in Tibet, and the practical details of goat husbandry. Most other representatives of the movement—the nuns and ministers and priests and rabbis who are now playing conspicuous roles—have come out of clerical backgrounds, especially from missionary orders and social-action ministries. Jim Corbett has come, literally, out of the desert.

For almost two decades he has had a special interest in the spiritual uses of wilderness. The Buddhist and Hindu and Taoist

traditions all include a theme, Corbett says, of the person who
goes off alone into wilderness (often a desert wilderness) for some
stretch of time, to strip away those aspects of misguided worldly
concern that Corbett calls "the social busyness." The Hebrews'
Sinai sojourn as described in Exodus served a similar purpose, he
says, though in that case it was not a lone individual but a whole
community seeking purgation. During the early 1970s Corbett
began to experiment with the same kind of sojourn himself. He
was teaching ecology and anthropology to students from a
Quaker school, and at the end of each semester he would lead
those teenagers out for a two-week stay in the desert. This was
not "survivalist training," he stresses. He hoped these students
would learn how to *be at home* in the desert, not how to conquer
it; and he hoped that, in the process, they might discover the
spiritual value of quietude.

Corbett and his students traveled light. They took sleeping
bags, a little other gear, but no food. Carrying food into this
landscape was unnecessary. Instead of food, they herded along a
few goats.

Later Corbett would write a book-length (still unpublished)
manuscript titled *Goatwalking,* an improbable gumbo of his
ranching and backcountry know-how and his philosophic and
political ideas. *Goatwalking* is a strange, intriguing document, the
quiet manifesto of a man who combines in himself some of the
more appealing aspects of Thoreau, Thomas Merton, and
Emiliano Zapata. It is a guidebook toward revolutionary simplicity and wildland dairying. He writes in the book that "goatwalking could be explained on a single page, as a menu. How about a
quart-and-a-half of [goat's] milk, another quart of yogurt, a side
dish of tumbleweed greens, some roasted mescal heart for sweets,
and four or five saguaro fruits for dessert? And put some *bellota*
[a type of desert acorn] in your shirt pockets for between-meal
snacks. I've discovered that it's not difficult to teach people to

eat, although they may prefer starvation to tasty but taboo foods such as grubs or grasshoppers."

But it's really much more than a desert-survival menu. Through this concept he calls "goatwalking," Corbett aligns himself with those nomadic pastoralists—of ancient Sinai or twentieth-century Tibet or wherever—who have come to the realization that "their livestock could provide the life-support and security associated with [planted crops] while also providing the mobility necessary to escape the state." In Corbett's usage, goatwalking is a potent synecdoche, representing exactly what the word says and also much more.

At the literal level it stands for the life of pastoral nomadism (tending and traveling with half-wild grazing animals), practiced on a wilderness landscape and, in Corbett's version, outside the purview but within the physical boundaries of the modern industrial state. The goats are allowed to go feral, habituating themselves to wilderness pasturage, and the goatwalker goes feral along with them, living on milk and wild plant foods. On a political level, this goatwalking life is recommended as what Corbett calls "the cimarron alternative." The Spanish word *cimarrón* has entered English with two definitions, and Corbett intends them both: Besides "feral animal," it also means "runaway slave."

The cimarron alternative in this sense is the act of stepping beyond societal constraints and into the wilderness of a purer moral freedom. The goatwalker is a runaway slave who knows how to live off the land. Naturally, therefore, he will feel sympathy for his fellow cimarrons—and Jim Corbett's own goatwalking has always had that dimension. "During the Indochina War," he says in *Goatwalking,* "I became a habitual criminal, frequently associated and conspired with fellow lawbreakers, and sometimes used an isolated ranch headquarters as a refuge and way-station for fugitives. Naturally enough, we occasionally speculated about the use of goatwalking as an escape technique. A small group of people who have mastered goatwalking can simply vanish, since their life-support is mobile and is also independent of the governmentally monitored commercial system." It was no big step from that sort of speculation to Corbett's later role in the sanctuary movement. His manuscript continues: "When a person or a group is faced with extermination, enslavement, or long-term imprisonment, going free may be a more responsible choice than attempting to resist. . . . If we are lucky, few of us will ever face political conditions that would make escape necessary for survival. . . . Maybe Latin American peasants or World War II partisans or pre-emancipation blacks might withdraw into the sierras, but the thought that anyone in today's United States might do so is absurd, isn't it? It is for those who don't know how."

Now this may all sound quixotic or woolly to you or me—but Jim Corbett happens to be the sort of stubborn Quaker moralist who turns quixotic notions into acts. *Goatwalking* was written in the late 1970s, several years before Corbett met his first Salvadoran refugee. Then when the need arose for a desert-smart guide who would lead terrified fugitives through wilderness and across a border, circumventing the armed minions of national policy (as distinct from law), he was decidedly ready. He knew how.

And there was one other element that seems to have figured in Jim Corbett's readiness, closely related to his cimarron sensibility, closely related also to his reading of Exodus: the tradition, common among nomadic peoples inhabiting harsh landscapes, of radical hospitality. For the Bedouin this was *dakhala.* Among the tribal nomads of Tibet—whose culture was for Corbett an important paradigm—the provider of *dakhala* finds a striking equivalent in the protective host known as *bDag Po.*

The Tibetan plateau is not a true desert but, with its drastically high elevations (even the valleys are above 10,000 feet), its rocky canyons, its thin air and poor soil and sudden shifts between heat and blizzard, it is certainly a land of extremity and denial. In such a place—lacking police, lacking inns and restaurants, lacking the forms of refuge that can be bought elsewhere with money

—no one goes visiting for frivolous reasons, and hospitality is limited to a high seriousness. When a *bDag Po* has offered shelter to a guest, he has also committed himself as a guardian and sponsor, guaranteeing against his own honor that the guest will be safe from danger and aided materially for the continued journey.

In an inclement land like Tibet or Arabia, the need for such human clemency is recognized as a sacred truth, because the need is always potentially mutual. Hospitality is understood vividly: as a matter of life and death. In the Sonoran Desert, where thirteen Salvadorans had already died, that's exactly how Jim Corbett came to understand it.

The trial began in October of 1985 and lasted until the following May. It was a long and expensive prosecution, with its full share of complex legal technicalities, its moments of true drama and melodrama, but the proceedings as they unfolded were perhaps more notable for what did *not* happen than for what did.

At the very start the presiding judge, Earl H. Carroll, issued several orders barring certain types of evidence: No testimony would be accepted concerning the political conditions or dangers in any foreign country; no testimony concerning the defendants' religious beliefs or motivations; no testimony related to the defendants' understanding of U.S. immigration laws; no evidence of the defendants' belief that those aliens they stood accused of helping were legitimate refugees. That list of exclusions covered nearly every defense that the defendants' attorneys had hoped to use. Evidence about the ninety-eight percent denial rate for Salvadoran asylum applicants was inadmissible. The 1980 Refugee Act was inadmissible.

Consequently the trial's outcome may have been virtually settled before the opening statements were made. But the trial went ahead anyway, with its other significant omissions. The chief INS investigator who had guided the undercover operation was never called by the prosecution to testify. The ninety-one tapes of supposedly conspiratorial sanctuary conversations were never (except for one half-hour set of excerpts, carefully selected by the prosecutor) played in court. The defense attorneys themselves fought for admission of the full tapes, hoping that way to show the defendants' activities in context, but the judge supported the prosecutor's decision to keep the jury ignorant of any such context. Three unindicted sanctuary workers and one refugee all refused to testify for the prosecution, despite subpoenas, and were therefore held in contempt, sentenced to house arrest until the trial ended. Of the refugees who *did* testify, seemingly under duress, the prosecutor complained that their memories were selective: They more readily recollected the deaths of their family members, the terror and violence they had fled, than whatever incriminating words had been uttered by John Fife or Darlene Nicgorski. One refugee witness, Alejandro Rodriguez, speaking of a middle-aged woman defendant, had another recollection: "She was the only person that offered me a roof over my head when I was most in need. People told me she had a good heart. I remember her with much love."

And finally the defendants themselves did not testify. In fact they literally presented no defense at all. On a Friday morning in the nineteenth week of the trial, with the prosecution having rested and the sanctuary lawyers now scheduled to begin calling witnesses, each of those lawyers stood up in turn and announced that the defense, too, rested its case. This seems to have been partly an act of strategy (if the defendants were forbidden to mention refugee law or religious motivations or anything else they considered significant, what value in giving the prosecution a chance to cross-examine them?) and partly an act of sheer protest.

Insofar as it was strategy, the strategy seems to have failed. Probably, given the judge's rulings, any strategy would have failed. On May 1 the jury came in with its verdicts.

*   *   *

Late one evening near the end of the trial, Reverend Fife sat in the living room of his home, exhausted from six months of courtroom tension, nursing a beer, and telling me about the large place held in his own Presbyterian heart by the spiritual traditions of the Papago Indians. It might sound as though he were digressing, but he was not.

In the unsparing terrain that is southwestern Arizona, the niche of Bedouin existence has for hundreds of years been filled by the Papago tribe. They are also known, to themselves and others, as the Desert People. The area they traditionally occupied, and within which their reservation now lies, is one of the most arid and least hospitable parts of even the Sonoran Desert —a landscape of flat valleys cobbled with wind-blown pebbles, sharp ridges that curl around confusingly like the walls of a labyrinth, arroyos and washes carved by torrential runoff and opening out blankly into dry basins, where nothing much grows except creosote bush. Drought is followed by flood, in Papago country, then again by drought; the desert blooms, briefly, then withers; the cycle of life for all living creatures entails unpredictable but ineluctable swings between extremes of abundance and dearth. Over the centuries the Papago adapted themselves to this cycle.

One of their adaptations was an ethic of radical hospitality. Under pressure of landscape, a Papago culture evolved in which great premium was placed on generosity, gift-giving of food and clothing, the sharing of surplus whenever there was any surplus. Wildly generous with each other, the Papago lived as though abundance were the rule, in a land where abundance was the exception. Today we might see them as existentialists of the desert—or perhaps just as hopelessly improvident. But in fact they were quite provident. The limitless mutual gift-giving was a survival strategy for a desert people.

That Papago ethos still informs the spirit of Southside Presbyterian Church, which was founded eighty years ago as a Papago mission in a Tucson ghetto that was then known as "Papagoville." It also goes far to explain the presence in Tucson of John Fife himself. Twenty years ago, fresh out of a seminary in Pittsburgh, Fife came down to spend a summer on the Papago reservation, where he fell in love with the people and the desert and the strange dynamic between those two. When the pastorship of a little Papago church in Tucson came open, six years later, he jumped for it.

"I've heard their stories," Fife told me. "We've spent a lot of time talking about traditions. I climb their sacred mountain, Baboquivari, every year. Try to get to I'itoi's cave." I'itoi is the chief Papago deity, believed to dwell at the moral center of Papago life and at the physical center of their lands, in a cave on the steep slope of Baboquivari. "I've been on that mountain when Papago folk had visions," Fife told me. "I didn't see anything— but they did." As he spoke, on the wall behind his head hung a characteristic piece of Papago coiled basketry, flat and circular, woven from tan and black fibers in the design of a concentric maze. At the entrance to the maze stood a small figure, itself woven in black, recognizably human. The large silver buckle on Reverend Fife's belt bore exactly the same pattern. The design is called *I'itoi Ki:*, and has strong resonance for the Papago. The pattern commemorates an episode, Fife explained, when I'itoi escaped from his enemies by leading them into such a maze.

The design is also understood allegorically. "The maze represents all the complexities and dead ends of life," Fife said. In the course of a lifetime a person must move through all those complexities, through all those tribulations and misleading paths, toward the center point, at which waits safety, fulfillment, Baboquivari. I was intrigued by this maze. Clearly it also represents the desert.

* * *

The sentencing of Reverend Fife and the seven other convicted refugee-smugglers was held in early July 1986, the same week as that great orgy of self-congratulation by which some Americans celebrated the centennial of the Statue of Liberty. Fife was eligible for as much as fifteen years in prison, and the other defendants faced between five and twenty-five. But each of them was given a suspended sentence and a period of probation. Evidently such treatment is usual for first-offense cases under the laws in question.

Still, it all seemed a little anticlimactic after such a notorious trial—and it properly *was* anticlimactic, since the real drama had always lain elsewhere. The real drama had always lain in Central America, where noncombatants are still being killed, and in the deportation policies enforced by our government against refugees of some nationalities but not others. The Tucson defendants had never forgotten that, and so they were relieved at the relative leniency they received, but not jubilant. There had been no leniency and no suspension of sentence, after all, for the terrified people who face deportation.

I did not intend this to be an idle rumination on the ecology and anthropology of arid lands. The moral ecology of the United States is what concerns me. As more and more Salvadorans and Guatemalans are deported, under the pretense that they are "economic migrants," more and more innocent people, America's rejects, may be abducted and tortured and murdered. Of course each of us will share responsibility with our government for those deportations. Some will try to believe that this country, with its poor sad stumbling economy, cannot afford any more refugees. Others will simply not want to be reminded about another group of abused, needy people. Most of us would prefer to forget the whole subject. The thing that we all need to remember is the same thing that John Fife and Jim Corbett have each learned: that sometimes hospitality is a matter of life and death. The desert, in this essay, is just a mnemonic device.

V
CHAMBERS
OF MEMORY

THE MIRACLE
OF THE GEESE

---

*A Bizarre Sexual Strategy
Among Steadfast Birds*

Listen: *uh-whongk, uh-whongk, uh-whongk, uh-whongk,* and then you are wide awake, and you smile up at the ceiling as the calls fade off to the north and already now they are gone. Silence again, 3 A.M., the hiss of March winds. A thought crosses your mind before you roll over and, contentedly, resume sleeping. The thought is: "Thank God I live here, right here exactly, in their path. Thank God for those birds." The honk of wild Canada geese passing overhead in the night is a sound to freshen the human soul. The question is why.

What makes the voice of that species so stirring, so mysteriously authoritative, to the ears of our own species?

It is more than a matter of beauty. It is more than the majesty of unspoiled nature. Listen again, to America's wisest poet:

> *Long ago, in Kentucky, I, a boy, stood*
> *By a dirt road, in first dark, and heard*
> *The great geese hoot northward.*
>
> *I could not see them, there being no moon*
> *and the stars sparse. I heard them.*

I did not know what was happening in my heart.

It was the season before the elderberry blooms,
Therefore they were going north.

The boy in Kentucky, seventy years ago, was Robert Penn Warren. The lines are from *Audubon: A Vision,* Warren's great medi-
tative poem on John James Audubon, the American wilderness,
and the nature of love and knowledge. What was happening that
evening in young Warren's heart? What is it that happens in
yours or in mine when we hear the same sound today? Presump-
tuously, I propose a theory.

Wild geese, not angels, are the images of humanity's own highest self. They show us the apogee of our own potential. They live
by the same principles that we, too often, only espouse. They
embody liberty, grace, and devotion, combining those three contradictory virtues with a seamless elegance that leaves us shamed
and inspired. When they pass overhead, honking so musically, we
are treated to (and accused by) a glimpse of the same sort of
sublime creaturehood that we want badly to see in ourselves.

The particularities that support this notion are many, and you
can find them in any study of the animal's biology and behavior.
Here I want to consider just one. Geese mate monogamously,
and for life.

Some thinkers would have us believe that monogamy and (still
more extreme) fidelity are masochistic inventions of human culture, artificial limitations inspired by superstition and religion,
and running counter to all natural imperatives of biology.
Doesn't biology dictate that males of any given species should try
to perpetrate their sperm as broadly as possible upon the female
population? Doesn't evolution require that a female advance her
own genes by selecting the strongest and smartest mate available
when she is first ready to breed, and by then selecting another, if

possible even stronger and smarter, the next time around in her cycle? Doesn't the Darwinian dynamic—the relentless competition for reproductive success and survival—entail an equally relentless flirtatiousness among all animal species, an unending lookout for the prospect of a new and better mate? Well, no, not always. The evolutionary struggle, it turns out, is somewhat more complicated than a singles' bar. Among geese, there is an ecological mandate for fidelity.

Geese live a lofty but difficult life, facing the problems of starvation and predation in forms that are acutely particular to them, traveling long distances each year between their wintering ranges and their breeding grounds, struggling each summer to hatch and raise and educate a brood of goslings. Amid these travails, they just can't afford to philander. They need one another there on the scene, male and female, each its chosen mate, at all times. They have committed themselves, by physiology and anatomy, to a life of mutual reliance in permanent twosomes.

Curiously, this commitment seems to derive straight from the two other characteristics that we humans most admire in them: their noble size and their impressive migrations.

Of the world's fifteen species of wild geese, all are confined to the northern hemisphere, and most populations of those species make formidable annual migrations (hundreds or thousands of miles and, in one species, over the Himalayas), traveling northward in spring to breed, south again in the fall. Many fly all the way to the Arctic. Canada geese (also known as Canadian honkers and, scientifically, *Branta canadensis*) are the largest and the most familiar on this continent, with populations that follow flyways on the East Coast and the West Coast and several other north-south routes in between. The particular population I happen to know spend their winters in Arizona and thereabouts, feeding busily to build up fat reserves that will be needed later, and then fly up the Rockies to a certain braided stretch of the Madison River here in Montana, where dozens of tiny islands separated by narrow channels give them a choice of ideal nesting sites. As with any animal migration, there are routine costs and acute dangers that must be faced by these journeying geese. Why the various populations migrate at all is not completely explicable, but flying up into the far northern summer does bring them to fresh food supplies (they eat grasses and other vegetation), to areas relatively empty of man and other predators, and to thawing wetlands that suit their needs for nesting. Also, the type of food they find by chasing spring northward is especially nutritious, since the young plant shoots they favor tend to hold high concentrations of protein and nitrogen. This last fact is quite important. Nutritionally, geese have to play every angle they can.

Their digestive system is damnably inefficient. Unlike other grazing herbivores, geese have no capacity to digest cellulose, which accounts for a large portion of plant tissue and holds the cellular juices (rich in sugar and protein) locked within cell walls. Most grazing animals digest cellulose with the help of bacteria that live in their guts. Along the upper digestive tract of a cow, for instance, is an extra stomach known as the rumen, wherein reside the cellulose-gobbling bacteria. But a Hereford is not obliged to cope with the delicate physics of flight. A goose, already large and heavy for a bird, and destined for long-distance flights, cannot tolerate the extra weight of a rumen. So a goose has no bacteria to help it with cellulose, and therefore no high rate of gastric efficiency. Much of the potential nutriment consumed passes straight through the bird without being utilized.

And it passes quickly. A huge full belly is also forbidden by aerodynamics, and so the whole alimentary process is accelerated. A meal of grass travels the length of a goose gut, top to bottom, in only about two hours. During such a short time, and with no chemical breakdown of cellulose, digestion is necessarily partial. In consequence, a goose needs to be constantly filling itself and, also constantly, emptying. Hence the expression "Loose as a goose."

Concerning the storage of fat reserves, it's the same problem once more. Some smaller birds that migrate to the Arctic can lay on as much as another full body weight before they head north to breed. But the laws of scale as applied to aerodynamics make that sort of provident fattening, for a goose, impossible. Already so large, a goose (despite its great strength) cannot let itself get much bulkier. Anything more than a twenty-five percent weight gain, during the winter months of serious feeding, will jeopardize its ability to get airborne.

Each of these limitations makes the life of a goose a little harder, the margin of survival a little slimmer. Combined, they dictate that a goose needs to spend every possible moment stuffing its gullet. Hours are precious, net benefit is low, and a goose must gorge steadily just to stay even, or to get slightly ahead for those lean and costly breeding months to come. This may be, in fact, another reason why geese migrate north in summer: Under the long northern hours of daylight, they can spend more time feeding.

And all those nutritional hardships of goosehood affect not just survival, but also procreation. A female goose will give away most of her own precious energy reserves—in the form of embryos and yolk—with the laying of a clutch of eggs. Then for almost a month she must incubate those eggs, scarcely leaving the nest to grab even one daily meal. During the incubation period she will regain some weight, but not much, since most of her time is spent sitting, supplying the motherly heat. Occasionally a female will even starve to death right on the nest. If she dies, the eggs will not hatch or the hatchlings will die also. The gander will be left a childless widower. Obviously, malnourishment of mama is bad for all concerned.

But time spent courting, each year, would be time stolen from eating. Energy spent on sexual coquetry would be energy that might have gone into eggs, or made the difference for survival of a female exhausted after laying. Geese have neither time nor energy to spare, so they take a long view. They commit themselves to endurance, to each other, to the future—and not to maximizing their sexual options.

Romance in the life of a goose begins during the second or third winter. A male and a female find one another on the wintering grounds or just after migration north; overtures are made, a modest neck-stretching dance is performed, then reciprocated, and before long an understanding has been struck. This arrangement is accomplished almost hastily, but destined to last. The new pair honk in mutual acknowledgment, then fly off to establish a nest, which will be only their first of many. Ducks, closely related to geese in the family Anatidae, go about things differently. Ducks tend toward elaborate courtship displays and garish plumage among the males, both of which serve toward distinguishing males of a given species from females, and males of one species from males of another, all to facilitate the pairing process, which in ducks is repeated each year. Not the geese. Choosing one mate for life and remaining (with rare exceptions) faithful, geese have no need for such fancy displays or flashy dimorphic costumes. They put their resources to other uses. They spurn narcissism and fickleness and that annual flirtatious skirmishing, in favor of economy and a dignified singlemindedness.

It takes the best efforts of two geese, working full time, to hatch and rear a brood of goslings. The female lays a clutch of eggs (five is the average number), and then sits on them throughout the chilling days and nights of April and early May. The male meanwhile stands watch. If a predator approaches, he warns her by honking, and together they fly to safety—or else she hunkers low on the nest and he takes flight alone, noisily, attempting to lead the danger away. After hatching, he is still there, standing sentinel so that the mother and young can devote their undivided attention to feeding—and now *he* loses weight, while his mate restores herself and the goslings grow. For two months the goslings are flightless, but good swimmers, and during that period they all travel their river or lake as a tight family group, the mother paddling in front, then a file of goslings, the father following close behind. In autumn they fly south again, still together, an inseparable family. Evidently the migration routes are not programmed instinctively, but must be taught by the parents to each new generation. On the winter feeding grounds they *still* stay together, with the father again mainly responsible for keeping watch while the others feed. Finally, after a full year, either the youngsters leave voluntarily or the male drives them away. He and his mate are now once again devoting themselves to each other, and to the prospect of a new brood. They fly north as a pair of old lovers, to Manitoba or British Columbia or Newfoundland, or to the channels of the Madison River in Montana.

Each year in May I take a boat down through the Madison channels and visit, as unobtrusively as possible, those nesting geese. In good years, when deadlines are distant and life is sane, I get down there more than once, catching the geese at various stages of their cycle. The first time I ever saw a brood of newborn goslings was also the first year I made the float in a kayak.

There were two of us, a woman and I, neither of us very familiar with kayak technique nor with each other. As we paddled past a small island, five balls of yellow fluff exploded hysterically out of a nest, straight into the river, and were swept immediately downstream. In the shock of the moment my friend's kayak went upside down; I was no help whatsoever, and it seemed suddenly that five young geese and a tall twenty-eight-year-old woman might all drown at once. But everyone survived. Now the woman and I are married and at least some of those five goslings, with decent luck, have long since flown back up in spring to become grandparents. The years intervening passed very quickly.

Monogamy and lifelong devotion, like an annual flight to the

Arctic and back, are not things accomplished easily. St. Paul told the Corinthians that "love does not come to an end," but the divorce rate among your friends and mine proves that St. Paul was either a liar or a fool. Considering all trends and pressures to the contrary, I was glad to find an ecological mandate for permanent partnership among animals so estimable as *Branta canadensis*. I was equally glad, recently, to come upon an interesting quote from the French novelist Marguerite Duras:

> Fidelity, enforced and unto death, is the price you pay for the kind of love you never want to give up, for someone you want to hold forever, tighter and tighter, whether he's close or far away, someone who becomes dearer to you the more you've sacrificed for his sake. This sacrificial relationship is precisely the one that exists in the Christian church between pain and absolution. It can survive outside the church, but it retains its ecclesiastical form. There can be no more violent, and beautiful, strategy than this for seizing time, for restoring eternity to life.

Geese figured it out for themselves. They know something about violence and beauty and time. Listen: *uh-whongk, uh-whongk, uh-whongk, uh-whongk, uh-whongk* . . .

SWAMP ODYSSEY

A Journey in Black Water and Time

My eighteenth high school reunion was held in the Okefenokee Swamp, seven hundred miles from the scene of the crime. One advantage of this arrangement was that only two of us showed up. There was the Red Ace and myself. He flew into Jacksonville on a sardine-class ticket aboard People Express and spent a miserable night on a bench at the airport, worst sleep he'd had since May of 1966 when we pulled a late one cramming Virgil together for a senior exam and he crashed until morning in my bedroom chair. This was back before the invention of software, the pocket calculator, possibly also fire. People still memorized Latin verbs. The Red Ace and I, however, must have been the only two high school seniors of even our generation so moronically dutiful as to lose a night's sleep over *The Aeneid* within ten days of graduation itself. More sensible souls were driving Chevies to the levee. All things considered, it was a miracle of Jesus that neither Red nor I ended up a priest or a lawyer. He went into professional tennis and I came out of grad school as a bartender and a fishing guide. Eighteen years later we rendezvoused at the Tahiti Motel in Folkston, Georgia, just outside the east entrance of the Okefenokee. Folkston, for those of you who remember *Pogo,* is not far from Fort Mudge.

I had ridden out from Savannah with an old boy named John Crawford, a.k.a. Crawfish, a wizard swamp guide who by a happy coincidence of compatibility was just six days younger than the Red Ace and had therefore gone to high school together with us separately in a different place at the same time, if you see what I mean. We're talking about the infamous mid-sixties, exactly those years stretching from "Louie, Louie" to the Gulf of Tonkin to the assassination of Malcolm X. Unmatchable for sheer dizziness and an overabundance of loud, nasty sounds. I had suggested the Okefenokee Swamp with a mind to peace and quiet. Also, I suspected it might be a wonderful place to visit.

This cheerful predisposition was based mainly on optimism and ignorance. Turned out I was right, but for all the wrong reasons.

I had imagined that five days of slogging across the Okefenokee Swamp would offer such heights of discomfort and travail that the experience would be exhilarating for its pure intensity. Tangled vegetation, oppressive heat, no solid ground for miles, fetid water, biting insects, ten thousand alligators, and the continent's foremost selection of poisonous snakes—that sort of thing. I had put it to Red like one of those old recruiting ads for the Peace Corps: "Bad pay and long hours, but at least you'll be hungry and in danger." The experts said that you should do your traveling in this swamp, if you had to do any, between February and April—that is, before the water dropped, the heat came up, and the mosquitoes appeared in sky-darkening multitudes. So of course I had us there at the end of May. Even Crawfish, who himself harbors a helpless and unstinting love for the Okefenokee, had told me by phone, "You know, this trip is liable to be hardship duty."

Our last stop in civilization was at a tourist concession on the very fringe of the swamp, a store and boat dock run by a third-generation swamper named Harry Johnson, from whom the Red Ace made last-minute purchases (our eight or ninth bottle of insect repellent) while Crawfish saw to food and I filled a five-gallon carboy with drinking water. At least I had been told we would drink it. But the water that came out of Harry Johnson's side tap was black, blacker than the coffee at the Folkston cafe. Johnson's dock sat on a blackwater cove at the end of a blackwater canal leading away into the depths of the swamp, and the faucet was evidently drawing on that selfsame blackness. Also, the stuff smelled like a shoe factory.

"Are we going to drink this?" I asked Crawfish, sloshing a bit out so he could see. Crawfish did not seem concerned.

"Isn't that a bit darker than usual?" he said to Harry Johnson.

Harry Johnson smiled benignly. "Got a little sulfur in there. Do you good. Keep the 'skeeters off you."

The Okefenokee Swamp is a great shallow saucer full of water and peat and vegetation, covering 400,000 acres near the eastern end of the border between Georgia and Florida. Thanks to a foresightful purchase by the U.S. government back in 1937, most of it is protected as the Okefenokee National Wildlife Refuge. It is closer to wilderness condition today than it was during the early decades of this century, when humans lived in it, hunting and fishing and timbering. Motorized travel is now restricted to the fringes of the swamp, and even canoe travel is controlled by the U.S. Fish and Wildlife Service, which grants a limited number of permits each year for the watery trails that lead to a limited number of campsites.

The Okefenokee is a relatively young ecological system, the wild vegetal growth and the buildup of peat (dead and decaying plant material) having begun about seven thousand years ago. The swamp holds a very large volume of water that is very gently in motion. Prevented from percolating downward by impermeable clays underneath, and slowed by the sponge-like peat and the network of living vegetation, the swamp water flows down an incline that varies by only ten feet of vertical drop from the northeastern edge of the swamp to the southwestern edge. It is drained away by two separate rivers headed toward two separate seas: the St. Marys River, emptying from the swamp's southeastern corner into the Atlantic, and the Suwanee River, meandering off from the western border of the swamp to the Gulf of Mexico. Within the swamp the divide between St. Marys flow and Suwanee flow is by no means clear cut, though a much larger share of the total finds its way into the Suwanee. The current of the Okefenokee itself moves in broad, shallow sheets more than in narrow channels, especially during times of high water, passing over and under and through the vast, filtering mass of vegetation and peat. For a number of complicated reasons related to ground-water seepage and the configurations of islands and troughs, as well as to the general incline, this current proceeds in a roughly circular pattern: a great mandala of dark water, moving around counterclockwise.

The submerged vegetation and peat strain out organic impurities, while also turning the water black with tannic acid. It's the same process that gives color to certain flatland jungle streams, like the Zabalo of eastern Ecuador or, most notably, the Rio Negro of Brazil. Plant life is burgeoning and dying within the drainage much faster than it can decay, much faster than the drowsy current can carry its products of decomposition away.

The result is an acidic blackwater tea, ideal medium for culturing cypress trees, carnivorous plants, alligators. On a bright day that blackwater tea casts back reflections of a complete swamp world seen upside down, as on a surface of polished and oiled ebony. And it's as potable, I learned eventually, as it is beautiful.

We set off from a point called Kingfisher Landing, the Red Ace and I paddling one canoe, Crawfish standing in the stern of the other, easing his boat along with what seemed to be effortless strokes of a twelve-foot bamboo pole. For an hour or three we moved down long tunnel-like corridors through thick brush, riding the current in a channel that was often no deeper than a bathtub and no wider than a sidewalk. In some places the brush arched overhead into a darkening canopy. In others it closed so tightly ahead that we had to spread branches by hand as we went through. Always the water beneath us was that lovely, inscrutable black. Crawfish led one detour to what he said was a typical gator hole—a small, muddy pond not far off our channel that had been scooped out of the peat by force of reptilian will. It was deeper than we could measure, more turbid than the channel, but apparently unoccupied. Crawfish probed his pole down into the center and made some strange muted yelping sounds into the end, like a drunken jazzman struggling with a clogged trumpet.

"That's it. Our guide has flipped. He thinks he's a sea lion," said the Red Ace. "We're doomed."

"Sometimes that brings them up," said Crawfish.

"Do we want them up?"

The first of the rains began, which seemed inconvenient only until we stopped trying to stay dry and surrendered ourselves to the cooling effect. A drenching in rainwater seemed preferable to a drenching in sweat, after all, and the temperature had plummeted right into the eighties. Then the sun returned, bringing with it the deerflies. Slim chartreuse vines groped outward like green snakes from the overhanging brush, slender stalks reaching for light, for support, for the brush on the opposite side of the channel, for a passing canoeist, striving to get hold and tighten down, to knit closed on daylight and motion. The vines were called smilax, Crawfish said. It was his swamp and he knew the names of everything. He said the buds and the terminal leaves of the vines were sweet and tasty.

"You can eat them."

"*You* can eat them," said the Red Ace.

My hands had started to swell from the deerfly bites. A curious new experience for me, who could not even spell anaphylactic shock. I remembered the tale Crawfish told about a city dude he was once required to evacuate out of the Okefenokee by moon-light. This fellow had coated his whole body with layer upon layer of the fiercest insect repellent; then, when the afternoon heat got serious, started dunking his terry-cloth hat and letting the cool runnels trickle down his face. Soon he had one eye full of *N-diethyl-meta-toluamide,* but the doctors just managed to save it. A little parable, Crawfish seemed to imply, about where insect repellent would get you.

We made camp an hour before dark at Maul Hammock Lake, a modest patch of open water clotted over only partly by water lilies and another big-leafed floating plant that Crawfish called spatterdock. Our appointed campsite was the Maul Hammock platform, a bare structure of planks and pilings just big enough for three tents and an Optimus stove and a billion mosquitoes. It looked like a little lakeside dock, the kind you would scamper down to from the summer cabin and use as a diving board if you were a kid—except here in the Okefenokee there was no real lake to dive into (unless you craved to pack your nostrils and ears full of peat), nor adjacent dry land on any side. The platform, at day's end, was it. Step off it, try to stride out into that tangle of floating shrubbery that passed for the landward side, and you would sink to your waist. Lie down in your sleeping bag on some comfortable patch of sphagnum moss, and you were liable to wake up drowned.

"Who would like wine?" said Crawfish.

"Yes, yes, yes!"

It was a pert but amusing Chablis in a large plastic jug bearing a label that read ANTIVENIN.

That night I thought and dreamed intermittently about missing digits. Thanks to the mysterious toxic deerflies of the Okefenokee, my hand had continued swelling and I had waited too long to transfer my wedding ring; now the ring was bound on at the base of a finger that looked bloated and pale as a boiled bratwurst. I did not want to see this particular ring, which means a lot to me, taken off with a Swiss Army hacksaw. But I had also begun wondering, more than idly, which would give first—the gold band or the blood flow to that finger. It put me in mind of a story Crawfish had told about the time he was snakebit and decided against seeing a doctor.

Crawfish, you must first understand, is one of those singular folk born with an incurable affinity toward reptiles. He is a self-taught herpetologist of professional rigor and a passionate admirer of the animals he knows. Every lizard, to him, is a creature of arresting beauty. Every alligator is like an old friend. Every snake is a poem. The particular poem in question here was a small copperhead.

He found it one day on the long woodland drive that led to his house. Captured it easily and, holding the snake in his left hand, resumed driving with his right. He had handled thousands of poisonous snakes over the years, including a pygmy rattler that lived in his bedroom when he was a kid. But this time, according to Crawfish, he got careless. Climbing out of the vehicle, he relaxed his grip slightly and the snake jerked back, nailing one fang into Crawfish's middle finger. "It was like a hot poker jammed in there," he told me. "Worst pain I've ever felt."

He turned down the horse-serum antivenin because a human body sometimes reacts drastically to that stuff; a friend of his once in the same situation had nearly died from it. He didn't even phone a doctor. "I like to let my body try and heal itself," Crawfish told me in the most unassuming and matter-of-fact manner; he would have dismissed the whole subject if I hadn't prodded him for details. "Heal itself *if possible,*" he added. "Within reason." On this occasion his arm swelled hugely, all the way up to the shoulder, and stayed swelled for three weeks. Evidently he judged that to be within reason. His finger puffed out bigger than he had imagined a finger could puff. Then it turned black. "I thought it would probably just fall off." But it didn't. After three months the finger was back to normal, except for the lingering numbness near the tip.

"What happened to the snake?" I asked.

"You mean did he get sick?"

"I mean what did you do to the sucker?"

"Oh, we kept him around as a pet," said Crawfish. "Just awhile. Then let him go."

So this was not a man you would wake from sound sleep with squeaky talk of evacuating your fat little finger. By midafternoon the next day, my ring could be quietly moved.

We paddled for several hours through an open area called Sapling Prairie, near the northern edge of the swamp. With clear lines of sight for miles across the horizon, and little chance that a predator can come up by surprise, Sapling Prairie is one of the favorite habitats of the swamp's biggest birds: three species of heron, several kinds of egret, several ibises, and a good population of sandhill cranes, whose loud ratchety calls sounded at three hundred yards like the complaint of a rusty barn hinge broadcast by loudspeaker.

When they say "prairie" in the Okefenokee what they mean is a large shallow marshy pond, a zone bare of trees and bushes but covered almost entirely by grasses and other small foliage such as spatterdock, floating hearts, a couple of species of orchid, the carnivorous sundews and bladderworts. In the prairies, water stands two or three feet deep over a substrate of peat, the current is nearly imperceptible, and the only pathways are those kept open by canoeists and alligators.

Large rafts of peat occasionally rise up from the prairie bottom, lifted by the buoyant force of methane gas, a by-product of anaerobic bacteria at work on the decomposition of the submerged plant muck. Sundews especially seem to favor these risen rafts, colonizing them early and supplementing the marginal diet of available nutrients with insects caught in their own sticky, fistlike leaves. After the sundews, other small plants and even pine saplings get aboard, stitching out a network of roots, until the raft may become a soft, anchored island.

In the distance across Sapling Prairie, giving a skyline to the flats, are another sort of island-like feature called cypress domes. Cypress is a water-loving hardwood with seeds that require long submersion (as well as a dry interval) before they will germinate, so the clusters of cypress originate without benefit of a raft, sometimes growing right up out of the peat through a layer of standing water. One tree takes hold, dropping seeds, offering some stability of conditions for other recruits, and a colony of cypress expands outward over the marsh, dome-shaped against the sky because the oldest and therefore largest trees are at the center. Eventually, such a stand will become carpeted at the base with a tussocky layer of mosses and peat and brush—almost but not quite like solid ground. The cypress may be joined by black gum trees and maple and several species of bay. Local slang refers to these patches of soggy forest as "houses," possibly because they provide habitat for a big share of the swamp's mammalian wildlife. But the Okefenokee, with its meager supply of real solid ground, is not nearly so hospitable to mammals as it is to birds and reptiles and amphibians. Most of the mammalian species are small: cotton mouse, gray squirrel, marsh rabbit, raccoon. Flying squirrel. Evening bat. Big-eared bat. Seminole bat. Animals that don't *need* much solid ground.

Swimming and flying are the optimal modes of travel here. Climbing is also an option. Walking is problematic. It's hard to imagine how even a small deer could support its seventy pounds over those tiny hoofs on a platform of floating peat. When a creature as large as a human strides through this terrain, the ground bounces and the tall trees shudder. The name *Okefenokee* itself comes from old Indian words—*ecunnau finocau*—that meant "the trembling earth."

* * *

"Watch out for cottonmouths above in the bushes," said Crawfish.

"You got it, buddy," said the Red Ace.

"And be careful when you step over fallen logs."

We were bushwhacking through the understory of a cypress dome, sunk to our knees in a lush patch of yellow-green sphagnum, clutching at saplings with each step to avoid sinking farther. In the softest places we had to knee-walk, using our shins like snowshoes. The water was warm, the sensation was surprisingly pleasant. Hiking this way, we could cover a mile in about two days. Crawfish was barefoot.

Lichens in four colors were wrapped like gaudy decals on the trunks of loblolly bay trees. There were some amazing shades and configurations of shelf fungi. In the center of the thicket we paused to admire one especially majestic cypress. It was a hundred feet tall, naked and straight along the trunk, its canopy hung with long beards of Spanish moss—very possibly it had been the patriarch of this whole dome. Then we slogged on in a wide loop back toward the boats. Suddenly Crawfish reversed course, backing hastily out from under the limb of a bush.

He was clutching the side of his face and wheezing in pain. By the time I got near him, though, he already seemed calm again. His left eye was beginning to swell shut.

"It's okay. Only a wasp. Yow. Stings pretty good, but what a relief," he said. "I thought I'd been tagged by a snake."

"What's the first aid when a cottonmouth bites into your eyeball?"

"I can't imagine." He looked at me cheerfully with one good eye and one gone slimy and red. "Just don't put a tourniquet on my neck."

His body would heal itself. Once after a trip in the Ogeechee River drainage, Crawfish had told me, he pulled fifty-two ticks off his body, every one of which had already gotten itself plugged in. Around that time, he suspected, he must certainly have had a case of tick fever. All the symptoms were there. But his body had healed itself.

No more rain, no more deerflies, no more oppressive heat and humidity—just mild sunshine and the gradual awareness that this swamp journey of ours was somehow being smiled upon.

The scenery had gotten even more exotically gorgeous after Sapling Prairie, when we turned south toward the very heart of the Okefenokee on a channel that led in and out among cypress domes. The cypress themselves seemed to thrive in this area; they were lofty and stark, exaggeratedly fat where they came out of the black water but tapering quickly down into long root-beam trunks, Spanish moss dangling all over the high branches. The smilax vines continued to reach out at us along narrow runs, but now Red and I were reaching back, letting navigational chores lapse while we snapped off those sweet little tips, popping them down like huckleberries. There was a noticeable current again, upon which we moved easily. The surroundings were halcyon, but best of all, for me, was having the Red Ace there in the front of the canoe, intermittently rummaging down into his bucket of cameras and zoom lenses and fancy filters, coming back up with some combination of that hardware in front of his face while he tracked the latest alligator on a leisurely swim along the channel before us, the latest heron on a laborious takeoff and then a slow graceful walk across the sky. I was glad to have Red here in the swamp because it had been too little and too long. I had barely seen him since 1972.

Certain people can make the most pleasant enterprise seem doleful; others can turn any grim misadventure into at least pretty good slapstick. The Red Ace is of the latter group. I had laughed through some of my life's dreariest moments in his company. I could describe the time he split my scalp open with one crack of an exploding all-day lollipop, an event that occurred onstage during a high-school-production melodrama in 1965. I bled on my Buster Brown suit while we went ahead and sang "Never Hit Your Grandma with a Shovel." I could tell you about the West Side of Chicago in 1968 and a neighborhood gang that was intent on frightening off a commune of do-gooder white boys. I could recount the one about The Man in the Towel, late at night in the labyrinthine corridors of the Penn Station YMCA, 1969, with the Red Ace and me literally barricaded up in a five-dollar room. And there were the few weeks he slept on the floor of my garret in England, during the winter of 1971, while he tried to decide whether to fly home and propose marriage to a certain lady and I groped for a plausible excuse to drop out of graduate school. But never mind all that. Just take my word. Space doesn't allow doing justice here to those episodes, and anyway this is a story about—at least mainly about—the Okefenokee Swamp.

During the past dozen years we had seen little of each other, Red and I. It was a matter of history and geography. Time and change. The movement of waters along an imperceptible gradient, dividing to follow different routes to different seas. Then again, though, it wasn't really so gentle as that implies. Something ended abruptly in 1972.

What was it that ended? Not the friendship. Not just our youth or his bachelorhood. Not just my romance with academia. It was the sixties themselves, according to my theory, that ended in 1972.

Now I know some pundits argue that the sixties ended at Altamont, in December of 1969, when a Mick Jagger song finally resulted in murder and the band played on. Others would claim that the true end came in April of 1975, at the moment the last U.S. helicopter lifted off the roof of a building that had been the American Embassy in a place now named Ho Chi Minh City. I assert otherwise. For me the definite and unmistakable end of the sixties—for whatever they had been worth, and God only knows

—came on that evening in November of 1972 when the network computers announced, just minutes after the polls had closed, that Richard Nixon had squashed an earnest, unfortunate man named George McGovern, on whose behalf I had gone AWOL from all aspects of my own life. And of course I was just one of many.

Me, I slept that night on a pile of leaflets in the back room of a McGovern storefront in suburban Chicago. I used my seersucker politico jacket for a pillow, next morning dropping that into a trash barrel. My reaction within ten days was to depart the civilized U.S., heading back to England and then to Africa and then eventually, still farther, to Montana.

Yes I was young, and yes my political metabolism was hysterical. I was angry and worried and saddened—everything but surprised. But I also count myself as having been lucky: The abrupt end of the sixties may have been one of the best things that ever happened to me, because Montana certainly was.

Neither Red nor I got back to southern Ohio for that fifth or tenth or (if there are such things) fifteenth high school reunion. I heard he was married and then later not and teaching tennis and then not. He was back East in a town that he himself had always celebrated for its grim ugliness. He was steady, but there were no giveaways of good fortune. He endured solitarily through a run of bad weather, of the personal variety, that went on just too damn long. It seemed to me like unfairness. I invited him, in a tone that verged on browbeating, to come out and fill his lungs with Montana air. But that never managed to happen. I suggested he move out permanently (although adding to the number of Montana residents, even by one, is a responsibility I don't take lightly). Moving wasn't on. Still he needed—and *deserved*, it seemed to me—to fill his lungs with a new sort of air. Any sort. Shuffle the deck, give a crank to the kaleidoscope, get some fresh alignments and juxtapositions. This was all unsolicited diagnosis by me, the Dutch uncle. A new sort of air.

Finally I said: *Meet me in south Georgia two months from to-day, and we'll go out and get lost in the Okefenokee Swamp.*
The Red Ace said: *How could I possibly refuse?*

Which brings me to another story that Crawfish told in the privacy of the swamp. He didn't push these stories forward, understand, as though he enjoyed talking about himself. On the contrary. No, it was simply a matter of memory doors opening and anecdotes emerging as a certain swamp-bound but genuine rapport grew up among the three of us. And Crawfish, I learned, was a man of multiple doors, with a luminous little memory behind each.

This one was about being electrocuted. It happened when he was fourteen. (A hard year for him, the same year he shot an arrow through his own wrist with a device called a Hawaiian sling. But that's a different story, and not one that illustrates the human body's capacity for self-healing.) The doctors in this case of electrocution honestly thought he had killed himself, at least temporarily. They suspected that his heart was not beating during the time he sailed through the air.

He was in the upper branches of a tree, doing merely the sort of foolhardy and routinely life-threatening things that fourteen-year-old boys used to do in trees. Leaning too far, he reached back for support and grabbed hold of a wire. The wire was carrying ten thousand volts. The tree was wet. Zap: legally dead, through that long dreamy moment while his body fell forty-five feet to the ground. "I had the sensation of floating," said Crawfish. "I *saw* myself floating there, my body in the air. Dead."

But he was a lucky young Crawfish, missing the picket fence by a full three feet and hitting the ground hard. That impact on landing—so the doctors hypothesized—must have started his heart beating again.

The moral, I suppose, is that if the tree had been smaller his death might have been more permanent. The moral is that you

never know what it might be, causing your lungs to fill with new
air. It might be Richard Nixon. It might be the Okefenokee
Swamp.

As late afternoon was turning to early evening, we came into
an area called Big Water, which is a lake by the Okefenokee
system of figuring, though in some ways seems more like a river,
yet, in real justice, should not and cannot be reduced to either of
those categories. Big Water is a thing of the swamp world, and
you would find its equivalent nowhere else. It was the loveliest
spot Red and I had seen or would see in the Okefenokee, and in
its own style probably one of the most magical wild places on the
continent. It was also high on Crawfish's private list of Okefenokee secrets, and though he presented it to us with quiet pride,
noncommittally, later we knew that he had been gratified by our
appreciation. Here in Big Water was where the alligators came
out to greet us.

What the maps call Big Water Lake is really a liquid canyon
through tall cypress, a long blade of open water running on for
three miles but never more than about forty yards wide. On each
side, beneath the cypress, are little coves of still water carpeted
over with spatterdock. The current moves north to south, steady
enough to carry a canoe but so smooth that the water never
forfeits its texture of polished ebony. With the light angled low,
we could see from thirty yards back the tiny wakes of whirligig
beetles as they proceeded before us along the surface. In the
course of a couple of miles, paddling quietly, we also saw the
wakes of a dozen alligators, wakes that were larger but not much
larger than those of the beetles: nothing but nostrils and eyes
protruding to cut the water, tail working powerfully but invisibly. Most of these alligators slid away as we approached, moving
off downstream and then, if we gained on them, diving; they
could easily stay down, if they had to, for half an hour. But some
were more curious.

In one of the spatterdock coves we stopped to explore the possibility of a fish dinner. Crawfish unwound the line from his cane pole and flopped out a hook baited with salami—the higher technology of angling has not yet come to the Okefenokee, nor is there any reason why it should. In a minute Crawfish's bobber was bobbing tentatively. I held our canoe below Crawfish's boat, in the tail of the eddy, giving him room, while the Red Ace's camera went clickety clickety. We found ourselves whispering. Last shards of sunlight breaking through the cypress, and we both felt the same tranquility and pagan reverence as if we had been sitting the afternoon away in the cathedral at Chartres. We watched Crawfish working his hook and line—and in that we weren't alone. A large alligator had come out of the spatterdock, sliding up quietly near Crawfish's canoe to see how the fisherman was faring.

Crawfish twitched the cane, then lifted a small sunfish up and into his boat. We whooped encouragingly, Crawfish said nothing, and the alligator came a couple of yards closer.

Only its eyeballs and snout were visible, but the spacing between those suggested an animal about seven feet long. It was holding position, patient and very attentive, less than ten feet off Crawfish's starboard bow. He could have tweaked it on the nose with his fishing pole. Instead he just ignored it. Caught another sunfish. The alligator moved still closer. I had thought at first, unavoidably, about Captain Hook and the croc-with-the-clock, but this alligator, it became clear, did not represent the slightest menace. It had more the demeanor of a shameless mutt at the back door of a butcher shop.

"He's waiting for a handout," Crawfish said across the quiet water. "Been around too many fishermen at this spot."

Crawfish offered the gator no handout. We understood why. That would have only reinforced its false and dangerous misapprehension of the nature of the human species. Still, it took a person of will as well as principle to say no to such a beautiful animal.

Another story, this one of will and principle.

Back in 1968, about the same time Red and I were being terrorized by that gang in Chicago, Crawfish was enrolled at Armstrong College in Savannah; he was also working part-time as a herpetologist for the Savannah Science Museum. Herpetology being his real true love, he gradually began to spend more time at the museum than at Armstrong. When this fact became known to the members of a certain civic body, John Crawford received a draft notice.

The year 1968 was of course a very lousy time to be drafted. Furthermore, Crawfish was opposed on grounds of conscience to the war in Vietnam.

So he enlisted in the Navy, thinking this might be a partial solution. He was trained, then assigned as an electrician's mate to a submarine support ship based in Bremerton, Washington. Pulled duty down through Panama, at the Guantánamo base on Cuba, and at a submarine base in Key West. His ship was still there in Key West when word filtered through the ranks that a large antiwar demonstration would be held soon, just outside the gates of the sub base. If he had leave that day, Crawfish thought, he would like to participate. He was in no position, at that point in his life, to foresee which way the waters would flow.

The Navy brass at Key West were concerned that there might be trouble from those demonstrators. So they planned to assign a few men to stand guard with rifles, just in case things got out of hand. A finger was pointed while a voice said, "You, you, you, and Crawford." It brought to Crawfish the clarification that until then had been muddled and delayed. He thought, "I can't do that. I might be asked to shoot my own friends." And not just friends, but people with whom he was in political and moral agreement. So he filed for status as a conscientious objector.

It was the wrong time to do that. Convincing the U.S. armed forces that you are a conscientious objector after you have already *enlisted* in the Navy—and with a Catholic upbringing, which is supposed to make you well fit religiously for war—is only a little more difficult than driving an alligator through the eye of a needle. While his application was pending, Crawfish took abuse from the noncom officers. He was given the nickname "Rabbit." He was razzed late at night by patriots stumbling in drunk. A large and solid fellow, Crawfish explained to them in his mild way that, though opposed to war, he had no objection whatever to fistfights. They backed off. And he argued his way successfully to the CO discharge.

Escaping the Navy at that juncture led him to a very different sort of life in the Florida Keys—a little commercial fishing, lots of diving, wildlife photography, lobster research, and eventually some free-lance biological consulting. That experience led back to Savannah, where in 1973 he and two friends started an enterprise called Wilderness Southeast, a nonprofit institution providing outfitted and guided wilderness trips with a strong emphasis on ecological education. Crawfish never suspected, early on, that he would ever earn a living from what he loved best: mucking around in places like the Okefenokee Swamp, one eye peeled for reptiles. But eleven years later the business was flourishing.

After the Red Ace agreed to come on a swamp odyssey, it was Wilderness Southeast that I called. "The Okefenokee," I said. "Have you got a good guide? Somebody who could show me the reptile life?"

They said, "Do we ever."

There was more. There was much more swamp and many more stories and quite a few other arrestingly beautiful reptiles. We drank all the antivenin. The Red Ace and I did a reprise of "Never Hit Your Grandma with a Shovel," first performance in eighteen years, and Crawfish, having sat through it, was made an honorary member of our high school class. Late at night, as we lay on a platform near Big Water, we heard the unforgettable bellow of a very large alligator, throaty and low and prolonged. It was a deep bass rumbling, so deep that we felt it through the planks of the platform almost as much as we heard it, and at first Red and I took it for the sound of a big outboard motor held at very low idle, in the distance at least a mile off. Then it was answered by another outboard, much nearer us. This wasn't anyone's low idle. It was a living sound, a sound with the same magisterial quality as a lion's roar heard after dark on the East African savanna. And for the Okefenokee, it was the precise equivalent: king of beasts.

After five days we had completed our loop and were headed out. Somewhere in one of the prairies south of Big Water we had turned against the current and begun paddling back upstream, toward the point of division between those waters destined for the Gulf of Mexico and those waters destined for the Atlantic— but it was impossible for us to know just where that divide stood. We never saw it. From where we sat, so close, this was a single mandala of black water, moving around counterclockwise. That's always the way it is at the time.

Finally, reluctantly, we swung the canoes out through a gap between bushes and onto a wide thoroughfare called the Suwanee Canal—which was, being man-made, the least attractive stretch we had seen in the swamp. The Suwanee Canal would carry us straight back to the blackwater cove at Harry Johnson's gift shop and boat landing.

The canal was too deep for Crawfish to pole against the bottom, so he was reduced at last to using a paddle. Paddling his canoe up beside ours, he told a last story:

In October of 1889 the Georgia legislature passed a bill that decreed that the Okefenokee Swamp be sold to the highest bidder. It went for twenty-six and a half cents an acre. The buyers were a consortium of businessmen calling themselves the Suwanee Canal Company. Their plan was to cut a canal from the east edge of the swamp to the St. Marys River, a monumental engineering feat that was supposed to result in draining the Okefenokee like an unclogged sink. The waters would rush out to the Atlantic, leaving behind thousands of acres and millions of dollars' worth of timber and fertile land. The digging began in 1891 and continued for four years. The main canal was cut thirty-two feet deep and eleven miles long, including the stretch along which we three were presently paddling.

Then in 1897 the work ceased. The project was abandoned, never to be revived. In those days some few things were still beyond the technological will of humankind. At roughly the point in the effort when water was expected to begin surging toward the St. Marys, toward the Atlantic, widening out its own channel with the inexorable force of its call to the sea, the opposite happened. The waters began flowing back into the swamp.

THE SIPHUNCLE

*Chambers of Memory
in the Ocean of Time*

The past is not dead, Faulkner told us, it is not even past. Or words to that effect. I'm quoting from memory. Memory believes before knowing remembers, Faulkner told us, another way of making the same point. It was his central and abiding theme: The past is not dead, is not gone, cannot ever be completely escaped or erased or forgotten; the past *is*. This of course was the heresy of a self-educated Mississippi crank, an axiom more Confederate than American, but probably (and despite the fact that Freud agreed) he was right. William Faulkner himself has been in his grave twenty-five years now, and *he* certainly isn't dead or gone. I got to thinking about—got to remembering—his words this week as I considered the chambered nautilus, an animal that carries its own past evermore forward through life and history, sealed off behind a wall of pearl.

For a living nautilus, the past literally provides balance and buoyancy. And the animal stays in touch with that past, remotely, inextricably, through a long tubular organ known as the siphuncle. This nautiloid siphuncle is a conduit of blood and memory.

The nautilus itself is a staggeringly ancient beast, a marine creature that has remained almost unchanged over 450 million

years, since before life on Earth had even climbed out of the
oceans. Five species within the genus *Nautilus* survive today, last
remnants of a line that once produced 10,000 different species to
dominate the ocean environment as emphatically—and at the
same time—as dinosaurs dominated the land. This ancestral line
was the chambered cephalopods, including nautiloids and their
close relatives the ammonoids. They seem to have been the first
successful marine predators, preceding such other cephalopod
predators as the squid and the octopus. Like the squid and the
octopus, though, nautiloids were soft-bodied animals with multiple tentacles. Long before backbones and toothy jaws and scales
came into fashion, the nautiloids and their kin had solved the
problems connected with making a living as carnivores in the
ocean depths. They did it by secreting ingenious shells.

The shells were most typically spiral in shape, flattened on
both sides and coiling gracefully outward from an axis, very
much like the shells of surviving *Nautilus* species. The animals
secreted these structures progressively as they themselves grew—
adding wider extensions to the spiral, vacating ever outward as
they needed more elbow room, living always in only the outer-
most chamber and closing each earlier chamber behind them
with a calcareous wall. Of course the shells afforded protection,
for the early nautiloids, but they also did something more. Like
the wings of the first true bird, those chambered shells allowed
nautiloids to rise up off the substrate, defying gravity.

Controlled buoyancy may seem a modest feat to us, by hind-
sight, but the extent to which it expanded nautiloid horizons
would be hard to overestimate.

The shells of living *Nautilus* species serve the same function
today. Actually they perform less like a bird's wing than like a
hot-air balloon. The successive chamber walls are known techni-
cally as *septa,* and behind every septum is a space filled with
either liquid or gas, or with some balance of both—depending on
whether the individual nautilus is seeking to rise or descend

through the levels of water. Behind every septum is a sealed chamber representing either ballast or lift. Behind every septum is a phase of the animal's history.

But the seal isn't absolute. At the center of every septum is a small hole. Only the siphuncle penetrates backward in space and time.

In July of 1962 William Faulkner died suddenly, under somewhat mysterious circumstances involving whiskey and a steep flight of stairs, possibly also a heart attack or a stroke. He was buried quickly and rather quietly (for a Nobel Prize winner) beneath blasting summer heat in the town of Oxford, Mississippi, where he had lived his life. Roughly a year later an article entitled "The Death of William Faulkner" appeared in *The Saturday Evening Post.* I remember seeing it. There was a photograph of a fierce-looking little man with a stiff mustache and the eyes and nose of a peregrine falcon: this person Faulkner, evidently, of whom I knew nothing. I was fifteen. In the background of the photo, I recall, was a house that looked imposing behind its tall neoclassic columns. I read the Ogden Nash in that issue of the *Post,* and probably much of the rest, and glanced at the cartoons, but I ignored the article about the dead man, whom I understood only vaguely to be some sort of notorious curmudgeon, maybe a segregationist governor. I was chiefly preoccupied at the time with football and bass fishing and the banjo, and no one had yet so much as forced me to read even "Barn Burning" or "The Bear," thank goodness. The article was by someone named Hughes Rudd, which fact I took note of not at all.

Six years later much had changed, and my life was spiraling around William Faulkner the way a miller spirals around a summer lantern. I had consumed all the novels and was well launched on an obsession that would go beyond appreciative rereading, beyond critical pedantry (and a graduate thesis describing "Centripetal and Contrapuntal Structural Patterns in William Faulkner's Major Novels"), beyond the demented self-assigned task of trying to translate *Absalom, Absalom!* into a film script; beyond all that, I say, and straight on into cultic veneration. Junior in college now. Late one evening I got a call from a buddy who said I should scutter right down to a certain bar and meet this wild man from CBS News, who was waving tumblers of Cutty Sark through the air and talking about my favorite subject, Faulkner. The man's name was Hughes Rudd.

It turned out that this Mr. Rudd was now a correspondent for CBS, and that he was leaving soon for Oxford, Mississippi, where he would film a documentary about Faulkner and Faulkner's country. Within the elapsed time of one Cutty Sark, I found myself hired. When I protested earnestly that I hadn't come to ask for a job, that I was just genuinely interested, that I didn't want to bust his budget, Hughes Rudd said: "Don't be a fool, David. CBS has money falling off it like dry leaves." And he fluttered his fingers through the air. "Dry leaves."

A few days later I was AWOL from college, camped at a motel in Oxford along with Hughes and a film crew. For two weeks there I lived the exalted life of an editorial consultant and gofer. I stood by while Hughes interviewed the chairman of the English Department at Ole Miss, a blindingly tedious man who considered himself chief curator of Faulkner's memory but whom Faulkner certainly would have loathed and Hughes had no patience for either. I stood by while Hughes talked with Faulkner's old hunting chums and the blacks who had tended his horses. I stood by throughout long days of filming inside the small ramshackle house on the south edge of town, beyond the driveway chain and the huge magnolias, the same house that from a distance looked so imposing behind its neoclassic columns. And sometimes, though not for many hours, I stayed at the motel to work on a script. But Hughes wasn't really shooting this program according to any script. He was shooting from his gut; he was shooting from his memory of what certain phrases, certain

scenes, certain novels could mean to a person's life. Clearly
Hughes himself was still a writer at heart, despite the CBS business, and he cared about Faulkner in a way that no mere TV
commentator ever would. Hughes Rudd was in those days (and
remained) an anomaly in the sleek world of network news—a
jowly man with a bloodshot glare and a fast, sardonic wit who
stubbornly worked the fringes of American culture, the flea circuses and hog-calling fests and tattooists' conventions by which
he could illuminate, with his dour deadpan, the important truth
that life itself was a benign but very ridiculous practical joke.
And the notion of putting a thoughtful contemplation of Faulkner and Faulkner's Mississippi before a prime-time CBS audience
was itself so mischievously improbable that it suited Hughes perfectly. Meanwhile there was no need for a script. Faulkner himself had written the script; it was *his* words we would use. For
now, Hughes just wanted to capture the flavor of Faulkner's
place—which happened to be rural and small-town Mississippi.
Get a shot of those mules. Get a shot of that kudzu. Get a shot of
this derelict plantation house with the roof fallen in and the columns awry and the thistles growing up between the porch planks.
I stood by.

We ate steaks every night and I learned to drink and Hughes
and I talked about Faulkner. We talked about writing, the craft
Hughes had abandoned and I was just hoping to begin. We talked
about sleekness versus fringes. It emerged that my real job on this
assignment was to keep Hughes good company and to prevent
him from getting himself into trouble—so Hughes said—when
the Cutty Sark piled up over his eyebrows. I was fired and re-
hired three times within the first week. One harrowing evening at
dinner I sat between Hughes and Faulkner's sister-in-law, a middle-aged woman still seething with outrage over something
Hughes wrote in that *Post* piece six years earlier, and I was
obliged to referee. Then it was over. I went back to college and

heard six months later that the whole project had been scrapped, because CBS News was a half million dry leaves over budget.

I visited Hughes once in New York, where he took me out to a dauntingly fancy lunch. Then for sixteen years I didn't see him again, except occasionally on the tube. Mississippi had been wild good fun, but for me it seemed a closed compartment of the past.

Beneath a soft fleshy hood that covers what might loosely be called its face, the nautilus has jaws like a parrot. With those jaws it crunches the carapaces of crabs and lobsters; in captivity it will feed like a geek on raw chicken. It gapes at the world through a pair of large empty eyes, almost as blank as Orphan Annie's. It has more arms than ten octopuses. It propels itself horizontally by jet power, farting water out through a flexible funnel and steering on sound Newtonian principles. A creature, then, of many bizarre charms—but none of these is so notable as its buoyancy system. The nautiloid buoyancy system is responsible for a seemingly paradoxical feat: allowing the animal to grow bigger and heftier without changing its weight.

The nautilus does grow more *massive* as it matures. But weight is a measure of gravitational force, not of mass, and for a nautilus that gravitational force depends on its own average density, relative to the density of seawater. The spiral shell is made of very dense material, and tends therefore to sink. The buoyancy system compensates, enabling the nautilus to levitate. The shell is constantly being enlarged, constantly getting heavier, and so every five or six weeks the nautilus slides its soft body toward the opening and secretes another septum behind, sealing off another abandoned chamber. Then it begins pumping heavy fluid out of that chamber, by means of its siphuncle, and refilling the same space with buoyant gas.

To rise toward the ocean surface, it replaces more fluid with gas. To descend again, it exchanges gas for fluid. None of these transfers is accomplished quickly. To build a new septum and empty the space behind it requires time and energy. To refill a chamber with ballast once it has been emptied was thought by scientists, until recently, to be impossible. Most of its life a nautilus spends in the middle depths, along the steep seaward slopes of drowned reefs in the Pacific, between a thousand and two thousand feet down, scavenging there along muddy ledges. Or simply hovering.

The pressure at those depths is enormous. A human body would be squashed. It might seem logical that such pressure would also drive seawater back in through the siphuncle, flooding all chambers of a nautilus shell despite any resistance the animal might try to offer.

This does not happen. A nautilus is immune to nostalgia.

For me there have been a number of compartmented phases, and a number of lucky fortuities. I was fortunate enough to escape the future that seemed to await me, quite manifestly, as an assistant professor of English whose turf was Faulkner. I was fortunate enough to get untangled from the ivy and sneak off without punching the dots for a doctorate. I evaded the looming Volvo and the corduroy jacket with leather elbows and the unfunny early marriage. Any complacency sensed here should be understood in the context that I managed to make my share of other good roaring mistakes instead. But at least those weren't manifest in advance. I spent three years at menial labor while writing a novel about the death of Faulkner, a novel that no one at the time or for years afterward wanted to publish, and by now I don't either. But it took much time and energy to seal that one behind a wall. Then for reasons of rent and groceries I drifted into being a science journalist, sort of. By what seemed an accident of disposition I found myself working the fringes, the flea circuses and hog-calling fests of the realm of natural history. Probably if you had asked me about influences, though, I would have mumbled the names Ardrey, McPhee, Gould.

Like a recovering alcoholic I can brag that it's now seven years, a record, since I last reread *Absalom, Absalom!* Life is short and eleven times is probably enough.

A few months ago I got a letter from Hughes Rudd. He had seen a small bit of my science writing in the *Washington Post* and called the editors for my address. He was now with ABC, Hughes told me, though planning to retire this autumn and move to France with his wife, Ann. He was glad to hear I had fetched up in the northern Rockies, of which he had fond memories from many years back, when he had rattled through Montana and Wyoming in his old Chevy pickup. "No gunrack but a WWII Walther P-38 in the glove compartment. I used to go out in the semi-desert around Rock Springs, Wyo., and fire it at rocks, pretending they were newspaper publishers or book publishers." It was vintage Hughes, the whole letter, and it made me smile widely. I had forgotten over the years how much I cherished this man. I had forgotten how much I had learned from him. Even owning a television might have been justified, possibly, on the merits of Hughes Rudd alone.

"I took Ann to Oxford four or five years ago," Hughes wrote, "so she could see the Faulkner house, and the ole burg didn't look the same at all: they were remodeling the courthouse! Insanity. When they get started they don't leave a fellow nothing, as Hemingway said somewhere." Hughes knew that I knew that in many ways that old courthouse, with its Confederate monument facing stubbornly South, had been a symbol of Faulkner's world and Faulkner's central idea. But of course the civic beavers who give face-lifts to historic courthouses can't obliterate the essence of recollection, and in even his cynical moments Hughes would admit it. "I've lost track of all the Faulkner relatives and friends I knew in those days," he added.

People come into our lives and then they go out again. The entropy law, as applied to human relations. Sometimes in their passing, though, they register an unimagined and far-reaching influence, as I suspect Hughes Rudd did upon me. There is no scientific way to discern such effects, but memory believes before knowing remembers. And the past lives coiled within the present, beyond sight, beyond revocation, lifting us up or weighting us down, sealed away—almost completely—behind walls of pearl.

THE SAME RIVER TWICE

Stenothermal Waters and
the Remorseless Flow of Time

I've been reading Heraclitus this week, so naturally my brain is full of river water.

Heraclitus, you'll recall, was the Greek philosopher of the sixth century B.C. who gets credit for having said: "You cannot step twice into the same river." Heraclitus was a loner, according to the sketchy accounts of him, and rather a crank. He lived in the town of Ephesus, near the coast of Asia Minor opposite mainland Greece, not far from a great river that in those days was called the Meander. He never founded a philosophic school, like Plato and Pythagoras did. He didn't want followers. He simply wrote his one book and deposited the scroll in a certain sacred building, the temple of Artemis, where the general public couldn't get hold of it. The book itself was eventually lost, and all that survives of it today are about a hundred fragments, which have come down secondhand in the works of other ancient writers. So his ideas are known only by hearsay. He seems to have said a lot of interesting things, some of them cryptic, some of them downright ornery, but his river comment is the one for which Heraclitus is widely remembered. The full translation is: "You cannot step twice into the same river, for other waters are continually flowing on." To most people it comes across as a nice resonant metaphor, a bit of philosophic poetry. To me it is that and more.

Once, for a stretch of years, I lived in a very small town on the bank of a famous Montana river. It was famous mainly for its trout, this river, and for its clear water and its abundance of chemical nutrients, and for the seasonal blizzards of emerging insects that made it one of the most rewarding pieces of habitat in North America, arguably in the world, if you happened to be a trout or a fly-fisherman. I happened to be a fly-fisherman.

One species of insect in particular—one "hatch," to use the slightly misleading term that fishermen apply to these impressive entomological events, when a few billion members of some mayfly or stonefly or caddisfly species all emerge simultaneously into adulthood and take flight over a river—one insect hatch in particular gave this river an unmatched renown. The species was *Pteronarcys californica,* a monstrous but benign stonefly that grew more than two inches long and carried a pinkish-orange underbelly for which it had gotten the common name "salmonfly." These insects, during their three years of development as aquatic larvae, could survive only in a river that was cold, pure, fast-flowing, rich in dissolved oxygen, and covered across its bed with boulders the size of bowling balls, among which the larvae would live and graze. The famous river offered all those conditions extravagantly, and so *P. californica* flourished there, like nowhere else. Trout flourished in turn.

When the clouds of *P. californica* took flight, and mated in air, and then began dropping back onto the water, the fish fed upon them voraciously, recklessly. Wary old brown trout the size of a person's thigh, granddaddy animals that would never otherwise condescend to feed by daylight upon floating insects, came up off the bottom for this banquet. Each gulp of *P. californica* was a major nutritional windfall. The trout filled their bellies and their mouths and still continued gorging. Consequently the so-called salmonfly so-called hatch on this river, occurring annually during two weeks in June, triggered by small changes in water temperature, became a wild and garish national festival in the fly-fishing year. Stockbrokers in New York, corporate lawyers in San Francisco, federal judges and star-quality surgeons and foundation presidents—the sort of folk who own antique bamboo fly rods and field jackets of Irish tweed—planned their vacations around this event. They packed their gear and then waited for the telephone signal from a guide in a shop on Main Street of the little town where I lived.

The signal would say: *It's started.* Or, in more detail: *Yeah, the hatch is on. Passed through town yesterday. Bugs everywhere. By now the head end of it must be halfway to Varney Bridge. Get here as soon as you can.* They got there. Cab drivers and schoolteachers came too. People who couldn't afford to hire a guide and be chauffeured comfortably in a Mackenzie boat, or who didn't want to, arrived with dinghies and johnboats lashed to the roofs of old yellow buses. And if the weather held, and you got yourself to the right stretch of river at the right time, it could indeed be very damn good fishing.

But that wasn't why I lived in the town. Truth be known, when *P. californica* filled the sky and a flotilla of boats filled the river, I usually headed in the opposite direction. I didn't care for the crowds. It was almost as bad as the Fourth of July rodeo, when the town suddenly became clogged with college kids from a nearby city, and Main Street was ankle deep in beer cans on the morning of the fifth, and I would find people I didn't know sleeping it off in my front yard, under the scraggly elm. The salmonfly hatch was like that, only with stockbrokers and flying hooks. Besides, there were other places and other ways to catch fish. I would take my rod and my waders and disappear to a small spring creek that ran through a stock ranch on the bottomland east of the river.

It was private property. There was no room for guided boats on this little creek, and there was no room for tweed. Instead of

tweed there were sheep—usually about thirty head, bleating in
halfhearted annoyance but shuffling out of my way as I hiked
from the barn out to the water. There was an old swayback horse
named Buck, a buckskin; also a younger one, a hot white-stockinged mare that had once been a queen of the barrel-racing cir-
cuit and hadn't forgotten her previous station in life. There was a
graveyard of rusty car bodies, a string of them, DeSotos and
Fords from the Truman years, dumped into the spring creek
along one bend to hold the bank in place and save the sheep
pasture from turning into an island. Locally this sort of thing is
referred to as the "Detroit riprap" mode of soil conservation;
after a while, the derelict cars come to seem a harmonious part of
the scenery. There was also an old two-story ranch house of
stucco, with yellow trim. Inside lived a man and a woman, married then.

Now we have come to the reason I did live in that town.
Actually there wasn't one reason but three: the spring creek, the
man, and the woman. At the time, for a stretch of years, those
were three of the closest friends I'd ever had.

This spring creek was not one of the most eminent Montana
spring creeks, not Nelson Spring Creek and not Armstrong, not
the sort of place where you could plunk down twenty-five dollars
per rod per day for the privilege of casting your fly over large
savvy trout along an exclusive and well-manicured section of water. On this creek you fished free or not at all. I fished free,
because I knew the two people inside the house and, through
them, the wonderful surly old rancher who owned the place.

They lived there themselves, those two, in large part because of
the creek. The male half of the partnership was at that time a
raving and insatiable fly-fisherman, like me, for whom the luxury
of having this particular spring creek just a three-minute stroll
from his back door was worth any number of professional and
personal sacrifices. He had found a place he loved dearly, and he
wanted to stay. During previous incarnations he had been a wire-

service reporter in Africa, a bar owner in Chicago, a magazine editor in New York, a reform-school guard in Idaho, and a timber-faller in the winter woods of Montana. He had decided to quit the last before he cut off a leg with his chain saw, or worse; he was later kind enough to offer me his saw and his expert coaching and then to dissuade me deftly from making use of either, during the period when I was so desperate and foolhardy as to consider trying to earn a living that way. All we both wanted, really, was to write novels and flyfish for trout. We fished the spring creek, together and individually, more than a hundred days each year. We memorized that water. The female half of the partnership, on the other hand, was a vegetarian by principle who lived chiefly on grapefruit and considered that anyone who tormented innocent fish—either for food or, worse, for the sport of catching them and then gently releasing them, as we did— showed the most inexcusable symptoms of arrested development and demented adolescent cruelty, but she tolerated us. All she wanted was to write novels and read Jane Austen and ride the hot mare. None of us had any money.

None of us was being published. Nothing happened in that town between October and May. The man and I played chess. We endangered our lives hilariously cutting and hauling firewood. We skied into the backcountry carrying tents and cast-iron skillets and bottles of wine, then argued drunkenly over whether it was proper to litter the woods with eggshells, if the magpies and crows did it too. We watched Willie Stargell win a World Series. Sometimes on cold clear days we put on wool gloves with no fingertips and went out to fish. Meanwhile the woman sequestered herself in a rickety backyard shed, with a small wood stove and a cot and a manual typewriter, surrounded by black widow spiders that she chose to view as pets. Or the three of us stood in their kitchen, until late hours on winter nights, while the woman peeled and ate uncountable grapefruits and the man and I drank whiskey, and we screamed at each other about literature.

The spring creek ran cool in summer. It ran warm in winter. This is what spring creeks do; this is their special felicity. It steamed and it rippled with fluid life when the main river was frozen over solid. Anchor ice never formed on the rocks of its riffles, killing insect larvae where they lived, and frazil ice never made the water slushy—as occurred on the main river. During spring runoff this creek didn't flood; therefore the bottom wasn't scoured and disrupted, and the eggs of the rainbow trout, which spawned around that time, weren't swept out of the nests and buried lethally in silt. The creek did go brown with turbidity during runoff, from the discharge of several small tributaries that carried meltwater out of the mountains through an erosional zone, but the color would clear again soon.

Insects continued hatching on this creek through the coldest months of the winter. In October and November, large brown trout came upstream from the main river and scooped out their spawning nests on a bend that curved around the sheep pasture, just downstream from the car bodies. In August, grasshoppers blundered onto the water from the brushy banks, and fish exploded out of nowhere to take them. Occasionally I or the other fellow would cast a tiny fly and pull in a grayling, that gorgeous and delicate cousin of trout, an Arctic species left behind by the last glaciation, that fared poorly in the warm summer temperatures of sun-heated meltwater rivers. In this creek a grayling could be comfortable, because most of the water came from deep underground. That water ran cool in summer, relatively, and warm in winter, relatively—relative in each case to the surrounding air temperature, as well as the temperature of the main river. In absolute terms the creek's temperature tended to be stable year-round, holding steady in a hospitable middle range close to the constant temperature of the groundwater from which it was fed. This is what spring creeks, by definition, do. The scientific jargon for such a balanced condition is *stenothermal:* temperatures in a narrow range. The ecological result is a stable habitat and a twelve-month growing season. Free from extremes of cold or heat, free from flooding, free from ice and heavy siltation and scouring, the particular spring creek in question seemed always to me a thing of sublime and succoring constancy. In that regard it was no different from other spring creeks; but it was the one I knew and cared about.

The stretch of years came to an end. The marriage came to an end. There were reasons, but the reasons were private, and are certainly none of our business here. Books were pulled down off shelves and sorted into two piles. Fine oaken furniture, too heavy to be hauled into uncertain futures, was sold off for the price of a sad song. The white-stockinged mare was sold also, to a family with a couple of young barrel-racers, and the herd of trap-lame and half-feral cats was divided up. The man and the woman left town individually, in separate trucks, at separate times, each headed back toward New York City. I helped load the second truck, the man's, but my voice wasn't functioning well on that occasion. I was afflicted with a charley horse of the throat. It had all been hard to witness, not simply because a marriage had ended but even more so because, in my unsolicited judgment, a great love affair had. This partnership of theirs had been a vivid and imposing thing.

Or maybe it was hard because two love affairs had ended—if you count mine with the pair of them. I should say here that a friendship remains between me and each of them. Friendship with such folk is a lot. But it's not the same.

Now I live in the city from which college students flock off to the Fourth of July rodeo in that little town, where they raise hell for a day and litter Main Street with beer cans and then sleep it off under the scraggly elm in what is now someone else's front yard—the compensation being that July Fourth is quieter up here. It is only an hour's drive. Not too long ago I was down there myself.

I parked, as always, in the yard by the burn barrel outside the stucco house. The house was empty; I avoided it. With my waders and my fly rod I walked out to the spring creek. Of course it was all a mistake.

I stepped into the creek and began fishing my way upstream, casting a grasshopper imitation into patches of shade along the overhung banks. There were a few strikes. There was a fish caught and released. But after less than an hour I quit. I climbed out of the water. I left. I had imagined that a spring creek was a thing of sublime and succoring constancy. I was wrong. Heraclitus was right.

PARTIAL SOURCES

Magazine formats generally do not allow for bibliographical acknowledgments or footnoting. This is too bad. Facts and quotes don't come out of thin air; they all have to be quarried or borrowed or stolen from somewhere, and most of us journalistic pirates would prefer whenever possible to credit our sources. For any essayist who publishes his work first in magazines, therefore, one of the good things about collecting the same pieces into a book is that, finally, proper acknowledgment can be made.

Still, even this bibliography is not complete. In addition to the sources listed below, for instance, I am indebted also to a number of scientists and others who gave me their thoughts over the telephone, and to broad reference works upon which I depend habitually. Foremost among the latter is *Grzimek's Animal Life Encyclopedia,* a monumentally useful work edited by Bernhard Grzimek and published by Van Nostrand Reinhold.

Besides giving credit where credit is due, the following list is also offered as a guide, to the zealous, for further reading. Within each chapter heading the individual works are listed in (roughly) the order of their importance to my own idiosyncratic purposes; that ordering doesn't necessarily coincide with either their full scientific value, or with chronology, or with the alphabet. The technical sources should be mainly distinguishable from the works of general interest by their titles. I haven't noted that distinction explicitly, because in some cases the supposedly technical papers are precisely the ones that deserve a wide general audience. Gold is where you find it. Pan for it here at your own leisure, according to your own intuition.

In the cases of books, each edition listed below is not necessarily the first edition, nor the most recent, but simply the one to which I happened to have access.

The Face of a Spider

The Black Widow Spider. Raymond W. Thorp and Weldon D. Woodson. New York: Dover Publications, Inc. 1976.

Biology of Spiders. Rainer F. Foelix. Cambridge: Harvard University Press. 1982.

The Religion of India. Max Weber. Translated and edited by Hans H. Gerth and Don Martindale. New York: The Free Press. 1967.

Mosquitoes, Malaria and Man. Gordon Harrison. New York: E. P. Dutton. 1978.

Thinking About Earthworms

The Formation of Vegetable Mould, Through the Action of Worms, with Observations on Their Habits. Charles Darwin. New York: D. Appleton & Co. 1896.

The Autobiography of Charles Darwin. Charles Darwin. Edited by Nora Barlow. New York: Harcourt, Brace & Co. 1958.

Earthworm Ecology: From Darwin to Vermiculture. Edited by J. E. Satchell. New York: Chapman and Hall, 1983.

Soil Biology. Edited by A. Burges and F. Raw. New York: Academic Press. 1967.

Soil Animals. D. Keith McE. Kevan. New York: Philosophical Library. 1962.

Living Earth. Peter Farb. New York: Harper & Brothers. 1959.

The Physiology of Earthworms. M. S. Laverack. New York: The Macmillan Co. 1963.

The Vision of the Past. Pierre Teilhard de Chardin. Translated by J. M. Cohen. New York: Harper & Row. 1966.

The Thing with Feathers

"*Archaeopteryx* and the Origin of Flight." John H. Ostrom. *The Quarterly Review of Biology,* Vol. 49. March 1974.

"Bird Flight: How Did It Begin?" John H. Ostrom. *American Scientist,* Vol. 67. January–February 1979.

"The Ancestry of Birds." John H. Ostrom. *Nature,* Vol. 242. March 9, 1973.

"The Evolutionary Origin of Feathers." Philip J. Regal. *The Quarterly Review of Biology,* Vol. 50. March 1975.

"Back to the Trees for *Archaeopteryx* in Bavaria." Michael E. Howgate. *Nature,* Vol. 313. February 7, 1985.

"The *Archaeopteryx* Flap." Stephen Jay Gould. *Natural History.* September 1986.

"The Flying Ability of *Archaeopteryx.*" D. W. Yalden. *Ibis,* Vol. 113. 1971.

"Speculations on the Origin of Feathers." Kenneth C. Parkes. *The Living Bird,* Vol. V. 1966.

"Volant Adaptation in Vertebrates." Richard S. Lull. *The American Naturalist,* Vol. XL, No. 476. August 1906.

"Flight Capability and the Pectoral Girdle of *Archaeopteryx.*" Storrs L. Olson and Alan Feduccia. *Nature,* Vol. 278. March 15, 1979.

The Age of Birds. Alan Feduccia. Cambridge: Harvard University Press. 1980.

Men and Dinosaurs. Edwin H. Colbert. Harmondsworth: Penguin Books. 1971.

Nasty Habits

A Natural History of Sex: The Ecology and Evolution of Sexual Behavior. Adrian Forsyth. New York: Charles Scribner's Sons. 1986.

"Homosexual Rape and Sexual Selection in Acanthocephalan Worms." Lawrence G. Abele and Sandra Gilchrist. *Science,* Vol. 197. July 1, 1977.

"Sperm Sharing in *Biomphalaria* Snails: A New Behavioural Strategy in Simultaneous Hermaphroditism." Warton Monteiro, José Maria G. Almeida, Jr., and Braulio S. Dias. *Nature,* Vol. 308. April 19, 1984.

Nature's Economy: A History of Ecological Ideas. Donald Worster. Cambridge, England: Cambridge University Press. 1985.

"Drafting the Bombardier Beetle." Natalie Angier. *Time.* February 25, 1985.

Evolution: The Challenge of the Fossil Record. Duane T. Gish. El Cajon: Creation-Life Publishers. 1985.

"The Scopes Trial in Reverse." Duane T. Gish. *The Humanist.* November–December 1977.

The Decade of Creation. Edited by Henry M. Morris and Donald H. Rohrer. San Diego: Creation-Life Publishers. 1981.

Science on Trial: The Case for Evolution. Douglas J. Futuyma. New York: Pantheon Books. 1983.

Scientists Confront Creationism. Edited by Laurie R. Godfrey. New York: W. W. Norton & Co. 1983.

Parasitic Insects. R. R. Askew. New York: American Elsevier Publishing Co. 1971.

Ecological Entomology. Edited by Carl B. Huffaker and Robert L. Rabb. New York: John Wiley & Sons. 1984.

Stalking the Gentle Piranha

The Fishes and the Forest: Explorations in Amazonian Natural History. Michael Goulding. Berkeley: University of California Press. 1980.

"Forest Fishes of the Amazon." Michael Goulding. In *Key Environments: Amazonia.* Edited by Ghillean T. Prance and Thomas E. Lovejoy. New York: Pergamon Press. 1985.

"A Fish in the Bush Is Worth . . ." Thomas H. Maugh II. *Science,* Vol. 211. March 13, 1981.

The Primary Source: Tropical Forests and Our Future. Norman Myers. New York: W. W. Norton & Co. 1984.

See No Evil

Spiders, Scorpions, Centipedes and Mites. J. L. Cloudsley-Thompson. London: Pergamon Press. 1968.

"Prey Detection by the Sand Scorpion." Philip H. Brownell. *Scientific American,* Vol. 251, No. 6. December 1984.

"A Short Review of Scorpion Biology, Management of Stings, and Control." Franklin Ennik. *California Vector Views,* Vol. 19, No. 10. October 1972.

"Biology of the Large Philippine Forest Scorpion." W. Schultze. *The Philippine Journal of Science,* Vol. 32, No. 3. March 1927.

"The Biology of Scorpions." Max Vachon. *Endeavour,* Vol. XII, No. 46. April 1953.

Scorpions of Medical Importance. Hugh L. Keegan. Jackson, Miss.: University Press of Mississippi. 1980.

Venomous Animals and Their Toxins. Gerhard G. Habermehl. New York: Springer-Verlag. 1981.

Venomous Animals and Their Venoms. Vol. III: *Venomous Invertebrates.* Edited by Wolfgang Bucherl and Eleanor Buckley. New York: Academic Press. 1971.

Dangerous to Man. Roger A. Caras. South Hackensack, N.J.: Stoeger Publishing Co. 1977.

"Courtship of the Scorpion." J. Henri Fabre. In *The Insect World of J. Henri Fabre.* With an introduction and interpretive comments by Edwin Way Teale. New York: Harper & Row. 1981.

Turnabout

Insectivorous Plants. Charles Darwin. New York: D. Appleton & Co. 1889.

The Carnivorous Plants. Francis Ernest Lloyd. Waltham, Mass.: The Chronica Botanica Co. 1942.

" 'The Most Wonderful Plant in the World': With Some Unpublished Correspondence of Charles Darwin." Frank Morton Jones. *Natural History,* Vol. XXIII. 1923.

"Pitcher Plants and Their Moths." Frank Morton Jones. *Natural History,* Vol. XXI. 1921.

"Carnivorous Plants." Yolande Heslop-Harrison. *Scientific American,* Vol. 238, No. 2. February 1978.

"Fly in the Sundew." Terry Ashley and Joseph F. Gennaro, Jr. *Natural History,* Vol. 80. December 1971.

"Observations on the Sundew." Mrs. Mary Treat. *The American Naturalist,* Vol. VII, No. 12. December 1873.

The Selfhood of a Spoon Worm

"When Is Sex Environmentally Determined?" Eric L. Charnov and James Bull. *Nature,* Vol. 266. April 28, 1977.

"Temperature-Dependent Sex Determination in Turtles." J. J. Bull and R. C. Vogt. *Science,* Vol. 206. December 7, 1979.

"Evolution of Environmental Sex Determination from Genotypic Sex Determination." J. J. Bull. *Heredity,* Vol. 47, No. 2. 1981.

"Monogamy and Sex Change by Aggressive Dominance in Coral Reef Fish." Hans Fricke and Simone Fricke. *Nature,* Vol. 266. April 28, 1977.

"Temperature of Egg Incubation Determines Sex in *Alligator mississippiensis."* Mark W. J. Ferguson and Ted Joanen. *Nature,* Vol. 296. April 29, 1982.

Intersexuality in the Animal Kingdom. Edited by R. Reinboth. New York: Springer-Verlag. 1975.

Sex Determination. Guido Bacci. New York: Pergamon Press. 1965.

Common Intertidal Invertebrates of the Gulf of California. Richard C. Brusca. Tucson: University of Arizona Press. 1980.

"Natural Selection of Parental Ability to Vary the Sex Ratio of Offspring." Robert L. Trivers and Dan E. Willard. *Science,* Vol. 179. January 5, 1973.

"Thermal Biology of Sea Turtles." N. Mrosovsky. *American Zoologist,* Vol. 20. 1980.

"Temperature Dependence of Sexual Differentiation in Sea Turtles: Implications for Conservation Practices." N. Mrosovsky and C. L. Yntema. *Biological Conservation,* Vol. 18. 1980.

"Adaptive Significance of Temperature-Dependent Sex Determination in a Fish." David O. Conover. *The American Naturalist,* Vol. 123, No. 3. March 1984.

The Descent of the Dog

Genetics and the Social Behavior of the Dog. John Paul Scott and John L. Fuller. Chicago: University of Chicago Press. 1965.

The Dog: Its Domestication and Behavior. Michael W. Fox. New York: Garland STPM Press. 1978.

"Canid Communication." Michael W. Fox and James A. Cohen. In *How Animals Communicate.* Edited by Thomas A. Sebeok. Bloomington, Ind.: Indiana University Press. 1977.

Canine Behavior. Michael W. Fox. With a foreword by J. P. Scott. Springfield, Ill.: Charles C Thomas, Publisher. 1965.

"On the Origin of the Domestication of the Dog." M. F. Ashley Montagu. *Science,* Vol. 96, No. 2483. July 31, 1942.

A History of Domesticated Animals. Frederick E. Zeuner. New York: Harper & Row. 1963.

The World of Dogs. Josephine Z. Rine. New York: Doubleday & Co. 1965.

Of Wolves and Men. Barry Holstun Lopez. New York: Charles Scribner's Sons. 1978.

"Acoustic Behaviour of Mammals." G. Tembrock. In *Acoustic Behaviour of Animals,* edited by R.-G. Busnel. New York: Elsevier Publishing Co. 1963.

"Wild Dogs and Tame—Past and Present." Edwin H. Colbert. *Natural History.* February 1939.

The Complete Dog Book. An official publication of the American Kennel Club. New York: Howell Book House. 1972.

Street Trees

"The Natural History of Urban Trees." Ervin H. Zube. *Natural History,* Vol. 82, No. 9. November 1973.

This issue of *Natural History* (11/73) contained an admirable special supplement, collectively titled "The Metro Forest," of which Zube's paper was part and which also included contributions by Saul Rich; Clark E. Holscher; Melvin B. Hathaway; Darrel L. Cauley and James R. Schinner; Paul E. Waggoner and George R. Stephens; Barry Gordon and Thomas G. Lambrix; Frederick Hartmann; Robert Arbib; Robert D. Williamson; and Brian R. Payne.

Likewise the *Journal of Forestry* devoted a block of space in its issue for August 1974 to the subject of urban forestry, with individual contributions by Norman A. Richards, Lee P. Herrington, Gordon M. Heisler, and Rod Cochran.

Nature in Cities. Edited by Ian C. Laurie. (Especially the chapters by Owen Manning, Michael Laurie, David Pitt, Kenneth Soergell II and Ervin Zube, and Rob Tregay.) New York: John Wiley & Sons. 1979.

Nature in the Urban Landscape: A Study of City Ecosystems. Don Gill and Penelope Bonnett. Baltimore: York Press. 1973.

A History of Landscape Architecture: The Relationship of People to Environment. G. B. Tobey. New York: American Elsevier Publishing Co. 1973.

The Ontological Giraffe

Walker's Mammals of the World. Ronald M. Nowak and John L. Paradiso. Vol. II. Baltimore: The Johns Hopkins University Press. 1983.

East African Mammals: An Atlas of Evolution in Africa. Jonathan Kingdon. Vol. III, Part B. New York: Academic Press. 1979.

The Lonesome Ape

The Red Ape: Orang-Utans and Human Origins. Jeffrey H. Schwartz. Boston: Houghton Mifflin Company. 1987.

"The Evolutionary Relationships of Man and Orang-Utans." Jeffrey H. Schwartz. *Nature,* Vol. 308. April 5, 1984.

The Ape Within Us. John MacKinnon. New York: Holt, Rinehart and Winston. 1978.

"The Behaviour and Ecology of Wild Orang-Utans (*Pongo pygmaeus*)." John MacKinnon. *Animal Behaviour,* Vol. 22, No. 1. 1974.

"The Relationships of *Sivapithecus* and *Ramapithecus* and the Evolution of the Orang-Utan." Peter Andrews and J. E. Cronin. *Nature,* Vol. 297. June 17, 1982.

"New Hominoid Skull Material from the Miocene of Pakistan." David Pilbeam. *Nature,* Vol. 295. January 21, 1982.

"Is the Orangutan a Living Fossil?" Roger Lewin. *Science,* Vol. 222. December 16, 1983.

"Is *Sivapithecus pilgrim* an Ancestor of Man?" William K. Gregory. *Science,* Vol. XLII, No. 1080. September 10, 1915.

"The Descent of Hominoids and Hominids." David Pilbeam. *Scientific American,* Vol. 250. 1984.

The Natural History of the Primates. J. R. Napier and P. H. Napier. Cambridge, Mass.: The MIT Press. 1985.

"Evolution of Type C Viral Genes: Evidence for an Asian Origin of Man." Raoul E. Benveniste and George J. Todaro. *Nature,* Vol. 261. May 13, 1976.

Stranger than Truth

"Cryptozoology: Interdisciplinary Journal of the International Society of Cryptozoology." J. Richard Greenwell, editor. Lawrence, Kan.: Allen Press, Inc. Vols. 1–4. 1982–85.

Searching for Hidden Animals. Roy P. Mackal. New York: Doubleday & Co. 1980.

On the Track of Unknown Animals. Bernard Heuvelmans. Translated by Richard Garrett. New York: Hill and Wang. 1959.

"Mammals and Cryptozoology." George Gaylord Simpson. *Proceedings of the American Philosophical Society,* Vol. 128, No. 1. 1984.

Deep Thoughts

"Heavenly Fire." George Greenstein. *Science 85.* July–August 1985.

The Fire Came By. John Baxter and Thomas Atkins. New York: Doubleday & Co. 1976.

"Was the Tungus Event Due to a Black Hole?" A. A. Jackson IV and Michael P. Ryan, Jr. *Nature,* Vol. 245. September 14, 1973.

"Possible Anti-matter Content of the Tunguska Meteor of 1908." Clyde Cowan, C. R. Atluri, and W. F. Libby. *Nature,* Vol. 206, No. 4987. May 29, 1965.

"Evidence from Crater Ages for Periodic Impacts on the Earth." Walter Alvarez and Richard A. Muller. *Nature,* Vol. 308. April 19, 1984.

"First Look at the Deepest Hole." Richard A. Kerr. *Science,* Vol. 225. September 28, 1984.

"Continental Drilling Heading Deeper" and "The Deepest Hole in the World." Richard A. Kerr. *Science,* Vol. 224. June 29, 1984.

The Discovery of Subatomic Particles. Steven Weinberg. New York: Scientific American Library. 1983.

Particles: An Introduction to Particle Physics. Michael Chester. New York: New American Library. 1980.

Island Getaway

"Cracking an Ecological Murder Mystery." Mark Jaffe. *The Philadelphia Inquirer.* June 4, 1985.

Geographical Ecology: Patterns in the Distribution of Species. Robert H. MacArthur. New York: Harper & Row. 1972.

Biogeography. James H. Brown and Arthur C. Gibson. St. Louis: The C. V. Mosby Co. 1983.

The Theory of Island Biogeography. Robert H. MacArthur and Edward O. Wilson. Princeton: Princeton University Press. 1967.

The Ecology of Invasions by Animals and Plants. Charles S. Elton. New York: John Wiley & Sons. 1958.

Biogeography: An Ecological and Evolutionary Approach. C. Barry Cox, Ian N. Healey, and Peter D. Moore. New York: John Wiley & Sons. 1973.

Island Populations. Mark Williamson. Oxford: Oxford University Press. 1981.

Island Biology. Sherwin Carlquist. New York: Columbia University Press. 1974.

Talk Is Cheap

Silent Partners: The Legacy of the Ape Language Experiments. Eugene Linden. New York: Times Books. 1986.

Apes, Men, and Language. Eugene Linden. New York: Penguin Books. 1976.

Language in Primates: Perspectives and Implications. Edited by Judith de Luce and Hugh T. Wilder. New York: Springer-Verlag. 1983.

In the Shadow of Man. Jane van Lawick-Goodall. Photographs by Hugo van Lawick. Boston: Houghton Mifflin Company. 1971.

Why Chimps Can Read. Ann J. Premack. Drawings by Robert Schneider. New York: Harper & Row. 1976.

Icebreaker

My information on the Senyavina incident came mainly from wire-service reports (Reuters, Associated Press, United Press International) that appeared in *The Philadelphia Inquirer* during February 1985. I also benefited from Serge Schemann's March 1985 story in *The New York Times*. Those articles reached me through an admirable clip service, devoted to environmental news, run by a Washington group called the Monitor Consortium. In addition:

The Book of Whales. Written and illustrated by Richard Ellis. New York: Alfred A. Knopf. 1980.

Sea Guide to Whales of the World. Lyall Watson. Illustrated by Tom Ritchie. New York: E. P. Dutton. 1981.

Whales: A Celebration. Edited by Greg Gatenby. Boston: Little, Brown & Co. 1983.

The Yevtushenko poem is reprinted in *Whales: A Celebration*. It was translated from the Russian "by John Updike with Albert C. Todd." Originally from *Stolen Apples,* Yevgeny Yevtushenko. New York: Doubleday & Co. 1968.

Beluga (Delphinapterus Leucas): Investigation of the Species. S. E. Kleinenberg, A. V. Yablokov, B. M. Bel'kovich, and M. N. Tarasevich. Moscow: Academy of Sciences of the USSR. 1964. Translated from the Russian: Israel Program for Scientific Translations, Jerusalem. 1969. Published for the Smithsonian Institution and the National Science Foundation, Washington, D.C., by the Israel Program for Scientific Translations.

The Blue Whale. George L. Small. New York: Columbia University Press. 1971.

The World's Whales: The Complete Illustrated Guide. Stanley M. Minasian, Kenneth C. Balcomb, III, and Larry Foster. Washington: Smithsonian Books. 1984.

The Ecology of Whales and Dolphins. D. E. Gaskin. London: Heineman. 1982.

Agony in the Garden

Biology and Geology of Coral Reefs. Edited by O. A. Jones and R. Endean. (Especially "Population Explosions of *Acanthaster planci* and Associated Destruction of Hermatypic Corals in the

Indo-West Pacific Region," by Robert Endean.) New York: Academic Press. 1973.

"Crown-of-Thorns Starfish on the Great Barrier Reef." Robert Endean. *Endeavour,* new series, Vol. 6, No. 1. 1982.

Australia's Great Barrier Reef. Robert Endean. St. Lucia: University of Queensland Press. 1982.

Perspectives in Ecological Theory. Ramón Margalef. Chicago: University of Chicago Press. 1968.

"The Crown-of-Thorns Starfish (*Acanthaster*) and the Great Barrier Reef." Frank H. Talbot and M. Suzette Talbot. *Endeavour,* Vol. 30, No. 109. January 1971.

"Acanthaster: A Disaster?" William A. Newman. *Science,* Vol. 167. February 27, 1970.

"Acanthaster: A Rarity in the Past?" Thomas F. Dana. *Science,* Vol. 169. August 28, 1970.

"Coral-Eating Sea Stars *Acanthaster planci* in Hawaii." J. M. Branham, S. A. Reed, Julie H. Bailey, and J. Caperon. *Science,* Vol. 172. June 11, 1971.

"Densities of *Acanthaster planci* in the Pacific Ocean." Peter J. Vine. *Nature,* Vol. 228. October 24, 1970.

"Locomotory Response of *Acanthaster planci* to Various Species of Coral." D. J. Barnes, R. W. Brauer, and M. R. Jordan. *Nature,* Vol. 228. October 24, 1970.

"Destruction of Pacific Corals by the Sea Star *Acanthaster planci."* Richard H. Chesher. *Science,* Vol. 165. July 18, 1969.

"Starfish Infestation: Hypothesis." J. L. Fischer. *Science,* Vol. 165. August 15, 1969.

"Fluctuations of Animal Populations, and a Measure of Community Stability." Robert MacArthur. *Ecology,* Vol. 36, No. 3. July 1955.

"A Note on Trophic Complexity and Community Stability." R. T. Paine. *The American Naturalist,* Vol. 103. January–February 1969.

The Poseidon Shales

Das Holzmadenbuch. Bernhard Hauff and Rolf Bernhard Hauff. Holzmaden, West Germany: privately printed (only in German). 1981.

"Museum Hauff in Holzmaden/Teck." A pamphlet. Holzmaden, West Germany: privately printed. No date.

The Successful Dragons: A Natural History of Extinct Reptiles. Christopher McGowan. Toronto: Samuel Stevens. (Available through University of Toronto Press.) 1983.

Water Reptiles of the Past and Present. Samuel Wendell Williston. Chicago: University of Chicago Press. 1914.

Vertebrate Paleontology. Alfred Sherwood Romer. Chicago: University of Chicago Press. 1966.

The Beautiful and Damned

"Genetic Basis for Species Vulnerability in the Cheetah." S. J. O'Brien, M. E. Roelke, L. Marker, A. Newman, C. A. Winkler, D. Meltzer, L. Colly, J. F. Evermann, M. Bush, and D. E. Wildt. *Science,* Vol. 227. March 22, 1985.

"The Cheetah Is Depauperate in Genetic Variation." Stephen J. O'Brien, David E. Wildt, David Goldman, Carl R. Merril, and Mitchell Bush. *Science,* Vol. 221. July 29, 1983.

The Cheetah: The Biology, Ecology, and Behavior of an Endangered Species. Randall L. Eaton. New York: Van Nostrand Reinhold Co. 1974.

East African Mammals: An Atlas of Evolution in Africa, Vol. III, Part A. Jonathan Kingdon. New York: Academic Press. 1977.

The Serengeti Lion: A Study of Predator-Prey Relations. George B. Schaller. Chicago: University of Chicago Press. 1972.

"Elephant Seals: Genetic Variation and Near Extinction." Michael L. Bonnell and Robert K. Selander. *Science,* Vol. 184. May 24, 1974.

"The Bottleneck Effect and Genetic Variability in Populations."

Masatoshi Nei, Takeo Maruyama, and Ranajit Chakraborty. *Evolution,* Vol. 29, No. 1. March 1975.
"Demography of Northern Elephant Seals, 1911–1982." Charles F. Cooper and Brent S. Stewart. *Science,* Vol. 219. February 25, 1983.

Provide, Provide

Gaia: A New Look at Life on Earth. J. E. Lovelock. Oxford: Oxford University Press. 1979.
"Atmospheric Homeostasis by and for the Biosphere: the Gaia Hypothesis." J. E. Lovelock and Lynn Margulis. *Tellus,* Vol. 26. 1973.
"Biological Modulation of the Earth's Atmosphere." Lynn Margulis and J. E. Lovelock. *Icarus,* Vol. 21. 1974.

The Flight of the Iguana

The Voyage of the "Beagle." Charles Darwin. London: J. M. Dent & Sons. 1959. (Originally published, 1845.)
The Origin of Species. Charles Darwin. New York: Avenel Books. 1979. (Reprint of the first edition, published 1859.)
The Theory of Island Biogeography. Robert H. MacArthur and Edward O. Wilson. Princeton: Princeton University Press. 1967.
Island Life. Alfred Russel Wallace. New York: AMS Press Inc. 1975. (Facsimile of the 1911 edition.)
Island Populations. Mark Williamson. Oxford: Oxford University Press. 1981.
Island Life. Sherwin Carlquist. Garden City: The Natural History Press. 1965.
Galápagos: A Natural History Guide. M. H. Jackson. Calgary: The University of Calgary Press. 1985.
Darwin and the Beagle. Alan Moorehead. Harmondsworth: Penguin Books Ltd. 1971.
Key Environments: Galápagos. Edited by R. Perry. Oxford: Pergamon Press. 1984.

Iguanas of the World. Edited by Gordon M. Burghardt and A. Stanley Rand. Park Ridge, N.J.: Noyes Publications. 1982.

The Galápagos: Proceedings of the Symposia of the Galápagos International Scientific Project. Edited by Robert I. Bowman. Berkeley: University of California Press. 1966.

Patterns of Evolution in Galápagos Organisms. Edited by Robert I. Bowman, Margaret Berson, and Alan E. Leviton. (Especially "An Ecological Study of the Galápagos Marine Iguana." P. Dee Boersma.) San Francisco: Pacific Division, AAAS. 1983.

"A Reappraisal of the Aquatic Specializations of the Galápagos Marine Iguana (*Amblyrhynchus cristatus*)." William R. Dawson, George A. Bartholomew, and Albert F. Bennett.

"Observations on Diving in the Galápagos Marine Iguana, *Amblyrhynchus cristatus* (Bell)." Edmund S. Hobson. *Copeia.* 1965, No. 2.

"A General Explanation for Insular Body Size Trends in Terrestrial Vertebrates." Ted J. Case. *Ecology,* Vol. 59, No. 1. Winter 1978.

"The Galápagos Giant Tortoises (*Geochelone elephantopus*); Part I: Status of the Surviving Populations." Craig G. MacFarland, José Villa, and Basilio Toro. *Biological Conservation,* Vol. 6, No. 2. April 1974.

"Galápagos Tomatoes and Tortoises." Charles M. Rick and Robert I. Bowman. *Evolution,* Vol. 15. December 1961.

"Species Number and Endemism: The Galápagos Archipelago Revisited." Michael P. Johnson and Peter H. Raven. *Science,* Vol. 179. March 2, 1973.

The Beaded Lizard

Interviews with Rev. John Fife, Jim Corbett, Phil Conger (now Willis-Conger), Father Ricardo Elford, Roger Wolf, Lupe Castillo, Duke Austin, Rabbi Joseph Weisenbaum, Sister Darlene Nicgorski, Dan Dale, "Lupe," "Roberto," and a number of other sanctuary activists, lawyers, public officials, and Central American refugees.

The Eliott Abrams quote comes from a videotaped interview with Mr. Abrams conducted by a crew from PBS television; portions of that interview were included within a segment of the PBS television series *Frontline;* the segment, with narration by Jessica Savitch, was produced and directed by Hector Galan under the auspices of WGBH Boston.

Among many printed sources drawn upon for this piece, some of the most valuable were:

"Immigration: Asylum Issues," an Issue Brief prepared for the Congressional Research Service by Sharon Masanz. Washington: Library of Congress. 1983.

"Illegal/Undocumented Aliens," an Issue Brief prepared for the Congressional Research Service by Joyce Vialet. Washington: Library of Congress. 1974.

"A Brief History of U.S. Immigration Policy," a report prepared for the Congressional Research Service by Joyce Vialet. Washington: Library of Congress. 1980.

"Salvadorans in the United States: The Case for Extended Voluntary Departure," a report prepared for the American Civil Liberties Union, under auspices of the National Immigration and Alien Rights Project, by Diana Bell, Kathryn Carovano, Stuart Gay, Sheila Murphy, Amit Pandya, and Cindy Peterson. Washington: ACLU. 1983.

No Promised Land: American Refugee Policies and the Rule of Law. Gary MacEoin and Nivita Riley. Boston: Oxfam America. 1982.

Basta!, newsletter and special supplements. Chicago: The Chicago Religious Task Force on Central America.

Public Law 96-212: Refugee Act of 1980. Washington. March 17, 1980.

The Deserts of the Southwest: A Sierra Club Naturalist's Guide. Peggy Larson, with Lane Larson. San Francisco: Sierra Club Books. 1977.

The North American Deserts. Edmund C. Jaeger. Stanford: Stanford University Press. 1957.

Drinking the Desert Juices

The Desert Smells Like Rain: A Naturalist in Papago Indian Country. Gary Paul Nabhan. San Francisco: North Point Press. 1982.

Gathering the Desert. Gary Paul Nabhan. Illustrations by Paul Mirocha. Tucson: University of Arizona Press. 1985.

Social Organization of the Papago Indians. Ruth Murray Underhill. New York: Columbia University Press. 1939.

Red Man's Religion: Beliefs and Practices of the Indians North of Mexico. Ruth M. Underhill. Chicago: University of Chicago Press. 1965.

"Man in Arid Lands: The Piman Indians of the Sonoran Desert." Bernard L. Fontana. In: *Desert Biology,* Vol. II. Edited by G. W. Brown, Jr. New York: Academic Press. 1974.

The Desert People: A Study of the Papago Indians. Alice Joseph, Rosamond B. Spicer, and Jane Chesky. Chicago: University of Chicago Press. 1949.

"Deceptive Barrenness." Richard S. Felger and Gary Paul Nabhan. *Ceres.* March–April 1976.

"Diabetes Research Focuses on Desert Tribe." Anonymous. *Research Resources Reporter.* May 1979.

"Saving the Bounty of a Harsh and Meager Land." Noel Vietmeyer. *Audubon,* Vol. 87. January 1985.

"Diabetes Incidence and Prevalence in Pima Indians: A 19-Fold Greater Incidence than in Rochester, Minnesota." William C. Knowler, Peter H. Bennett, Richard F. Hamman, and Max Miller. *American Journal of Epidemiology,* Vol. 108, No. 6. 1978.

"Diabetes Mellitus in American (Pima) Indians." Peter H. Bennett, Thomas A. Burch, and Max Miller. *The Lancet.* July 17, 1971.

"Hypertension in the Papago Indians." Charles H. Strotz and Gregory I. Schorr. *Circulation*, Vol. XLVIII. December 1973.

"Gallbladder Disease in Pima Indians: Demonstration of High Prevalence and Early Onset by Cholecystography." Richard E. Sampliner, Peter H. Bennett, Leonard J. Comess, Frederick A. Rose, and Thomas A. Burch. *The New England Journal of Medicine*, Vol. 283, No. 25. December 17, 1970.

"Congenital Anomalies and Diabetes in the Pima Indians of Arizona." L. J. Comess, P. H. Bennett, T. A. Burch, and Max Miller. *Diabetes*, Vol. 18, No. 7. July 1969.

"Nutrient Intake of Pima Indian Women: Relationships to Diabetes Mellitus and Gallbladder Disease." Jeanne M. Reid, Sandra D. Fullmer, Karen D. Pettigrew, Thomas A. Burch, Peter H. Bennett, Max Miller, and G. Donald Whedon. *The American Journal of Clinical Nutrition*, Vol. 24. October 1971.

"Diabetes Mellitus: A 'Thrifty' Genotype Rendered Detrimental by 'Progress'?" James V. Neel. *The American Journal of Human Genetics*, Vol. 14. 1962.

"Ascorbic Acid Deficiency Among Papago Indians." M. Pijoan, C. A. Elkin, and C. O. Eslinger. *The Journal of Nutrition*, Vol. 25, No. 5. 1943.

"Effects of Locust Bean Gum on Glucose Tolerance, Sugar Digestion, and Gastric Motility in Rats." Alan C. Tsai and Becky Peng. *Journal of Nutrition*, Vol. 111. 1981.

Insects as Human Food. F. S. Bodenheimer. The Hague: Junk. 1951.

Man and the Biology of Arid Zones. J. L. Cloudsley-Thompson. Baltimore: University Park Press. 1977.

The Desert Is a Mnemonic Device

This essay was informed by all of the interview and printed sources cited above for "The Beaded Lizard." It benefited likewise from the Underhill, Nabhan, and Fontana books cited for "Drinking the Desert Juices." It drew also upon a telephone interview with Eliott Abrams, further private conversations with John Fife and Jim Corbett, the collected *samizdat* letters of Corbett, and talks with Bob Hirsh, Peggy Hutchison, Sister Darlene Nicgorski, Phil (now) Willis-Conger, Ellen Willis-Conger, Father Tony Clark, Wendy LeWin, Mary Kay Espinoza, Don Reno, and others. Another invaluable source were the weekly summary-bulletins on the progress of the Tucson trial, issued by the press office of the sanctuary defense team. In addition:

Goatwalking. Jim Corbett. Unpublished manuscript. Copyright Los Cabreros Andantes, 1979.

Fields on the Hoof: Nexus of Tibetan Nomadic Pastoralism. Robert B. Ekvall. New York: Holt, Rinehart and Winston. 1968.

Wilderness and Paradise in Christian Thought: The Biblical Experience of the Desert in the History of Christianity and the Paradise Theme in the Theological Idea of the University. George H. Williams. New York: Harper and Brothers.

The Arab of the Desert. H. R. P. Dickson. Edited and abridged by Robert Wilson and Zahra Freeth. London: George Allen & Unwin. 1983.

The Desert Bible: Nomadic Tribal Culture and Old Testament Interpretation. Morris S. Seale. New York: St. Martin's.

Escape! Aron Spilken. New York: New American Library. 1983.

Sanctuary: A Resource Guide for Understanding and Participating in the Central American Refugees' Struggle. Edited by Gary MacEoin. New York: Harper & Row. 1985.

Sanctuary: The New Underground Railroad. Renny Golden and Michael McConnell. Maryknoll, N.Y.: Orbis Books. 1986.

Of Earth and Little Rain: The Papago Indians. Bernard L. Fontana with photographs by John P. Schaefer. Flagstaff, Ariz.: Northland Press. 1981.

The Tarnished Door: The New Immigrants and the Transformation of America. John Crewdson. New York: Times Books. 1983.

The Miracle of the Geese

"Canada Goose Production and Water Level Relationships on the Madison River, Montana." Donald Arthur Childress. Unpublished master's thesis. Bozeman, Mont.: Montana State University. 1971.

Wild Geese. M. A. Ogilvie. Illustrated by Carol Ogilvie. Vermillion, S.D.: Buteo Books. 1978.

Canada Goose Management: Current Continental Problems and Programs. Edited by Ruth L. Hine and Clay Schoenfeld. Madison, Wisc.: Dembar Educational Research Services, Inc. 1968.

Honker. C. S. Williams. Princeton: D. Van Nostrand Company, Inc. 1967.

"Nesting Canada Geese on the Upper Snake River." Frank C. Craighead, Jr., and John J. Craighead. *Journal of Wildlife Management,* Vol. 13, No. 1. January 1949.

"Breeding Habits of Canada Geese Under Refuge Conditions." Charles W. Kossack. *The American Midland Naturalist,* Vol. 43, No. 3. 1950.

The Marguerite Duras quote comes from an essay that appeared originally in a special issue of *Le Nouvel Observateur* devoted to the subject of love. A portion of the essay, including the quoted paragraph, was reprinted in the April 1986 issue of *Harper's,* in a translation by Christopher Benfey.

Swamp Odyssey

The Suwanee River: Strange Green Land. Cecile Hulse Matschat. New York: Farrar & Rinehart. 1938.

The Natural Environments of Georgia. Charles H. Wharton. Atlanta: Georgia State University. A report produced under a grant from the Georgia Department of Natural Resources.

"The Okefenokee, Land of the Trembling Earth," a pamphlet. Dot Rees Gibson. Waycross, Ga.: Dot Gibson Publications. 1974.

"Okefenokee Swamp Origin: Review and Reconsideration."
F. K. Parrish and E. J. Rykiel. *Journal of the Elisha Mitchell
Scientific Society,* Vol. 95, No. 1. 1979.
Other information, especially on the history of the Suwanee Canal Company, came from a draft paper by C. T. Trowell, 1982,
which reached me in its unpublished form. But because that
paper was self-proclaimed as an unfinished draft, Mr. Trowell
is not to be held responsible for any individual facts or, certainly, any conclusions or innuendos that appear in my essay.
*The Last of the Ruling Reptiles: Alligators, Crocodiles and Their
Kin.* Wilfred T. Neill. New York: Columbia University Press.
1971.

The Siphuncle

"The Death of William Faulkner." In *My Escape from the CIA,
and Other Improbable Events.* Hughes Rudd. New York: E. P.
Dutton. 1966.
*The Curves of Life: Being an Account of Spiral Formations and
Their Application to Growth in Nature, to Science, and to Art,
with Special Reference to the Manuscripts of Leonardo Da
Vinci.* Theodore Andrea Cook. New York: Dover Publications.
(A reprint of the original London edition of 1914.) 1979.
"The Buoyancy of the Chambered Nautilus." Peter Ward, Lewis
Greenwald, and Olive E. Greenwald. *Scientific American,* Vol.
243. October 1980.
"The Extinction of the Ammonites." Peter Ward. *Scientific
American,* Vol. 249. October 1983.
On Growth and Form. D'Arcy Wentworth Thompson. Abridged
edition, edited by John Tyler Bonner. Cambridge: Cambridge
University Press. 1961.
"A Magic Ratio Recurs Throughout Art and Nature." William
Hoffer. *Smithsonian.* December 1975.
"Nautilus: Have Shell, Will Float." Peter D. Ward. *Natural His-
tory.* October 1982.

"Not to Be or to Be?" Neil H. Landman. *Natural History.* August 1984.

"Chasing the Chambered Nautilus." Richard Conniff. *International Wildlife.* March–April 1985.

The Same River Twice

Heraclitus. Philip Wheelwright. Princeton: Princeton University Press. 1959.

The Art and Thought of Heraclitus. Charles H. Kahn. Cambridge: Cambridge University Press. 1979.

An Introduction to Early Greek Philosophy. John Mansley Robinson. Boston: Houghton Mifflin Co. 1968.

The Ecology of Running Waters. H. B. N. Hynes. Toronto: University of Toronto Press. 1970.

"Flow, Temperature, Solar Radiation, and Ice in Relation to Activities of Fishes in Sagehen Creek, California." Paul R. Needham and Albert C. Jones. *Ecology,* Vol. 40, No. 3. July 1959.

"Effects of Thermal Fluctuations on the Relative Survival of Greenthroat Darter Young from Stenothermal and Eurythermal Waters." Clark Hubbs. *Ecology,* Vol. 45, No. 2. Spring 1964.

"On the Zoogeography of Springs." Anker Nielsen. *Hydrobiologia,* Vol. 2. 1949–50.

Aquatic Productivity. W. D. Russell-Hunter. New York: Macmillan. 1970.

"Animal Ecology of a New Mexico Springbrook." Martha S. Noel. *Hydrobiologia,* Vol. 6. 1954.

"Trophic Structure and Productivity of Silver Springs, Florida." Howard T. Odum. *Ecological Monographs,* Vol. 27, No. 1. January 1957.

"Community Metabolism in a Temperate Cold Spring." John M. Teal. *Ecological Monographs,* Vol. 27, No. 3. July 1957.

River Ecology. Edited by B. A. Whitton. Berkeley: University of California Press. 1975.

Ecology of Inland Waters and Estuaries. George K. Reid. New York: Reinhold Publishing Corp. 1961.

The Living River. Charles E. Brooks. New York: Nick Lyons Books. 1979.